USMLE, 미국연수
그리고 영주권

USMLE, 미국연수 그리고 영주권

은종렬 지음

동국대학교출판부

은 종 렬

- 1997. 2 영남대학교 의과대학 졸업
- 1997-2002 영남대학교병원 인턴 및 레지던트
- 1999-2012 영남대학교 석사 및 경북대학교 박사
- 2002-2005 군위군보건소 및 안동성소병원 내과(공중보건의)
- 2005-2013 영남대학교병원 소화기내과 전임의, 전임강사, 조교수, 부교수
- 2012.3-2014.10 UC 데이비스 메디컬 센터 연수
- 2014.11-2024.2 명지병원 소화기내과 임상교수
- 2024.3-현재 동국대학교일산병원 소화기내과 교수
- 2011년 USMLE Step 1 & 2CK 합격
- 2012년 USMLE Step 2CS 합격, 영주권 신청 및 승인
- 2013년 USMLE Step 3 합격 및 PTAL, 영주권 발급
  미국 내과 레지던트 매치 지원(인터뷰 1개)
- 2014년 첫 번째 매치 실패, 재도전(인터뷰 2개 후 귀국)
- 2015년 3월 두 번째 매치 실패
- 2016년 8월 가족들 귀국

차례

프롤로그

2024년은 한국 의료시스템이 붕괴되는 해로 기록될 것 같습니다. 값싼 전공의의 노동력을 갈아 넣어 굴러가던 한국 의료시스템이 그대로 무너져 내렸습니다. 결국 꾸역꾸역 굴러오던 병든 의료시스템이 곪아 터진 것입니다. 저 역시 전공의 시절에 하루 2시간 자고 일주일에 100시간 이상 일하는 것을 당연하게 생각했습니다. 이제야 그것이 잘못된 것이었음을 깨닫습니다.

2025년 여름, 한국 의료는 이제 이전으로 돌아가기는 어렵고, 앞으로는 아마도 각자도생의 시대가 될 것 같습니다.

제가 미국으로 떠날 결심을 한 것은 사회나 제도에 불만 같은 거창한 이유가 있었던 것은 아니고 순전히 개인적인 이유였습니다. 물 흐르듯 레지던트를 마치고 공중보건의를 다녀와서 펠로우를 하라니 했고, 대학에 남으라니 남았습니다. 지금 생각해 보면 주체적이지 못한, 시키는 대로 움직이는 허수아비 같은 생활이었습니다. 어느새 마흔이 되어가는 나를 보니 수면제 없이는 잠을 이룰 수 없는, 피폐해질 대로 피폐해진 정신과 육체만 남아 있었습니다. 그때 현실 도피처로 선택한 것이 미국이었습니다.

2011년 3월, 미국행을 결심하고 USMLE 준비를 시작했습니다. 그리고 내 모든 것을 쏟아 부었습니다. 그러나 결국 좌절과 패배감만 안고 2014년 10월, 다시 한국으로 돌아왔습니다. 그 후 하루하루 정신없이 살다 보니 10여 년이 훌쩍 지나버렸습니다. 미국의사 도전과 실패는 제 인생에서 가장 뼈아픈 경험입니다. 당시에는 힘들고 예민해져서 아내와 많이 싸우기도 했지만, 뒤돌아보니 미국에서 가족과 함께 보냈던 시간이 가장 행복했다는 것을 이제는 알겠습니다.

제가 가장 존경하고 부러워하는 사람은 미국에 정착한 선생님들입니다. 물론 그분들도 나름대로 힘든 일들이 있겠지만, 제 입장에서는 가보지 못한 길이라 더욱 부러운 마음이 드는 것 같습니다. 이제는 이런 부끄럽고 고통스러운 기억을 추억으로 만들어 보려고 합니다.

주변에 성공담은 쉽게 찾아볼 수 있습니다. 안 좋은 스펙을 극복하고 불굴의 의지로 매치된 이야기, 언어장벽을 극복하고 미국 병원에서 레지던트 과정을 무사히 마친 이야기, 미국에 정착해서 일가를 이룬 이야기들 말입니다. 그러나 저처럼 실패한 선생님들도 많을 텐데, 실패한 이야기는 잘 들리지 않습니다. 성공 스토리는 자랑스러운 일이므로 많이 소개되지만 실패한 이야기는 묻히기 때문이 아닐까 생각합니다. 그래서 용기를 내서 제 이야기를 해보려고 합니다. 이 이야기가 미국행을 생각하는 의대생이나 선생님들께 혹여 도움이 될 수도 있지 않을까 싶어서 부끄럽지만 제가 USMLE를 준비한 과정, 인터뷰, 미국연수와 미국생활 그리고 NIW 영주권을 취득한 과정을 소개합니다. 아무쪼록 미국행을 준비하시는 의대생과 의사 선생님들께 행운이 함께하기를 기원합니다. 끝으로 책이 나오기까지 도움을 주신 동국대학교 출판문화원 박기련 대표와 관계자 여러분께 감사를 전합니다.

2025년 12월

동국대학교일산병원 소화기내과 은종렬

나아갈 결심

모든 일에는 동기가 가장 중요한 것 같다. 2002년 내과전문의를 취득하고 보건소에서 보낸 공중보건의 시절은 난생처음 경험해 보는 황금 같은 휴식기였다. 월드컵 분위기를 온전히 즐겼고 집사람을 만나 결혼도 했다. 너무 심심해서 USMLE(United States Medical Licensing Examination)를 잠시 생각했던 적이 있다. 그러나 동기와 목적이 전혀 없다 보니 접수의 벽을 넘지 못하고 포기했다. 3년간의 공중보건의를 마치고 자연스럽게 모교 병원에 전임의로 복귀했다. 시키는 대로 전임강사가 되고 조교수가 되었다. 같이 펠로우를 한 선생님들은 봉직의를 거쳐 개업의의 길을 가고 있었다. 그렇게 인생과 진로에 대한 고민 없이 대충 살던 나는 인생의 난관에 봉착했다.

나의 개인사를 일일이 설명할 필요는 없을 것 같다. 다만 심신은 피폐해졌고, 수면제 없이는 잠을 이룰 수 없는 지경이 되었다. 그때의 소원은 병원을 떠나는 것이었다. 일반 직장생활도 다르지 않겠지만 인간관계로 얽혀 있는 좁은 지역 의사 사회에서 매끄럽게 사직이나 이직을 하는 것도 중요했다. 물론 나의 사직 과정이 매끄러웠던 것은 아니다.

탈출구로 생각한 것이 USMLE와 미국연수였다. 시험을 봐야겠다고 결심한 때가 2011년 3월이다. 퍼스트 에이드First Aid Step 1을 구입해서 훑어보기 시작했다. 이번에는 공중보건의 때와는 다르게 포기하지 않았고 점점 가속이 붙었다. 미국연수 준비도 병행하고, 영주권도 알아보면서 시험공부를 해야 했기 때문에 매우 바쁜 한 해를 보냈다.

당시 내년(2012년)에 연수를 가겠다고 선언한 것만으로 나는 대역 죄인이 되었다. 그래도 어쨌든 나는 병원생활과 연수 준비를 함께 해야 했다. 꾸역꾸역 병원생활을 버티고 2012년 2월 25일 금요일 오전, 마지막 진료를 하고 28일 미국행 비행기에 몸을 실었다.

큰 산,
USMLE 접수

결심하고 나면 다음으로 넘어야 하는 큰 산이 접수다. 준비할 서류도 많고 막막할 수도 있지만 본인의 결심이 확고하다면 이후는 하나씩 헤쳐 나가면 되는 것 같다. 역사가 깊은 정보공유 사이트 usmlekorea.com에서 필요한 정보를 대부분 얻을 수 있었다. 요즘도 가끔 들어가는데, 그냥 OB들의 생활을 엿보면서 미국에 정착한 선생님들을 마음속으로 부러워하다가 나온다. 지금 준비하려는 선생님들도 usmlekorea.com에서 도움을 받아 차근차근 준비해 나가면 될 것 같다. 필요한 자료는 자료실에 대부분 있다. 맨 상단을 클릭하면 이렇게 접수 관련 자료들이 모여 있다.

시험 접수의 첫 단계는 www.ecfmg.org에 들어가서 USMLE ID와 임시 비밀번호를 받는 것이다. 다음은 사이트 첫 화면이다.

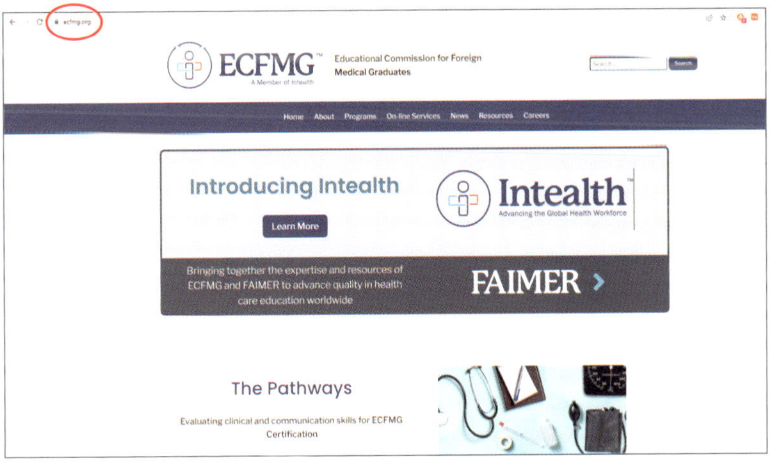

사이트 하단에 있는 IWA를 클릭하여 접수 절차를 밟는다.

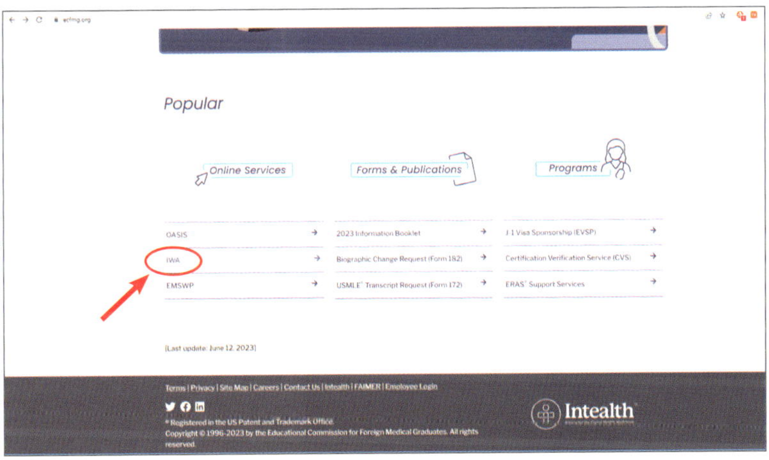

USMLE/ECFMG ID를 받기 위해서는 아래 표시된 부분을 클릭하고 기본 정보를 입력해야 한다.

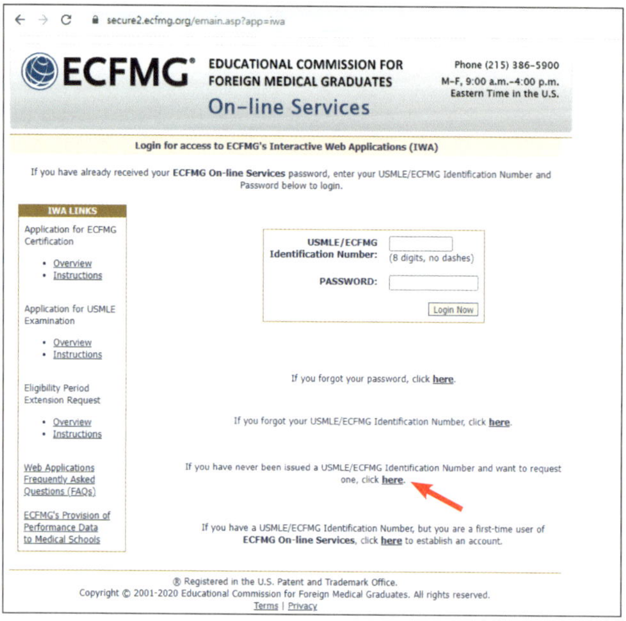

입력하고 하루 정도 기다리면 이메일로 ID를 받을 수 있다.

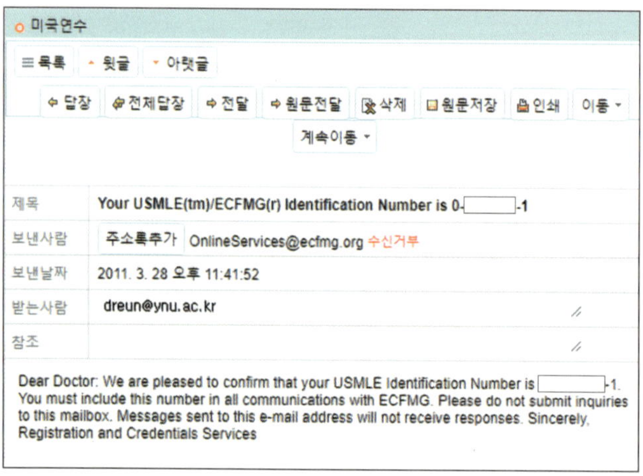

이제 본격적으로 온라인 지원서를 작성한다.

입력하다 보면 본인 학교가 인정 학교인지 묻는데, 우리나라 의과대학은 모두 Yes로 표기하면 된다. 인정 의대인지는 아이콘을 클릭해서 확인하면 알 수 있다.

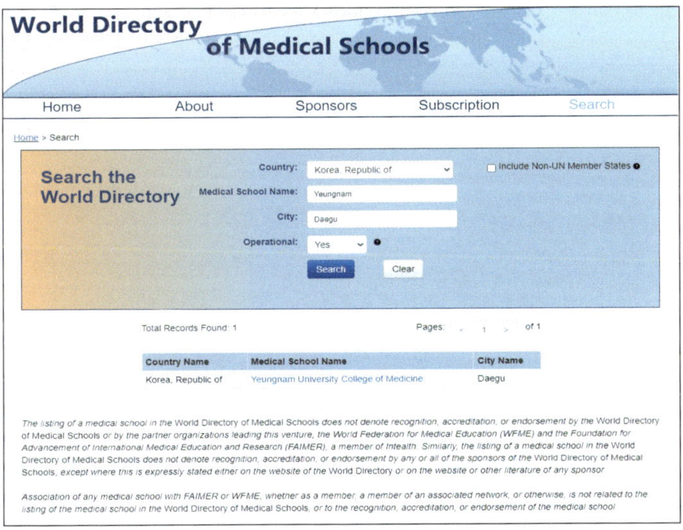

이렇게 입력을 완료했다.

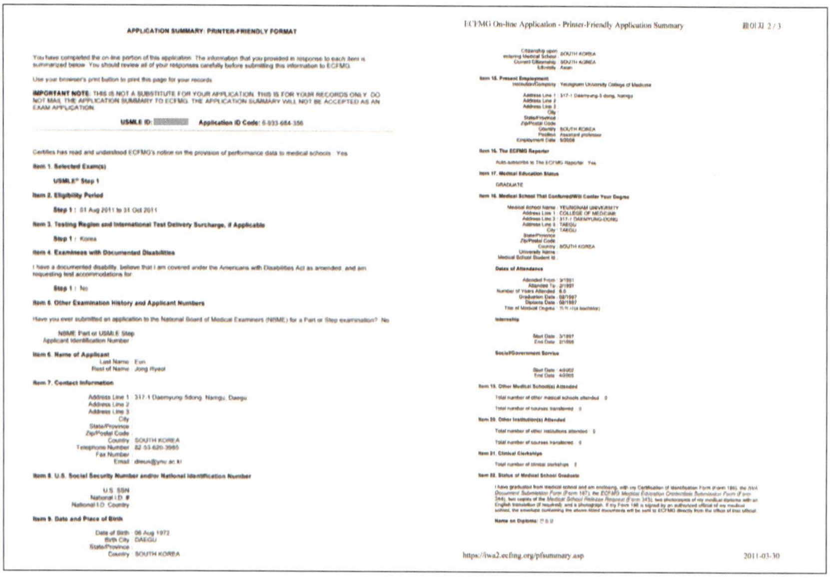

APPLICATION SUMMARY: PRINTER-FRIENDLY FORMAT

You have completed the on-line portion of this application. The information that you provided in response to each item is summarized below. You should review all of your responses carefully before submitting this information to ECFMG.

Use your browser's print button to print this page for your records.

IMPORTANT NOTE: THIS IS NOT A SUBSTITUTE FOR YOUR APPLICATION. THIS IS FOR YOUR RECORDS ONLY. DO NOT MAIL THE APPLICATION SUMMARY TO ECFMG. THE APPLICATION SUMMARY WILL NOT BE ACCEPTED AS AN EXAM APPLICATION.

USMLE ID: ▒▒▒▒ **Application ID Code:** 5-933-684-356

Certifies has read and understood ECFMG's notice on the provision of performance data to medical schools : Yes

Item 1. Selected Exam(s)

USMLE® Step 1

Item 2. Eligibility Period

Step 1 : 01 Aug 2011 to 31 Oct 2011

Item 3. Testing Region and International Test Delivery Surcharge, if Applicable

Step 1 : Korea

Item 4. Examinees with Documented Disabilities

I have a documented disability, believe that I am covered under the Americans with Disabilities Act as amended, and am requesting test accommodations for:

Step 1 : No

Item 5. Other Examination History and Applicant Numbers

Have you ever submitted an application to the National Board of Medical Examiners (NBME) for a Part or Step examination? No

NBME Part or USMLE Step
Applicant Identification Number

Item 6. Name of Applicant

Last Name : Eun
Rest of Name : Jong Ryeol

Item 7. Contact Information

Address Line 1 : 317-1 Daemyung-5dong, Namgu, Daegu
Address Line 2 :
Address Line 3 :
City :
State/Province :
Zip/Postal Code :
Country : SOUTH KOREA
Telephone Number : 82-53-620-3985
Fax Number :
Email : dreun@ynu.ac.kr

Item 8. U.S. Social Security Number and/or National Identification Number

U.S. SSN
National I.D. #
National I.D. Country

Item 9. Date and Place of Birth

Date of Birth : 06 Aug 1972
Birth City : DAEGU
State/Province :
Country : SOUTH KOREA

ECFMG On-line Application - Printer-Friendly Application Summary 페이지 2 / 3

Citizenship upon entering Medical School : SOUTH KOREA
Current Citizenship : SOUTH KOREA
Ethnicity : Asian

Item 15. Present Employment

Institution/Company : Yeungnam University College of Medicine

Address Line 1 : 317-1 Daemyung-5 dong, Namgu
Address Line 2 :
Address Line 3 :
City :
State/Province :
Zip/Postal Code :
Country : SOUTH KOREA
Position : Assistant professor
Employment Date : 9/2006

Item 16. The ECFMG Reporter

Auto-subscribe to The ECFMG Reporter : Yes

Item 17. Medical Education Status

GRADUATE

Item 18. Medical School That Conferred/Will Confer Your Degree

Medical School Name : YEUNGNAM UNIVERSITY
Address Line 1 : COLLEGE OF MEDICINE
Address Line 2 : 317-1 DAEMYUNG-DONG
Address Line 3 : TAEGU
City : TAEGU
State/Province :
Zip/Postal Code :
Country : SOUTH KOREA
University Name :
Medical School Student Id :

Dates of Attendance

Attended From : 3/1991
Attended To : 2/1997
Number of Years Attended : 6.0
Graduation Date : 02/1997
Diploma Date : 02/1997
Title of Medical Degree : 의학사(a bachelor)

Internship

Start Date : 3/1997
End Date : 2/1998

Social/Government Service

Start Date : 4/2002
End Date : 4/2005

Item 19. Other Medical School(s) Attended

Total number of other medical schools attended : 0

Total number of courses transferred : 0

Item 20. Other Institution(s) Attended

Total number of other institutions attended : 0

Total number of courses transferred : 0

Item 21. Clinical Clerkships

Total number of clinical clerkships : 2

Item 22. Status of Medical School Graduate

I have graduated from medical school and am enclosing, with my Certification of Identification Form (Form 186), the IWA Document Submission Form (Form 187), the ECFMG Medical Education Credentials Submission Form (Form 344), two copies of the Medical School Release Request (Form 345), two photocopies of my medical diploma with an English translation (if required), and a photograph. If my Form 186 is signed by an authorized official of my medical school, the envelope containing the above-listed documents will be sent to ECFMG directly from the office of that official.

Name on Diploma: 은종열

https://iwa2.ecfmg.org/pfsummary.asp 2011-03-30

입력한 내용은 다음과 같다.

Item 1. USMLE step 1
Item 2. Eligibility Period Step 1: 01 Aug 2011 to 31 Oct 2011 (3개월 구간설정)
Item 3. Testing Region and International Test Delivery Surcharge, if Applicable
  Step 1: Korea (시험 장소는 한국으로 선택)
Item 4. Examinees with Documented Disabilities No (장애가 없으므로 No)
Item 5. Other Examination History and Applicant Numbers
  Have you ever submitted and application to the National Board of Medical Examiners (NBME) for a Part of Step examinations? No
Item 6. Name of Applicant
  Last Name: Eun
  Rest of Name: Jong Ryeol
Item 7. Contact Information
  Address LIne 1: 317-1 Daemyung-5dong, Namgu, Daegu
  Address Line 2:
  Address Line 3:
  City: (시티 기입 안 했다고 수정 메일 받았음)

State/Province:
Zip/Postal Code:
Country: SOUTH KOREA
Telephone: 82-53-620-3985
Fax number:
Email: dreun@ynu.ac.kr (입력한 이메일로 연락이 옴)

Item 8. U.S. Social Security Number and/or National Identification Number
U.S.SSN: (SSN 없으므로 비워둔)
National I.D. #:
National I.D.Country:

Item 9. Date and Place of Birth
Date of Birth: 06 Aug 1972
Birth of City: DAEGU
State/Province:
Country: SOUTH KOREA

Item 10 - 14. Other Biographic info
Gender: Male
Native Language: Korean
Other Languages Spoken:
Citizenship at Birth: SOUTH KOREA
Citizenship upon entering Medical School: SOUTH KOREA
Current Citizenship: SOUTH KOREA
Ethnicity: Asian

Item 15. Present Employment
Institution/Company: Yeungnam University College of Medicine
Address Line 1: 317-1 Daemyung-5dong, Namgu
Address Line 2:
Address Line 3:
City: (시티 누락되었다고 이메일 받음)
State/Province:
Zip/Postal Code:
Country: SOUTH KOREA
Position: Assistant professor
Employment Date: 09/2006

Item 16. The ECFMG Reporter
Auto-subscribe to The ECFMG Reporter: Yes

Item 17. Medical Education Status
GRADUATE (졸업한 상태이므로 GRADUATE)

Item 18. Medical School That Conferred/Will Confer Your Degree
Medical School Name: YEUNGNAM UNIVERSITY
Address Line 1: COLLEGE OF MEDICINE

Address Line 2: 317-1 DAEMYUNG-DONG
ADDRESS LINE 3: DAEGU
City: DAEGU
State/Province:
Zip/Postal Code:
Country: SOUTH KOREA
University Name:
Medical School Student Id:
Dates of Attendance
Attended From: 3/1991
Attended to: 2/1997
Number of Years Attended: 6.0
Graduation Date: 02/1997
Diploma Date: 02/1997
Title of Medical Degree: 의학사(a bachelor)
Internship
Start Date: 3/1997
End Date: 2/1998
Social/Government Service
Start Date: 4/2002
End Date: 4/2005
Item 19. Other Medical School(s) Attended
Total number of other medical schools attended: 0
Total number of courses transferred: 0
Item 20. Other Institution(s) Attended
Total number of other institutions attended: 0
Total number of courses transferred: 0
Item 21. Clinical Clerkships
Total number of clinical clerkships: 2
Item 22. Status of Medical School Graduate

I have graduated from medical school and am enclosing with my Certification of Identification Form (Form 186), the *IWA Document Submission Form* (Form 187); the *ECFMG Medical Education Credentials Submission Form* (Form 344); two copies of the *Medical School Release Request* (Form 345); two photocopies of my medical diploma with an English translation (if required): and a photograph. If my Form 186 is signed by an authorized official of my medical school, the envelope containing the above-listed documents will be sent to ECFMG directly from the office of that official.

Name on Diploma: 은종렬

* Form 186 (상기 출력한 것), 그 외 Form 187, Form 344, Form 345, 의학사 학위증 2부, 성적표, 증명사진이 필요하며, 상기 서류에 의과대학 공식 사인을 받아서 ECFMG로 보내라는 내용이다.

입력을 마치면 마지막에 결제창이 뜬다. 이제부터 단계마다 돈이 많이 들어간다.

ECFMG On-line Application - Printer-Friendly Application Summary 페이지 3 / 3

Item 23. Certification By Applicant

Certifies has met requirements and has read and understood materials . Yes

Summary of Fees

Step 1		
Examination Fee	$780.00	
International Test Delivery Surcharge (Korea)	$170.00	
Total Step 1 Fees		$950.00
Total Due		**$950.00**

결제를 끝으로 온라인 지원서 신청을 마쳤다. 2011년 3월 30일이었다. 온라인 접수되었다는 이메일을 받았다. 이제 심사를 기다리는 시간이다. 진행 상황은 오아시스On-Line Application Status and Information에서 확인할 수 있다는 메일이 온다.

제목	Application for ECFMG Certification
보낸사람	주소록추가 onlineservices@ecfmg.org 수신거부
보낸날짜	2011. 3. 29 오전 10:20:37
받는사람	dreun@ynu.ac.kr
참조	

Dear Doctor: We are pleased to confirm that your Application for ECFMG Certification has been completed and received by ECFMG. A summary of your Application for ECFMG Certification can be accessed using the On-Line Applicant Status and Information System (OASIS), available from the ECFMG website at www.ecfmg.org You may now proceed with the Interactive Web Applications (IWA) for the USMLE examination(s). Please do not submit inquiries to this mailbox. Messages sent to this e-mail address will not receive responses. Sincerely, Registration and Credentials Services

다음날, 주소에 시티City를 쓰지 않았다고 바로 이메일을 받았다. 하나라도 빠지면 진행이 되지 않는다.

제목	0- **No city**
보낸사람	주소록추가 Frommer, Debbie<DFrommer@ECFMG.org> 수신거부
보낸날짜	2011. 3. 30 오후 11:27:54
받는사람	dreun@ynu.ac.kr<dreun@ynu.ac.kr>

March 30, 2011

Dear Dr. Eun,

ECFMG has received your on-line USMLE Step 1 application, submitted 3/30/11. It appears that your address is incomplete. You entered:

317-1 Daemyung-5dong, Namgu, Daegu
SOUTH KOREA

You have neglected to include the City.

It is essential to have a complete address of record to ensure that you receive all future correspondence and documents from ECFMG.

Please respond to this email with the necessary information to enter a complete address for your records. Once the information is received, processing will continue on your Step 2 CK application. Thank you.

Sincerely,
Debbie Frommer
Certification Specialist
ECFMG

시티 칸에 '대구'라고 써 넣었다. 온라인 접수가 잘 되었다는 이메일을 받았다.

제목	**Your USMLE(tm)/ECFMG(r) Identification Number is 0**
보낸사람	주소록추가 OnlineServices@ecfmg.org 수신거부
보낸날짜	2011. 3. 31 오후 9:56:31
받는사람	dreun@ynu.ac.kr
참조	

Dear Doctor: We are pleased to confirm that the On-Line part of your USMLE Step 1 application (Application Identification Code 6-) has been received by ECFMG. Your USMLE/ECFMG Identification Number is listed in the Subject line of this message. You must use this number in all communications with ECFMG Once your application has been reviewed, ECFMG will notify you of the outcome of your application. ECFMG typically processes on-line USMLE applications within 3 weeks of receipt of both the on-line part and the Certification of Identification Form (Form 186). You may track the status of your application by using ECFMG's On-line Applicant Status and Information System (OASIS). Access OASIS on the ECFMG website at oasis.ecfmg.org. Please do not submit inquiries to this mailbox. Messages sent to this e-mail address will not receive responses. Sincerely, Registration and Credentials Services

<필요한 서류>

1) 의학사 학위증Eui Hak Sa Diploma

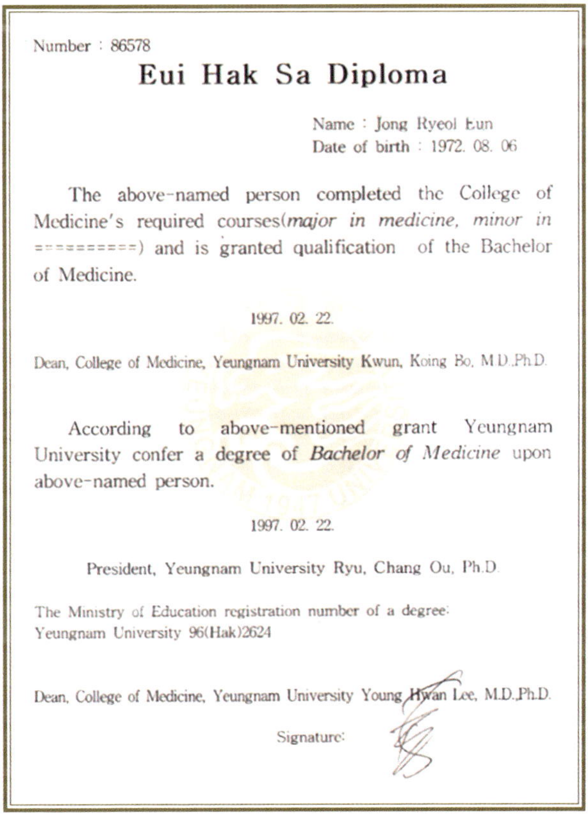

Number : 86578

Eui Hak Sa Diploma

Name : Jong Ryeol Eun
Date of birth : 1972. 08. 06

The above-named person completed the College of Medicine's required courses(*major in medicine, minor in* ==========) and is granted qualification of the Bachelor of Medicine.

1997. 02. 22.

Dean, College of Medicine, Yeungnam University Kwun, Koing Bo, M.D.,Ph.D.

According to above-mentioned grant Yeungnam University confer a degree of *Bachelor of Medicine* upon above-named person.

1997. 02. 22.

President, Yeungnam University Ryu, Chang Ou, Ph.D.

The Ministry of Education registration number of a degree:
Yeungnam University 96(Hak)2624

Dean, College of Medicine, Yeungnam University Young Hwan Lee, M.D.,Ph.D.

Signature:

2) 성적증명서 Transcript

성적증명서는 학장님 서명이 필요하다.

ISSUE NO. : 117675
DATE OF ISSUE : MARCH 08, 2013

YEUNGNAM UNIVERSITY
280 Daehak-Ro, Gyeongsan, Gyeongbuk 712-749, Republic of Korea

ACADEMIC RECORD

NAME : EUN JONG RYEOL	DATE OF BIRTH : AUGUST 06, 1972	SEX : MALE
DATE OF (TRANSFERRED)ADMISSION : MARCH 02, 1991	DATE OF GRADUATION : FEBRUARY 22, 1997	

COLLEGE OF MEDICINE/DEPARTMENT OF MEDICINE

DEGREE : BACHELOR OF MEDICAL SCIENCE

COURSES : DESCRIPTIVE TITLE	*GR	CR	COURSES : DESCRIPTIVE TITLE	*GR	CR
- 2ND SEMESTER 1993 -			PEDIATRICS	87	3
ANATOMY	76	9	PLASTIC SURGERY	91	2
BEHAVIORAL SCIENCE	86	2	PSYCHIATRY	92	3
BIOCHEMISTRY	80	10	SURGERY	90	4
EMBRYOLOGY	86	1	THERAPEUTIC RADIOLOGY	92	1
HISTOLOGY	83	5	THORACIC SURGERY	96	2
MICROBIOLOGY	91	9	UROLOGY	93	2
NEUROANATOMY	78	3			
PARASITOLOGY	92	2	- 2ND SEMESTER 1996 -		
PHYSIOLOGY	84	10	ANESTHEESIOLOGY CLINICAL PRACTICUM	70	1
			CLINICAL PATHOLOGY CLINICAL PRACTICUM	84	1
- 2ND SEMESTER 1994 -			CLINICAL PRACTICE OF EMERGENCY MEDICINE	90	1
CLINICAL PATHOLOGY	83	4	CLINICO-PATHOLOGIC CONFERENCE	95	2
DENTISTRY	93	1	DERMATOLOGY CLINICAL PRACTICUM	92	1
DEPARTMENT OF DIAGNOSTIC RADIOLOGY	89	1	DIAGNOSTIC RADIOLOGY CLINICAL PRACTICUM	90	1
DIAGNOSTIC RADIOLOGY	74	1	E.N.T CLINICAL PRACTICE	81	1
FORENSIC MEDICINE	90	1	INTERNAL MEDICINE CLINICAL PRACTICUM	76	7
GENERAL CONSIDERATIONS OF SURGERY	87	2	NEURO SURGERY PRACTICE	93	2
INTERNAL MEDICINE	87	8	NEUROLOGY CLINICAL PRACTICUM	98	1
NEURO SURGERY	94	1	OBSTETRICS CLINICAL GYNECOLOGY CLINICAL	75	3
NEUROSCIENCE	80	2	PRACTICUM		
OBSTETRICS & GYNECOLOGY	86	2	OPTHALMOLOGY CLINICAL PRACTICUM	82	1
ORTHOPEDIC SURGERY CLINIC	87	1	ORTHOPEDIC SURGERY CLINICAL PRACTICUM	81	2
PATHOLOGY	92	12	PEDIATRICS CLINICAL PRACTICUM	79	3
PEDIATRICS	86	3	PLASTIC SURGERY CLINICAL PRACTICUM	87	1
PHARMACOLOGY	90	8	PREVENTIVE MEDICINE & PUBLIC HEALTH LABORATORY	83	1
PHYSICAL DIAGNOSIS	83	2	PSYCHIATRY CLINICAL PRACTICUM	85	2
PREVENTIVE MEDICINE	89	8	PUBLIC HEALTH LAW	82	1
PSYCHIATRY	90	2	SURGERY CLINICAL PRACTICUM	82	5
SURGERY	85	2	THERAPEUTIC RADIOLOGY CLINICAL PRACTICUM	94	1
THERAPEUTIC RADIOLOGY	84	1	THORACIC SURGERY CLINICAL PRACTICUM	87	1
			UROLOGY CLINICAL PRACTICUM	89	1
- 2ND SEMESTER 1995 -					
ANESTHESIOLOGY	88	2	TOTAL OF EARNED CREDITS : 191/160		
DEPARTMENT OF DIAGNOSTIC RADIOLOGY	94	1	GPA : 3.40/4.50		
DERMATOLOGY	86	2	AVERAGE : 85.83/100		
E. N. T	87	2	RANK IN HIS/HER DEPARTMENT : 8/68		
INTERNAL MEDICINE	87	4			
NEURO SURGERY	92	2			
NEUROSCIENCE	81	1			
OBSTETRICS & GYNECOLOGY	89	3			
OPTHALMOLOGY	86	2			
ORTHOPEDIC SURGERY CLINIC	84	2			

*GR. REFERS TO GRADE
A+(4.5), A(4.0), B+(3.5), B(3.0), C+(2.5), C(2.0), D+(1.5), D(1.0), P(PASSING)
THE LOWEST PASSING GRADE IS D

Dean.
Young Hwan Lee

Seok Kyun Noh, Ph. D.
PRESIDENT

This certificate may be confirmed with the original copy on www.[illegible].com or using the QR code smartphone App.
The Smart verifier can be search or download from the App store or App market.

위·변조방지용
원본대조코드

3) Form 187

ECFMG | **IWA Document Submission Form**
Form 187

Applicant's Name ____
Last First Middle

USMLE®/ECFMG® Identification Number ☐-☐☐☐-☐☐☐-☐

Use this form to submit documents required to complete your USMLE exam application. This form is a transmittal form only and does not substitute for the separate form(s) required for the specific types of submissions outlined below. You must complete and attach any applicable form(s).

The *IWA Document Submission Form* (Form 187) facilitates more efficient processing of your application by ensuring that any additional documents are matched with the on-line part of your application. **Do not send Form 187 if there are no additional documents required to complete your application or if you are submitting a *Certification Statement* (Form 183) or *Certification of Identification Form* (Form 186) only.**

Important Instructions:

Use this form to submit documentation for any one or more of the following reasons:

Medical Education Credentials, including the final medical diploma (Form 344)
Medical School Release Request (Form 345)
Transcript(s) to Document Transferred Credits (Form 344)

- Include your name and USMLE/ECFMG Identification Number in the spaces above.
- Follow the instructions specific to each type of submission outlined on the following pages.
- The completed and signed *IWA Document Submission Form*, any additional form(s), and all required documents must be sent to ECFMG in one envelope.
    - If this includes a *Certification Statement* (Form 183) or a *Certification of Identification Form* (Form 186) that is signed by an authorized official of your medical school, this envelope must be sent to ECFMG directly from the office of that official. See *Applying for Examination* in the ECFMG *Information Booklet*.
    - If this includes a *Certification of Identification Form* (Form 186) that is certified **only** by a Consular Official, Notary Public, First Class Magistrate, or Commissioner of Oaths, this envelope can be sent to ECFMG by you. See *Applying for Examination* in the ECFMG *Information Booklet*.

These forms and documents must be sent to:
IWA
ECFMG
3624 Market Street, 4th Floor
Philadelphia, PA 19104-2685 USA

- Direct questions to ECFMG by telephone at (215) 386-5900.

Form 187

Documents submitted: **(Please circle YES or NO for each document type)**

1. MEDICAL EDUCATION CREDENTIALS **YES NO**

- Access the *ECFMG Medical Education Credentials Submission Form* (Form 344) on the Publications page of the ECFMG website at www.ecfmg.org.
- Complete and sign Form 344 as instructed.
- Attach required documents as instructed on Form 344.
- Attach the completed Form 344 and required documents to the *IWA Document Submission Form* (Form 187).
- Attach your *Certification of Identification Form* (Form 186), if applicable.
- Place all forms and documents required to complete your application in one envelope.
  - If you are required to complete a *Certification of Identification Form* (Form 186) and that form is signed by an authorized official of your medical school, this envelope must be sent to ECFMG directly from the office of that official.
  - If you are required to complete a *Certification of Identification Form* (Form 186) and that form is certified **only** by a Consular Official, Notary Public, First Class Magistrate, or Commissioner of Oaths, this envelope can be sent to ECFMG by you.
  - If you are not required to complete a *Certification of Identification Form* (Form 186), this envelope can be sent to ECFMG by you.

2. MEDICAL SCHOOL RELEASE REQUEST **YES NO**

- Access the *Medical School Release Request* (Form 345) on the Publications page of the ECFMG website at www.ecfmg.org.
- Complete and sign Form 345 as instructed.
- Attach required documents and *ECFMG Medical Education Credentials Submission Form* (Form 344).
- Attach the *IWA Document Submission Form* (Form 187), Form 344, and Form 345, along with all required documents.
- Attach your *Certification of Identification Form* (Form 186), if applicable.
- Place all forms and documents required to complete your application in one envelope.
  - If you are required to complete a *Certification of Identification Form* (Form 186) and that form is signed by an authorized official of your medical school, this envelope must be sent to ECFMG directly from the office of that official.
  - If you are required to complete a *Certification of Identification Form* (Form 186) and that form is certified **only** by a Consular Official, Notary Public, First Class Magistrate, or Commissioner of Oaths, this envelope can be sent to ECFMG by you.
  - If you are not required to complete a *Certification of Identification Form* (Form 186), this envelope can be sent to ECFMG by you.

3. TRANSCRIPT(S) TO DOCUMENT TRANSFERRED CREDITS **YES NO**

- Access the *ECFMG Medical Education Credentials Submission Form* (Form 344) on the Publications page of the ECFMG website at www.ecfmg.org.
- Complete and sign Form 344 as instructed.
- Attach required documents as instructed on Form 344.
- Attach the completed Form 344 and required documents to the *IWA Document Submission Form* (Form 187).
- Attach your *Certification of Identification Form* (Form 186) or *Certification Statement* (Form 183), if required.
- Place all forms and documents required to complete your application in one envelope.
  - If you are required to complete a *Certification Statement* (Form 183) or you are required to complete a *Certification of Identification Form* (Form 186) and that form is signed by an authorized official of your medical school, this envelope must be sent to ECFMG directly from the office of that official.
  - If you are required to complete a *Certification of Identification Form* (Form 186) and that form is certified **only** by a Consular Official, Notary Public, First Class Magistrate, or Commissioner of Oaths, this envelope can be sent to ECFMG by you.
  - If you are not required to complete a *Certification Statement* (Form 183) or a *Certification of Identification Form* (Form 186), this envelope can be sent to ECFMG by you.

Signature (in Latin characters) Date

Form 187, Rev. SEP 2010
Page 2 of 2

4) Form 345

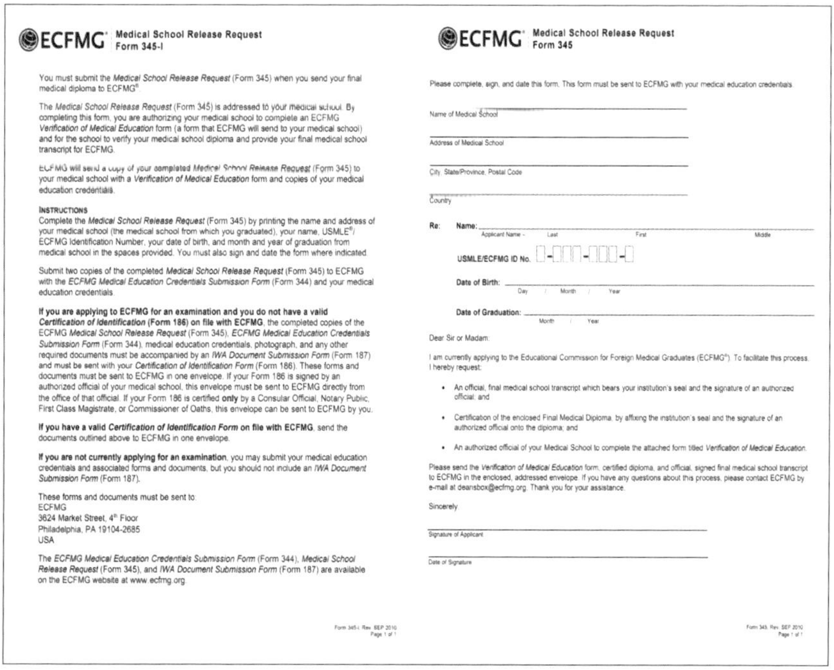

ECFMG® **Medical School Release Request**
Form 345-I

You must submit the *Medical School Release Request* (Form 345) when you send your final medical diploma to ECFMG®.

The *Medical School Release Request* (Form 345) is addressed to your medical school. By completing this form, you are authorizing your medical school to complete an ECFMG *Verification of Medical Education* form (a form that ECFMG will send to your medical school) and for the school to verify your medical school diploma and provide your final medical school transcript for ECFMG.

ECFMG will send a copy of your completed *Medical School Release Request* (Form 345) to your medical school with a *Verification of Medical Education* form and copies of your medical education credentials.

INSTRUCTIONS
Complete the *Medical School Release Request* (Form 345) by printing the name and address of your medical school (the medical school from which you graduated), your name, USMLE®/ECFMG Identification Number, your date of birth, and month and year of graduation from medical school in the spaces provided. You must also sign and date the form where indicated.

Submit two copies of the completed *Medical School Release Request* (Form 345) to ECFMG with the *ECFMG Medical Education Credentials Submission Form* (Form 344) and your medical education credentials.

If you are applying to ECFMG for an examination and you do not have a valid *Certification of Identification* (Form 186) on file with ECFMG, the completed copies of the ECFMG *Medical School Release Request* (Form 345), *ECFMG Medical Education Credentials Submission Form* (Form 344), medical education credentials, photograph, and any other required documents must be accompanied by an *IWA Document Submission Form* (Form 187) and must be sent with your *Certification of Identification Form* (Form 186). These forms and documents must be sent to ECFMG in one envelope. If your Form 186 is signed by an authorized official of your medical school, this envelope must be sent to ECFMG directly from the office of that official. If your Form 186 is certified **only** by a Consular Official, Notary Public, First Class Magistrate, or Commissioner of Oaths, this envelope can be sent to ECFMG by you.

If you have a valid *Certification of Identification Form* on file with ECFMG, send the documents outlined above to ECFMG in one envelope.

If you are not currently applying for an examination, you may submit your medical education credentials and associated forms and documents, but you should not include an *IWA Document Submission Form* (Form 187).

These forms and documents must be sent to:
ECFMG
3624 Market Street, 4th Floor
Philadelphia, PA 19104-2685
USA

The *ECFMG Medical Education Credentials Submission Form* (Form 344), *Medical School Release Request* (Form 345), and *IWA Document Submission Form* (Form 187) are available on the ECFMG website at www.ecfmg.org.

Form 345-I, Rev. SEP 2010
Page 1 of 1

ECFMG® **Medical School Release Request**
Form 345

Please complete, sign, and date this form. This form must be sent to ECFMG with your medical education credentials.

Name of Medical School

Address of Medical School

City, State/Province, Postal Code

Country

Re: Name: ______
Applicant Name - Last / First / Middle

USMLE/ECFMG ID No. □-□□□-□□□-□

Date of Birth: ______
Day / Month / Year

Date of Graduation: ______
Month / Year

Dear Sir or Madam:

I am currently applying to the Educational Commission for Foreign Medical Graduates (ECFMG®). To facilitate this process, I hereby request:

- An official, final medical school transcript which bears your institution's seal and the signature of an authorized official; and
- Certification of the enclosed Final Medical Diploma, by affixing the institution's seal and the signature of an authorized official onto the diploma; and
- An authorized official of your Medical School to complete the attached form titled *Verification of Medical Education*.

Please send the *Verification of Medical Education* form, certified diploma, and official, signed final medical school transcript to ECFMG in the enclosed, addressed envelope. If you have any questions about this process, please contact ECFMG by e-mail at deansbox@ecfmg.org. Thank you for your assistance.

Sincerely,

Signature of Applicant

Date of Signature

Form 345, Rev. SEP 2010
Page 1 of 1

필요한 서류를 준비하여 행정실에 가서 학장님 서명을 받았다. 병원 근처 우체국에서 등기로 ECFMG에 서류를 발송했다. 4월 15일 Form 186을 받았다는 메일을 받았다.

제목	Your USMLE(tm)/ECFMG(r) Identification Number is 0-
보낸사람	주소록추가 OnlineServices@ecfmg.org 수신거부
보낸날짜	2011. 4. 15 오전 3:27:08
받는사람	dreun@ynu.ac.kr
참조	

Dear Doctor: We are pleased to confirm that your Certification of Identification Form (Form 186) has been received by ECFMG. Your USMLE/ECFMG Identification Number is listed in the Subject line of this message. You must use this number in all communications with ECFMG. ECFMG typically processes on-line USMLE applications within 3 weeks of receipt of both the on-line part and the Certification of Identification Form (Form 186). You may track the status of your application by using ECFMG's On-line Applicant Status and Information System (OASIS). Access OASIS on the ECFMG website at oasis.ecfmg.org. Please do not submit inquiries to this mailbox. Messages sent to this e-mail address will not receive responses. Sincerely, Registration and Credentials Services

그런데 4월 29일, 문제가 있어 진행할 수 없다는 이메일을 받았다. 보낸 서류를 ECFMG가 검증verification하기 위해 의과대학으로 보냈는데 답을 받지 못했다고 한다. 의과대학에 검증을 의뢰했는데 회신을 못 받아 진행이 안 된다는 것이다. 돌이켜 보니 접수 과정에서부터 우여곡절이 많았던 것 같다. 내가 다니던 의과대학에서는 USMLE 경험이 거의 없어서 진행에 대해 잘 몰랐던 것 같다. 직접 행정실로 찾아가서 ECFMG로부터 온 우편이 있는지 확인하고 내가 직접 챙길 수밖에 없었다. 바로 의과대학 직인을 받아 발송인을 의과대학으로 해서 ECFMG로 다시 보냈다.

<진행이 안 되고 있다는 이메일>

제목	Your USMLE(tm)/ECFMG(r) Identification Number is 0-1
보낸사람	주소록추가 OnlineServices@ecfmg.org 수신거부
보낸날짜	2011. 4. 29 오전 12:00:49
받는사람	dreun@ynu.ac.kr
참조	

Dear Doctor: ECFMG is unable to process your recent USMLE application. Please refer to the attached letter for details on the specific reason the application can not be processed and for instructions on reapplication. Registration and Credentials Services ECFMG

· 첨부파일 일괄다운로드	CIFDemotionLetter.pdf (55.52KB) 다운로드

<진행이 안 되는 이유 상세 설명>

ECFMG® EDUCATIONAL COMMISSION FOR FOREIGN MEDICAL GRADUATES

3624 Market Street
Philadelphia PA 19104-2685 USA
215-386-5900 | 215-386-9767 Fax
www.ecfmg.org

April 28, 2011

Jong Ryeol Eun
Dept. of Internal Medicine
Yeungnam Univ. Hosp. 8th fl.
317-1 Daemyung-5dong, Namgu, Daegu City
SOUTH KOREA

USMLE™/ECFMG® Identification Number:

Dear Dr. Eun:

The Educational Commission for Foreign Medical Graduates (ECFMG®) has received your final medical diploma.

ECFMG medical education credential policy requires that ECFMG send a copy of the final medical diploma to the medical school for verification by the appropriate officials. When ECFMG sends your medical diploma to the medical school for verification, ECFMG will request the medical school to include your final medical school transcript when the school returns the verification of your medical diploma to ECFMG. Your credentials will not be considered complete until ECFMG receives verification of your medical diploma and final medical school transcript directly from the medical school.

ECFMG wrote to your medical school on April 28, 2011 to request verification of the diploma and a final medical school transcript. The request included a copy of the diploma, a photograph of you to assist in identification, a verification form, a copy of your "Medical School Release Request" or the Certification Page from your application and a return envelope addressed to ECFMG.

The medical school has been requested to complete the verification, include your final medical school transcript, in English if possible, and return the form and documents to ECFMG as soon as possible. ECFMG will not send the verification form to the applicant for transmittal to the medical school and ECFMG will accept the verification only if it is received directly from the medical school.

Once the verification has been received by ECFMG, you will be notified. If the transcript provided by your medical school is not in English, ECFMG will have the transcript translated into English by an independent translation service and will charge your ECFMG financial account US $205 for the translation. If ECFMG does not receive a response within the anticipated time period, subsequent verification requests will be sent and you will be notified.

You can check the status of your medical education credentials through the ECFMG On-line Applicant Status and Information System (OASIS) on the ECFMG website at www.ecfmg.org.

Sincerely,

Medical Education Credentials Department
By: RKALULE

Form N341-AS
Rev. JUL 2005

ECFMG | EDUCATIONAL COMMISSION FOR FOREIGN MEDICAL GRADUATES | 3624 Market Street Philadelphia PA 19104-2685 USA 215-386-5900 | 215-386-9767 Fax www.ecfmg.org

NOTICE OF DEFICIENT CERTIFICATION OF IDENTIFICATION FORM

USMLE™/ECFMG® Identification Number: 0-825-176-1

April 28, 2011

Dr. Jong Ryeol Eun
Dept. of Internal Medicine
Yeungnam Univ. Hosp. 8th fl.
317-1 Daemyung-5dong, Namgu, Daegu City
SOUTH KOREA

Dear Doctor:

The Educational Commission for Foreign Medical Graduates (ECFMG) is unable to process the Certification of Identification Form (Form 186) for your on-line application submitted March 30, 2011 for the reason described below.

Your Certification of Identification Form (Form 186) must be signed by an appropriate official as outlined below.

Therefore, to be registered for the USMLE Step you requested, you must reapply by submitting a new Certification of Identification Form (Form 186) completed in its entirety.

If you are a medical school graduate, your Certification of Identification Form (Form 186) must be signed and dated, in ink, by a Consular Official, First Class Magistrate, Notary Public or Commissioner of Oaths. The official's formal title and institution must also be listed. English translations must be provided for all information that is not in English. The stamp or seal must cover a portion of your photograph **and** the Certification of Identification Form (Form 186).

If you are having your Certification of Identification Form (Form 186) certified by the medical school from which you graduated, your Certification of Identification Form (Form 186) must be signed and dated, in ink, by an authorized official of your medical school. The signature of the medical school official must match an authorized signature that is on record at ECFMG. The Certification of Identification Form (Form 186) must also contain the official seal of the medical school. **The seal must cover a portion of your photograph and the Certification of Identification Form (Form 186).** The medical school seal must match the seal for your medical school that is on record at ECFMG. The official's title and institution must also be listed.

- Sign and date the Certification of Identification Form (Form 186) in the presence of an authorized official of your medical school. The medical school official must sign and date the Certification of Identification Form (Form 186) and provide his/her name, official title, and the institution name. The signature of the medical school official must match an authorized signature that is on record at ECFMG. The official must place the medical school seal so that it covers a portion of your photograph and the Certification of Identification Form (Form 186). The signature of the medical school official must be current; the official must have signed the Certification of Identification Form (Form 186) within four months of the date that it is received at ECFMG.

- Have the medical school official who certified the Certification of Identification Form (Form 186) send the form directly to ECFMG.

ECFMG must be able to determine that the Certification of Identification Form (Form 186) was sent directly from the office of the medical school official who certified the Certification of Identification Form (Form 186). If ECFMG, in its judgment, determines that the Certification of Identification Form (Form 186) may not have been sent directly from the office of the medical school official who certified the Certification of Identification Form (Form 186), it will not be accepted.

ECFMG has recently sent a request to your medical school for a list of the medical school officials who are currently authorized to certify Certification of Identification Forms (Form 186) and Certification Statements (Form 183). Contact your medical school to explain the importance that the school provide the list of authorized medical school officials to ECFMG immediately. If your medical school has any questions concerning the certification of Form 186, the school should contact ECFMG at deansbox@ecfmg.org. This email address is for the use of medical school officials only.

To be registered, you must submit a new Certification of Identification Form (Form 186) with any appropriate documentation as outlined above. You can do this by accessing the Interactive Web Application (IWA) at www.ecfmg.org. Under On-Line Services, click on IWA. At the next screen enter your USMLE/ECFMG Identification Number and your on-line services password. Next, choose **Login Now**. Under Print/ Reprint Documents, choose *Reprint your Certification of Identification Form (Form 186)*.

We will hold the on-line part of your application until March 30, 2012. This deadline date is twelve months from the **original** date the CIF was created. If we do not receive a properly completed Certification of Identification Form (Form 186) by **March 30, 2012** any application submitted up to **March 30, 2012** will be rejected.

If the on-line part of your application includes a request to extend a USMLE eligibility period, the properly completed Certification of Identification Form (Form 186) must be received and processed by the published deadline date, which is earlier than twelve months. You may review the current ECFMG *Information Booklet* and USMLE *Bulletin of Information* from the ECFMG website at www.ecfmg.org.

Should you require further assistance, please contact ECFMG Applicant Information Services at info@ecfmg.org or call (215) 386-5900.

Sincerely,

Registration and Credentials Services

접수 과정에서 의과대학 행정실을 자주 들락거렸다. 그나마 우리 학교는 의과대학 행정실이 병원과 붙어 있어서 다행이었다. 학교를 멀리 떠난 사람은 행정실과의 소통에 상당히 불편할 수 있겠다는 생각이 들었다. 수시로 행정실에 드나들면서 행정실 직원에게 ECFMG로부터 오는 서류가 누락되지 않도록 확인해 달라고 부탁했다. 6월 21일 Form 186이 제대로 접수되었고, 7월 5일 접수가 수락accept되었다는 메일을 받았다. 접수에 걸린 시간은 꼬박 3개월이었다.

<드디어 Form 186을 받았다는 이메일>

제목	Your USMLE(tm)/ECFMG(r) Identification Number is 0-
보낸사람	주소록추가 OnlineServices@ecfmg.org 수신거부
보낸날짜	2011. 6. 21 오전 2:55:26
받는사람	dreun@ynu.ac.kr
참조	

Dear Doctor: We are pleased to confirm that your Certification of Identification Form (Form 186) has been received by ECFMG. Your USMLE/ECFMG Identification Number is listed in the Subject line of this message. You must use this number in all communications with ECFMG. ECFMG typically processes on-line USMLE applications within 3 weeks of receipt of both the on-line part and the Certification of Identification Form (Form 186). You may track the status of your application by using ECFMG's On-line Applicant Status and Information System (OASIS). Access OASIS on the ECFMG website at oasis.ecfmg.org. Please do not submit inquiries to this mailbox. Messages sent to this e-mail address will not receive responses. Sincerely, Registration and Credentials Services

<접수가 수락되었다는 이메일>

제목	Your USMLE(tm)/ECFMG(r) Identification Number is 0-[ ]
보낸사람	주소록추가 OnlineServices@ecfmg.org 수신거부
보낸날짜	2011. 7. 5 오후 11:20:51
받는사람	dreun@ynu.ac.kr
참조	

Dear Doctor: Your Certification of Identification Form submitted 03/30/2011 has been accepted. This form will remain on file and be valid for a period of five years. The validity dates are as follows: 07/05/2011 through 07/05/2016. The Certification of Identification Form is processed independently of the on-line application. Acceptance of the Certification of Identification Form does not automatically guarantee acceptance of the application. Once your application has been reviewed, ECFMG will notify you of the outcome of your application. ECFMG typically processes on-line applications within three weeks of the receipt of both the on-line part and the Certification of Identification Form Processing will now continue on the on-line part of your application. Sincerely, Registration and Credentials Services

<Step 1 신청이 완료되었다는 이메일>

보낸사람	주소록추가 onlineservices@ecfmg.org 수신거부
보낸날짜	2011. 7. 6 오후 10:31:16
받는사람	dreun@ynu.ac.kr
참조	

Dear Doctor:

The processing of your USMLE Step 1 application is complete. You have been registered for the Aug 01, 2011 - Oct 31, 2011 eligibility period in the Korea testing region. ** Please see BELOW for details on the option to submit a request to have the exam results for this Step 1 withheld from your medical school**.

The eligibility period assigned to you for this exam may be different from the one you selected on your application for one of the following reasons:

- If you selected an eligibility period that has already begun and your application was not processed in time to assign the eligibility period you selected, you have been assigned the next eligibility period.

- USMLE policy states that you may not take the same Step more than four times in any 12-month period. If you have already taken this exam and the eligibility period you selected on your application does not comply with these requirements, you have been assigned to the first eligibility period that does meet these requirements.

The National Board of Medical Examiners(r) (NBME(r)) will issue your permit, which contains information on contacting Prometric to schedule a testing appointment. (If your assigned eligibility period begins more than six months from now, your permit will be issued approximately six months before the beginning of your assigned eligibility period.) Only electronic permits will be generated for Step 1/Step 2 CK, applicants will access their electronic permits using ECFMG's Interactive Web Application (IWA). You will not receive a paper permit by postal mail. In about one week you will receive another email from ECFMG to notify you that your permit is available. This message will include instructions for accessing the electronic permit using IWA. Although your permit will be issued by NBME, you should contact ECFMG by email at info@ecfmg.org or by phone or fax if you have questions or concerns about this document. You must print a copy of the electronic permit and bring it to the test center on your exam date. Your permit is a very important document, and you should be careful not to lose it. You cannot schedule your testing appointment or take the exam without it. If you lose your permit, you may print another one by using IWA. Your permit will be available on IWA until the LAST day of your eligibility period. However, ECFMG recommends that you print your permit as soon as it is available to you and keep it in a safe place. Upon accessing your permit, you should check that your name as it appears on the permit is spelled correctly. If the name on your permit is incorrect, you must contact ECFMG immediately. Name changes or corrections to your name must be received and processed by ECFMG no later than seven business days prior to your scheduled testing appointment.

If you cannot take a Step during your assigned three-month eligibility period, you may request an extension. There is a fee for this service. You may request an extension on-line using ECFMG's Interactive Web Application (IWA) or by submitting to ECFMG a completed Request to Extend a USMLE Step 1 / Step 2 CK Eligibility Period (Form 176). For information, access IWA or FORM 176 on the ECFMG website.

For current information on test centers in your testing region, visit the Prometric website at www.prometric.com or contact Prometric. Sample test materials for all Steps and Step Components are available on the USMLE website at www.usmle.org

Please refer to the ECFMG Information Booklet and USMLE Bulletin of Information FOR detailed information on scheduling your testing appointment and taking the exam. BOTH publications are available on the ECFMG website.

Instructions on how to withhold your exam results from your medical school

ACCESS the IWA home page at www.ecfmg.org. SELECT the exam administration for which you want to withhold your exam results from your medical school under "Request to Withhold Exam Results from Medical School". Be sure you read and understand the conditions before you authorize ECFMG to withhold your exam results.

Sincerely,

Registration and Credentials Services

<Step 1 일정을 잡으라는 이메일>

제목	Your Scheduling Permit is Available
보낸사람	주소록추가 onlineservices@ecfmg.org 수신거부
보낸날짜	2011. 7. 9 오후 2:31:30
받는사람	dreun@ynu.ac.kr
참조	

Name: Jong Ryeol Eun
USMLE ID: 0

Your STEP 1 SCHEDULING PERMIT IS NOW AVAILABLE on the ECFMG Interactive Web Applications (IWA) website.

YOU MUST PRINT YOUR SCHEDULING PERMIT AND BRING IT WITH YOU TO THE TEST CENTER ON YOUR SCHEDULED DATE. You will not be able to take the test if you do not bring your Scheduling Permit to the test center. Note: You will NOT receive an orange Scheduling Permit for this exam in the mail.

To access your Scheduling Permit, go to IWA at https://iwa2.ecfmg.org, login, and select "Print/Reprint your USMLE Step 1 Scheduling Permit." Your permit will open in a new browser window. Use your browser's "Print" function to print the permit.

If you have any questions, contact ECFMG Applicant Information Services at info@ecfmg.org or call (215) 386-5900.

Sincerely,

ECFMG

험난했던 접수를 완료했다. Step 1 공부는 계속하고 있었다. 이제 공부에 몰입할 시간이었다. USMLE 과정에서 많은 선생님께 도움을 구했고 내 경험을 전해주기도 했다.

접수와 관련해서 내가 다른 선생님께 답했던 이메일이다.

2012년 6월 27일 (수) 오후 9:33
pch216에게

제 멜은 dreun@ynu.ac.kr을 아직 사용하고 있으나 gmail로 바꾸는 중입니다.
USMLE의 첫 관문이 접수이고, 이 과정이 만만치 않아 Step 0이라고 하기도 합니다.
저도 접수 한 번 reject되고 재접수하여 accept되는 데 3개월 걸렸습니다.
행정실에서 USMLE 접수 경험이 있으면 가장 좋은 데 그렇지 않은 것 같군요.
의학사(Eui-Haksa diploma) 학위증을 발급받는 것과 필요한 양식에 기입 후 학장님 사인을 받는 것이 가장 중요했던 것 같습니다. 학장 사인은 ACGME(?) 등록된 사인과 같지 않으면 reject 당하므로 학장 사인을 받기 전에 담당자에게 어느 학장님 사인이 등록되어 있는지 확인하셔야 합니다(학장이 바뀌면 얼마 후 업데이트 되지만 최근 바뀐 경우는 전임 학장님으로 등록되어 있을 수 있습니다). 그나저나 미국에서 서류 준비하시려면 힘드시겠습니다.
누군가 대신 서류를 준비해 주면 좋을 텐데요. 저는 작년에 준비해서 행정실이 가까이 있어서 몇 번 들락거렸습니다. 학위증 사본을 첨부했던 것 같기도 한데, 저희는 학위증명서를 자동발급기에서 영문 또는 한글로 모두 발급받을 수 있어서 저는 필요할 때마다 수시로 자동발급기에서 발급받고 있습니다. 그나저나 연수기간이 다 되어 가시지 않나요? 교수님들이 USMLE를 생각하시는 게 흔치는 않은 것 같은데 암튼 뜻밖이고 반갑습니다. 저도 아직 갈 길이 멀고 Step 2CS를 시작하려니 막막하기도 하고 그렇습니다. 궁금하신 것 있으면 제가 아는 범위에서 답해 드리겠습니다.

은종렬 올림

미약한 한 걸음
USMLE Step 1

지금은 Step 1이 PASS/FAIL로 바뀐 것 같다. Step 1은 기초의학에 관한 시험이므로 해부학, 생리학, 생화학 등을 다시 공부해야 하는 부담이 있었다. 시작은 막막했다. 우선 퍼스트 에이드First Aid를 구입해서 시작했다. 일기장에 2011년 3월 25일부터 공부를 시작했다고 적혀 있다. 5월 23일에 본격적으로 암기파일을 만들기 시작해, 10월 10일 마지막 파일이 만들어진 것을 보니 공부 기간이 대략 7개월이었던 것 같다.

내분비	2011-05-23 오후 1:03	한컴오피스 한글 ...	16KB
미생물학	2011-05-24 오후 12:34	한컴오피스 한글 ...	29KB
행동과학(문제)	2011-05-27 오전 8:54	한컴오피스 한글 ...	48KB
생화학I	2011-05-30 오전 10:47	한컴오피스 한글 ...	29KB
약리학	2011-05-31 오후 5:28	한컴오피스 한글 ...	22KB
소화기학	2011-06-07 오후 7:24	한컴오피스 한글 ...	24KB
병리학	2011-06-19 오후 2:08	한컴오피스 한글 ...	20KB
순환기	2011-06-19 오후 9:01	한컴오피스 한글 ...	23KB
신경계	2011-06-27 오전 9:24	한컴오피스 한글 ...	37KB
신장학	2011-06-27 오후 3:29	한컴오피스 한글 ...	23KB
비뇨생식계	2011-06-27 오후 4:34	한컴오피스 한글 ...	31KB
생화학II	2011-07-03 오후 2:11	한컴오피스 한글 ...	14KB
행동과학	2011-07-03 오후 5:17	한컴오피스 한글 ...	20KB
발생학	2011-07-04 오후 7:03	한컴오피스 한글 ...	29KB
면역학	2011-07-10 오전 1:06	한컴오피스 한글 ...	25KB
혈액종양	2011-07-17 오후 12:59	한컴오피스 한글 ...	30KB
근골격계	2011-07-18 오후 7:33	한컴오피스 한글 ...	28KB
정신과	2011-07-25 오전 9:07	한컴오피스 한글 ...	27KB
호흡기학	2011-07-30 오후 5:20	한컴오피스 한글 ...	26KB
행동과학(답지)	2011-07-31 오후 7:43	한컴오피스 한글 ...	23KB
생화학II(답지)	2011-08-03 오후 7:15	한컴오피스 한글 ...	27KB
생화학I(답지)	2011-08-05 오후 8:30	한컴오피스 한글 ...	44KB
미생물학(답지)	2011-08-07 오후 4:03	한컴오피스 한글 ...	51KB
면역학(답지)	2011-08-08 오후 8:19	한컴오피스 한글 ...	32KB
FA Q & A 정리	2011-08-15 오후 8:57	한컴오피스 한글 ...	27KB
신경계(답지)	2011-08-24 오후 5:12	한컴오피스 한글 ...	51KB
정신과(답지)	2011-08-25 오전 7:56	한컴오피스 한글 ...	31KB
비뇨생식계(답지)	2011-09-17 오후 11:32	한컴오피스 한글 ...	39KB
Kaplan Qbook 정리	2011-09-22 오후 5:27	한컴오피스 한글 ...	78KB
소화기학(답지)	2011-09-24 오후 10:37	한컴오피스 한글 ...	31KB
UW 정리	2011-09-26 오전 11:59	한컴오피스 한글 ...	262KB
근골격계(답지)	2011-09-26 오후 7:29	한컴오피스 한글 ...	35KB
병리학(답지)	2011-09-27 오후 10:15	한컴오피스 한글 ...	27KB
혈액종양(답지)	2011-09-27 오후 10:17	한컴오피스 한글 ...	35KB
순환기(답지)	2011-09-28 오후 9:36	한컴오피스 한글 ...	30KB
신장학(답지)	2011-09-29 오후 6:14	한컴오피스 한글 ...	28KB
호흡기학(답지)	2011-09-30 오후 10:34	한컴오피스 한글 ...	28KB
약리학(답지)	2011-09-30 오후 11:04	한컴오피스 한글 ...	34KB

계획을 짜고 계획표대로 공부했다. 진료를 마치고 밤에 연구실에 남아 공부했던 기억, 주말에 밤샘했던 기억, 여름휴가 때도 공부했던 기억이 난다. 아무튼 다시는 못할 정도로 열심히 공부했다.

날짜	요일	FA	Kaplan QBOOK
2011-06-11	토	행동과학, 생화학	
2011-06-12	일	발생학	
2011-06-13	월	미생물학	
2011-06-14	화		p87-109
2011-06-15	수		p111-132
2011-06-16	목	면역학	
2011-06-17	금	병리학, 약리학	
2011-06-18	토	순환기학	
2011-06-19	일		p133-185
2011-06-20	월		p187-238
2011-06-21	화	내분비, 소화기	
2011-06-22	수	혈액종양, 근골격	
2011-06-23	목	신경계(1)	
2011-06-24	금	신경계(2)	
2011-06-25	토	정신과	
2011-06-26	일		
2011-06-27	월	신장,비뇨생식,호흡기	
2011-06-28	화		p239-286
2011-06-29	수		p287-331
2011-06-30	목		p333-377
2011-07-01	금		p379-424
2011-07-02	토		p425-446
2011-07-03	일	행동,생화학,발생	
2011-07-04	월	미생물,면역,병리	
2011-07-05	화	약리,순환기,내분비	
2011-07-06	수	소화기,혈종,근골격	
2011-07-07	목	신경계,정신,신장	
2011-07-08	금	비뇨생식,호흡기	

날짜	요일	FA	Kaplan QBOOK	FA Q&A	UW	누적
2011-08-01	월	행동과학			46	46
2011-08-02	화		행동과학	행동과학	46	92
2011-08-03	수	생화학			46	138
2011-08-04	목	생화학			46	184
2011-08-05	금		생화학	생화학	0	184
2011-08-06	토	발생학	발생학	발생학	46	230
2011-08-07	일	미생물학	미생물학	미생물학	46	276
2011-08-08	월	면역학		면역학	46	322
2011-08-09	화		면역학		46	368
2011-08-10	수	병리학			46	414
2011-08-11	목		병리학		46	460
2011-08-12	금			병리학	0	460
2011-08-13	토	약리학	약리학	약리학	46	506
2011-08-14	일	순환기	순환기	순환기	46	552
2011-08-15	월	내분비	내분비	내분비	46	598
2011-08-16	화	소화기			46	644
2011-08-17	수		소화기		46	690
2011-08-18	목			소화기	46	736
2011-08-19	금	혈액종양			0	736
2011-08-20	토		혈액종양	혈액종양	46	782
2011-08-21	일	근골격계	근골격계	근골격계	46	828
2011-08-22	월	신경계			46	874
2011-08-23	화		신경계		46	920
2011-08-24	수			신경계	46	966
2011-08-25	목	정신과			46	1012
2011-08-26	금		정신과	정신과	0	1012
2011-08-27	토	신장학	신장학	신장학	46	1058
2011-08-28	일	생식계	생식계	생식계	46	1104
2011-08-29	월	호흡기	호흡기	호흡기	46	1150
2011-08-30	화			test block1,2,3	46	1196
2011-08-31	수			test block4.5	46	1242
2011-09-01	목			test block6,7	46	1288
2011-09-02	금	순환기보충			0	1288
2011-09-03	토	내분비보충			46	1334
2011-09-04	일	신장학보충			46	1380
2011-09-05	월	생식보충			46	1426
2011-09-06	화	호흡기보충			46	1472
2011-09-07	수	기타보충			46	1518
2011-09-08	목	기타보충			46	1564
2011-09-09	금	기타보충			46	1610

그림 같은 것은 노트를 만들었고, 단답형은 FA 암기파일을 만들었다.

Muscle contraction

근육은 fascicle -> fiber -> myofiber -> myofibril로 이루어진다. Myofibril은 actin(thin) filament와 myosin(thick) filament로 이루어져 있다. Z disc와 Z disc 사이를 sarcomere라 하고, actin과 myosin이 겹치는 부분을 A band, 겹치지 않는 부분을 I band라 한다.

Acetylcholine이 synaptic cleft로 방출되어 sarcolemma의 ACh receptors에 결합하면 action potential이 sarcolemma를 따라 T-tubule 아래로 전파된다. Action potential은 SR의 terminal cistern으로부터 Ca^{2+}을 방출토록 한다(Ryanodine receptor). 방출된 Ca^{2+}은 troponin C에 결합하여 형태변화를 초래하는데, tropomyosin blocking action이 사라지고 actin active sites가 노출되도록 한다. Myosin cross bridges가 actin에 결합하여 actin filaments를 sarcomere center로 당김으로서 근육수축이 일어나는데, 이 과정에는 ATP hydrolysis(->ADP+iP)를 통하여 에너지가 방출된다.

FA Q&A 정리

생화학

1. Xeroderma pigmentosa (AR) - excision repair defect
   -> thymidine dimers repair 장애
2. Citrate: Acetyl-CoA carboxylase를 활성화하고, PFK-1을 억제한다.
   Citrate는 ATP에 의해 억제된다.
3. Methyl group을 전달하는 유일한 아미노산? Methionine
   cf. SAM(S-adenosyl-L-methionine) is a very common methyl group donor.
4. Calcium은 정상적으로 세포밖에 고농도로 유지된다. 세포내에서는 특정구역(mitochondria)에. 만약 세포내로 자유롭게 들어오면 여러 가지 효소들을 활성화시켜 심각한 세포손상을 초래한다.
   문제) 세포내 칼슘농도가 증가할 때 세포손상을 일으키는 기전? enzyme activation
   cf. 활성화되는 enzymes: APTase, phospholipase
5. 변이부위를 확인하는 것? sequencing
6. Linezolid mechanism: **23S rRNA 결합**하여 initiating complex와 상호용하여 단백합성을 방해
7. 50S subunit는 peptide bond를 형성하도록 하는데, 23S rRNA strand에 의해서 수행
8. Hypothalamic hormones 모두는 phospholipase C -> IP3를 통해 작용한다.
   예외, CRH : adenylate cyclaase -> cAMP
9. Calcium-calmodulin complex activates **myosin light chain kinase(MLCK)**.
   -> myosin를 phosphorylation시켜 actin과 결합하도록 한다.
10. F1P -> DHAP(dihydroxyacetone-**phosphate**) + glyceraldehyde
    aldolase B 결핍시 F1P은 liver에 축적되고, free phosphate는 결핍된다.
    phosphate 결핍되면 ATP생성을 못한다.

면역학

11. 면역반응이 더 이상 필요없게 되었을 때 immune response를 약화시키는데 관여하는 cvtokine? TGF-β

카플란 Q북Kaplan Qbook도 구입해서 공부했는데 도움은 별로 안 되었다. 결과적으로 성적이 좋지 않았다. 암기에 치중하고 문제 풀이를 충분히 하지 못했기 때문인 듯하다. 기본 내용들의 암기도 필요하지만, 시험은 종합적 사고를 요구하는 임상 문제에 가까운 것들이어서 최대한 짧은 시간에 암기를 마치고 많은 시간을 문제풀이를 통해 이해력과 실전 능력을 키우는 것이 중요하다.

Kaplan Qbook 정리 (I)

1. 금식 장기간(3일 이상) 할 때의 brain의 glucose source?
   amino acids (특히 muscle protein)
2. Duodenal ulcer에서 fasting serum gastrin 농도는 정상치이다.
3. Angiogenic factor = VEGF, bFGF
   Angiostatic factor = endostatin or angiostatin
4. GFR = $(U/P)_{inulin}$ x V = C_{inulin}
5. $R \propto 1/r^4$, $Q = \Delta P/R$ 직경이 2배 증가하면 저항은 16배 감소한다.
   그러면 blood flow는 16배 증가한다.
   cf. Q=cardiac output, R=total peripheral resistance(TPR)
6. cardiac cycle은 systolic time 1/3, diastolic time 2/3이다. 따라서 HR가 매우 빨라지면 diastolic time이 매우 짧아지고, systolic time은 약간 짧아진다.
7. Aortic arch -> Vagus afferent. Carotid sinus -> Glossopharyngeal afferent
   (A-10, C-9)
8. serum과 plasma의 차이? fibrinogen의 유무
9. Auditory pathway
   organ of Corti -> Spiral ganglion -> VIII nerve -> Cochlear N (dorsal & ventral)
   -> superior olivary complex -> lateral lemniscus -> inf. colliculus
   -> medial geniculate body -> termporal lobe
10. 착상은 대략 배란 7일째이다. 이때는 blastocyst상태.
11. Space constant가 증가하면 action potential의 전파속도는 빨라진다.
    cf. space constant : 신호 감쇄가 일어나는 거리
12. 골수의 구성 Myeloid:Erythroid=3:1
    Granulocyte precursors(60%), Erythroid precursors(20%),
    Lymphocytes, monocytes, and their precursors(10%), 기타(10%)
13. oogenesis에서 meiosis process는 출생전에 시작하여 사춘기까지는 prophase I에 멈춰있다. spermatogeneisis는 사춘기까지 시작하지 않는다.

94. type 1 DM에서 insulin이 부족하면 지방조직에서의 hormone-sensitive lipase가 활성화하여 혈중으로 TG가 방출된다. 이는 나중에 retina에 침착하게 된다.

95. TCA cycle에서 riboflavin이 사용되는 곳은?

succinate -----> fumarate (succinate dehydrogenase)

FAD FADH$_2$

riboflavin은 FAD의 원료이다.

96. PKU ; phenylalanine 함유 식품(**aspartame**)을 피해야 한다.

97. 서로 다른 유전자 변이로 질병의 발생 = locus heterogeneity

98. Tardive dyskinesia 부작용이 생겼을 때 사용할 수 있는 atypical antipsychotics?
clozapine = EPS s/e가 없다.

99. 배우자를 학대하는 남편은 자존감를 확립하고하는 방편으로 학대를 이용한다.
학대는 communication의 한 방편이다: **feeling of inadequacy**

100. Reactive attachment disorder of infancy: 부모-아기 관계가 끊어짐
cf. Mobius syndrome (=congenital facial diplegia)
: face expressionless, ocular palsy

Kaplan Qbook 정리 (II)

1. Tarasoff I decision: 환자가 다른 사람에게 위해를 가할 것으로 생각되면 예상되는 피해자에게 알려야 한다.
Tarasoff II decision: 의사가 비록 예상되는 피해자에게 경고할지라도, 의사는 또한 위해로부터 환자를 보호해야 한다.
cf. Irresistible impulse rule: 행동이 자발적이었는지 아니면 통제할 수 없는 상황이었는지를 보는 것. 범죄기소때 insanity defenses에 관련.

7월 9일, USMLEWORLD를 결제했다.

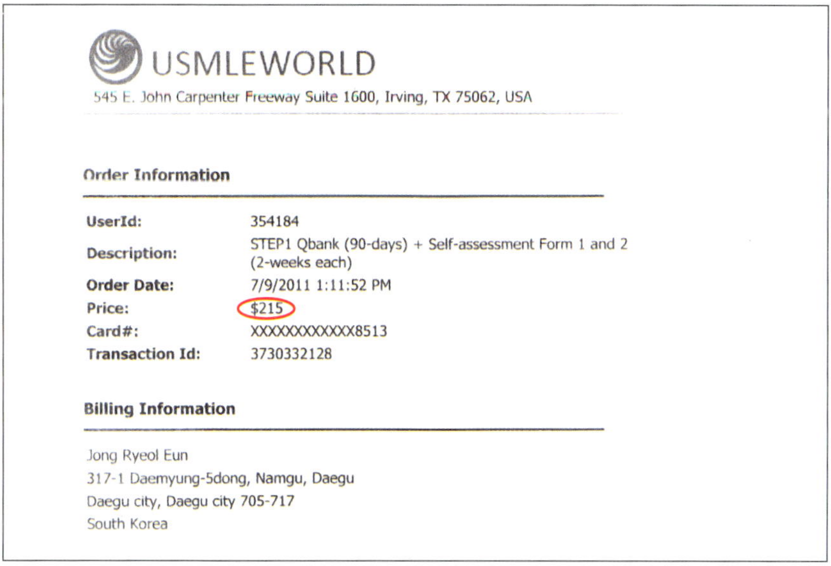

USMLEWORLD

545 E. John Carpenter Freeway Suite 1600, Irving, TX 75062, USA

Order Information

UserId:	354184
Description:	STEP1 Qbank (90-days) + Self-assessment Form 1 and 2 (2-weeks each)
Order Date:	7/9/2011 1:11:52 PM
Price:	$215
Card#:	XXXXXXXXXXXX8513
Transaction Id:	3730332128

Billing Information

Jong Ryeol Eun
317-1 Daemyung-5dong, Namgu, Daegu
Daegu city, Daegu city 705-717
South Korea

당시 215달러를 결제했는데 지금 UW에 들어가 보니 439달러로 2배나 올랐다.

UW 암기사항 992개를 만든 파일도 외장하드에 남아 있다. 이런 걸 공부했었나 싶을 만큼 기억이 가물가물하다.

UW 정리 (I)

1. Hemophilia A, B = X-linked recessive.
   어머니가 carrier일 경우 딸이 carrier일 확률 = 1/2
   어머니가 carrier일 경우 아들이 disease일 확률 = 1/2
   어머니가 carrier일 경우 자녀들(성별구분없이)이 disease일 확률 = 1/4
2. Vitiligo: melanocyte 결핍
   Albinism: melanin pigment 결핍 (=tyrosinase deficiency)
3. Mycobacterium avium complex(MAC)의 치료
   : Clarithromycin or Azithromycin. D4 cell <50에서 주 1회 Azithromycin prophylaxis
4. Cryptococcus neoformans의 polysaccharide capsule을 확인하기 위해 사용하는 염색법 2가지: (1) Mucicarmine stain(red-stained capsule확인)
   (2) Grocott's Methenamine silver stain(GMS)
   - fungal organism의 screening에 사용(carbohydrate staining)
5. AZT(Zidovudine)은 reverse transcriptase inhibitor로 RNA->cDNA 과정에서 경쟁적으로 억제한다. 다른 기전으로는 thymidine analog로 viral genome에 incorporation한다. AZT은 3-OH기가 없으므로 5'->3' phosphodiester linkage formation을 방해한다.
6. Hydrocephalus ex vacuo: brain atrophy 때문에 생기고, CSF pressure증가는 없다.
   예. Alzheimer, HIV, Pick's disease
7. Tachyphylaxis : 반복 투여시 약제반응성이 감소하는 것
   Permissive effect: 단독으로는 효과 없고 다른 약의 효과를 증강
   Synergistic effect: 1+1 = 5, Additive effect: 1+1=2
8. Strawberry hemangioma: 점차 커지다가 사춘기 전에 regress. 1-3세에 사라지기 시작하여 7세까지 대부분 사라짐.
   uncapsulated aggregates of closely packed, thin-walled capillaries
9. RBC는 mitochondria가 없으므로 TCA cycle에 의해 에너지 생성을 하지 못한다.
   그러면 에너지 생성의 major pathway? Glycolysis
   O2-Hb 결합을 조절하는데 중요한 조절인자는 2,3-BPG이다.
   2,3-BPG는 1,3-BPG로부터 생성되는 glycolysis의 부산물이다.
   1,3-bisphosphoglycerate ------------->2,3-BPG
   phosphoglycerate mutase
10. Horseshoe kidney의 대부분은 lower pole fusion. 위로 IMA가 지나가서 compression시키면 hydronephrosis가 생길 수 있다.

94. α-glucosidase inhibitor(acarbose, miglitol)

; intestinal brush border의 membrane-bound disacchariddeases activity↓

95. MS -> LAE -> Lt recurrent laryngeal N. impingement (Ortner syndrome)

= hoarseness

96. Visceral obesity as measured by waist-to-hip ratio is an important determinant of insulin resistance.

97. Huntington's disease; caudate nucleus, putamen loss

98. PSGN 예후인자; age

아이 95% 회복 (1% RPGN) 성인 60%만 회복(나머지는 CGN or RPGN)

99. Chronic lymphedema is an risk factor for the development of angiosarcoma. (Radical mastectomy후)

100. <50세, hypercoagulability의 유전적 원인

= factor V Leiden mutation

: activated protein C에 의해 factor Va inactivation안됨

atypical vein thrombosis의 약 20%

UW 정리 (IX)

1. Lepromin skin test

(+) = Tuberculoid leprosy = strong CD4+ Th1 cell-mediated immune response

(-) = Lepromatous leprosy

2. Celiac disease

IgA anti-tissue transglutaminase, IgA anti-endomysial Ab

3. mal. mesothelioma

nodular or smooth pleural thickening

EM: gold standard for Dx |

long slender microvilli & abundant tonofilaments

(cf. adenoca; short, plump microvilli)

4. Cerebral amyloid angiopathy = advanced age

2011년 6월 14일에 Step 1 시험을 접수한 후 7월 6일에 접수가 수락되었고, 10월 13일에 시험을 보았다.

oasis2.ecfmg.org/appinfo.asp

ECFMG® EDUCATIONAL COMMISSION FOR FOREIGN MEDICAL GRADUATES

On-line Services

Phone (215) 386-5900
M-F, 9:00 a.m.-4:00 p.m.
Eastern Time in the U.S.

OASIS General Information | Personal Settings | Log Out

USMLE/ECFMG ID: 0-825-176-1

Name: Jong Ryeol Eun

Applicant Contact Information
Application For ECFMG Certification Information
USMLE® Application Information
Financial Account Summary
Score Report Information

USMLE Exams

Your Most Recent USMLE Step 1 Application

Date Received: 14 Jun 2011
Processing Status: Accepted
Date Accepted: 06 Jul 2011
Eligibility Period: 01 Aug 2011 - 31 Oct 2011
Testing Region: Korea

United States Medical Licensing Examination®
Step 1 SCHEDULING PERMIT
IMPORTANT DOCUMENT - TAKE TO TEST CENTER

Name: Jong Ryeol Eun
USMLE#: 0-[ ]-1
Program: STEP1
Exam: STEP1
Scheduling #: 020914100
(for appointment scheduling)
Testing Region: Korea

Eligibility Begins: August 01, 2011
Eligibility Ends: October 31, 2011
 # Test Days: 1
CIN (Candidate ID #): QHJG062XDQY
(for use on test date only to access your exam)

This Scheduling Permit authorizes you to sit for Step 1 during the period noted above. **You must print and take this permit to the test center in order to take your exam.** Review the *USMLE ® Bulletin of Information* at www.usmle.org for specific procedures.

1. **SCHEDULE A TEST DATE:** Using the information above, schedule a test date via the Prometric website at www.prometric.com/USMLE or call +82-1566-0990 located in Seoul, Korea, available M-F 8:30AM-7PM (local time). Provide a valid telephone number and email address when scheduling so Prometric can email you a Confirmation Notice and contact you in the event that your appointment must be rescheduled. The Confirmation Notice contains a Prometric Confirmation Number -- You need this number to **confirm or change** your appointment.
2. **CONFIRM OR CHANGE APPOINTMENT:** Confirm your appointment using your Prometric Confirmation Number one week before your appointment at www.prometric.com/USMLE or by calling the telephone number above. You may change (e.g., reschedule, cancel, change test center location) your appointment within the eligibility period noted above. **To avoid an appointment change fee, you must change your appointment 31 or more days before (but not including) the first day of your scheduled test date.** All deadlines are calculated using local time in Seoul, Korea. If you reschedule your appointment or change your test center location within 30 days, you must pay a fee to Prometric at the time you make the change. If you u el your appointment within 30 days or do not test as scheduled, before you can schedule a new appointment, you must **call** Prometric at +82-1566-0990 to pay a fee to reinstate your eligibility record. Refer to your Confirmation Notice for specific fee information.
3. **ELIGIBILITY PERIOD EXTENSION**: If you are unable to test within your eligibility period, contact ECFMG to inquire about a one-time, contiguous three-month eligibility period extension. A fee is charged for this service. Visit ECFMG's website for more information. If you do not take the test within your original or extended eligibility period and wish to take it in the future, you must reapply by submitting a new application and fee(s).
4. **PRACTICE SESSION:** To take a Practice Session at a Prometric Test Center for a fee payable to Prometric, register on the USMLE website, www.usmle.org, using the Scheduling # and CIN from this permit. You will be issued a Practice Session Scheduling Permit within seven business days of registering. Upon receipt of your permit, you may contact Prometric to pay the fee and schedule an appointment.

5. **ADMISSION TO THE TEST CENTER:** You **must** bring this Scheduling Permit and an unexpired, government-issued form of ID (such as a driver's license or passport) that includes both your recent photograph and signature. **The name on your ID must match the name on this permit exactly.** The only acceptable differences are variations in capitalization; the presence of a middle name, middle initial or suffix on one document and its absence on the other; or the presence of a middle name on one and middle initial on the other. The name on your ID must appear in the Latin alphabet, i.e., in "English language letters." If the names on your ID and permit differ, contact ECFMG immediately. **You cannot make a name change or correction within seven business days of your scheduled test date.** If you are required to carry a Permanent Residency Card, be sure to bring it with you along with the other required form of ID as noted above.
6. **TEST DAY:**
   - **ARRIVAL:** Report to the test center 30 minutes before your scheduled appointment. You must sign in and your photograph will be taken. If you arrive later than your scheduled appointment, you **may not** be admitted. If you arrive **more than 30 minutes after your scheduled appointment**, you **will not** be admitted to the testing center.
   - **PERSONAL ITEM STORAGE: You must place all of your personal items, including cell phones, pagers, watches, wallets, food, and beverages in a small locker.** Pagers and cell phones must be turned off.
   - **TESTING:** The Test Center Administrator (TCA) will instruct you to write your name and CIN listed above on a laminated writing surface provided for making notes. The TCA will then collect the permit and escort you to the testing room. You will enter your CIN into the computer at your workstation to initiate your exam and to resume testing after breaks. **Do not erase your name and CIN** from the laminated writing surface until the end of your test day. If you are scheduled to take a **multiple-day** exam, **ask the TCA to return your permit** to you at the end of your test day since you will need to repeat this process on the following test day(s).
7. **END OF TEST DAY:** The TCA will provide you with a printout that confirms you appeared for that day's testing session. Once you leave the test center, Prometric cannot reproduce the printout.

Appointment Summary PROMETRIC

print close

Your appointment request has been confirmed with the following confirmation number(s):

8868000000828587

Candidate's Name:	Jong Ryeol Eun
Candidate's Address:	C/2906 Trumpworld Apartment, Dusang-dong Suseong-Gu Daegu KOR
Home (Evening) Phone:	+82-53-766-2173
Work/Day Phone:	+82-10-4811-2173
Program Name:	STEP1
Exam Name:	STEP 1 - United States Medical Licensing Examination
Site Number:	8693 - SEOUL MAPO-GU 8693, KOREA #12
Site Address:	KAEC, FULBRIGHT BUILDING MAPO-GU, YOMNI-DONG, 168-15
Site City:	SEOUL
Site Country:	KOR
Site Phone #:	1566-0990
Appointment Date:	13 Oct 2011
Appointment Time:	9:00 AM
Appointment Duration:	8:00
E-mail:	dreun@yu.ac.kr

Your appointment information is very important, so please save the information by either printing this page or writing it down. Additionally, you will receive an e-mail within 15-minutes containing your appointment confirmation details.

The Prometric web site, www.prometric.com, is available 24 hours a day, seven days a week for you to reschedule, cancel or confirm your appointment. Additionally, if you have questions, comments or suggestions for Prometric, please visit www.prometric.com, choose your testing program, and then choose the appropriate link from the "Questions?" section.

Thank you,

Prometric

시험 장소는 마포에 있었다. 미리 휴가를 내고, 시험 전날 올라가 시험장을 답사했다. 신촌에 있는 모텔에서 자고 당일 아침 시험장으로 향했다. 시험장에는 USMLE 외에 다른 시험을 보러 오는 사람들도 많았다. USMLE 공부를 몰래 해서 주변 사람들은 아무도 몰랐다. 집사람도 어렴풋하게 짐작만 했을 뿐이다.

시험은 무척 어려웠다. 지문도 길어서 시간 부족으로 풀지 못한 문제도 있었다. 화장실 가는 시간도 시험시간에 포함되었던 것 같은데, 아무튼 주어진 시간은 짧고 문제는 정말 길고 어려웠던 기억이 난다. 시험을 다 마쳤을 때는 탈진하기 일보직전이었다. 겨우 시험 종료 안내장을 받고 대구로 내려왔다.

시험이 끝나니 다음과 같은 안내장을 주었다.

NAME: Jong Ryeol Eun
DATE: 10/13/2011
CENTER: 8693

Your testing session for USMLE® Step 1 has ended.*

Each day of USMLE Step 1 must be taken in order, according to the schedule previously sent to you. Otherwise, the examination may be considered incomplete. Please note that incomplete examinations may be counted by licensing jurisdictions that set a limit to the number of times a candidate can sit for the examination.

Results for Step 1 examinations are typically available within three to four weeks after your test date. However, delays are possible for various reasons. Do not call about your scores unless more than 8 weeks have elapsed.

Scores are not provided by telephone or facsimile to anyone, including examinees.

See the *USMLE Bulletin of Information* for further information on score reporting. Changes to USMLE procedures will be published at the USMLE website.

Please remember: reproducing and/or disseminating examination material by any means (including reconstruction from memory) is considered irregular behavior by USMLE. If you are found to have engaged in irregular behavior, your score report and transcripts will include this finding, and you may be barred from taking USMLE in the future.

See the *USMLE Bulletin of Information* for further information regarding irregular behavior.

Thank you for participating in the United States Medical Licensing Examination®.

** Please note: This notice certifies that you appeared for today's testing session for Step 1; it does NOT imply that you have completed all test sections within today's session.*

사법고시나 행정고시가 어떤지는 모르겠지만 나에게 USMLE는 그 어떤 시험보다도 공부의 양과 스트레스가 상당한 시험이었다고 생각한다. 11월 2일, 결과가 나왔다는 이메일이 왔다.

제목	Your Score Report is Available
보낸사람	주소록추가 onlineservices@ecfmg.org 수신거부
보낸날짜	2011. 11. 2 오후 10:17:07
받는사람	dreun@ynu.ac.kr
참조	

Name: Jong Ryeol Eun
USMLE Id:

Your 13 Oct 2011 STEP 1 score report is NOW AVAILABLE on the ECFMG(r) On-line Applicant Status and Information System (OASIS) website.

To access your score report, you must enter OASIS at https://oasis2.ecfmg.org. On the OASIS homepage, choose the "Go to OASIS" button and then log into your personal account by entering your USMLE/ECFMG identification number and password.

Once you have entered your personal OASIS account, you must select the "Score Report Information" link on the left-hand side of the screen. Your electronic score report will then appear at the top of the screen available in PDF format. When you access the score report through this hyperlink, the score report will open in a new browser window. You may then use your PDF Viewer's "print" option to print your score report from this browser.

Our records indicate that you read the notice in IWA that ECFMG now provides performance data to international medical schools.

At this time please be advised your 13 Oct 2011 Step 1 score report will also be made available to your medical school via EMSWP unless your school is not currently enrolled in EMSWP or you chose to withhold your scores when you were given the opportunity.

You may access and print/reprint the score report for a period of 120 days from the date the score report is made available. After this time, examination results will be made available only in the form of an official paper USMLE transcript.

If you have any questions, contact ECFMG Applicant Information Services at info@ecfmg.org or by telephone at 215.386.5900.

두근거리는 마음으로 성적표를 열어보았는데 결과는 실망스러웠다.

US·MLE
United States
Medical
Licensing
Examination ®

UNITED STATES MEDICAL LICENSING EXAMINATION ®

STEP 1 SCORE REPORT

This score report is provided for the use of the examinee.
Third party users of USMLE information are advised to rely solely on official USMLE transcripts.

Eun, Jong Ryeol

USMLE ID: 0-825-176-1 **Test Date: October 13, 2011**

The USMLE is a single examination program consisting of three Steps designed to assess an examinee's understanding of and ability to apply concepts and principles that are important in health and disease and that constitute the basis of safe and effective patient care. Step 1 is designed to assess whether an examinee understands and can apply important concepts of the sciences basic to the practice of medicine, with special emphasis on principles and mechanisms underlying health, disease, and modes of therapy. The inclusion of Step 1 in the USMLE sequence is intended to ensure mastery of not only the sciences underlying the safe and competent practice of medicine in the present, but also the scientific principles required for maintenance of competence through lifelong learning. Results of the examination are reported to medical licensing authorities in the United States and its territories for use in granting an initial license to practice medicine. These scores represent your results for the administration of Step 1 on the test date shown above.

PASS	This result is based on the minimum passing score recommended by USMLE for Step 1. Individual licensing authorities may accept the USMLE-recommended pass/fail result or may establish a different passing score for their own jurisdictions.
223	This score is determined by your overall performance on Step 1. For recent administrations, the mean and standard deviation for first-time examinees from U.S. and Canadian medical schools are approximately 222 and 24, respectively, with most scores falling between 140 and 260. A score of 188 is set by USMLE to pass Step 1. The standard error of measurement (SEM)‡ for this scale is six points.
82	This score is also determined by your overall performance on the examination. A score of 75 on this scale, which is equivalent to a score of 188 on the scale described above, is set by USMLE to pass Step 1. The SEM‡ for this scale is one point.

INFORMATION PROVIDED FOR EXAMINEE USE ONLY

The Performance Profile below is provided solely for the benefit of the examinee.
These profiles are developed as self-assessment tools for examinees only and will not be reported or verified to any third party.

USMLE STEP1 PERFORMANCE PROFILE

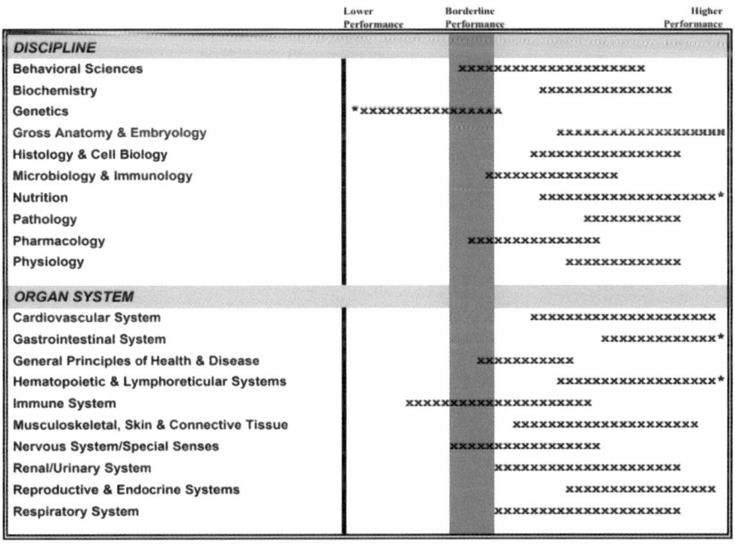

The above Performance Profile is provided to aid in self-assessment. The shaded area defines a borderline level of performance for each content area; borderline performance is comparable to a HIGH FAIL/LOW PASS on the total test.

Performance bands indicate areas of relative strength and weakness. Some bands are wider than others. The width of a performance band reflects the precision of measurement: narrower bands indicate greater precision. The band width for a given content area is the same for all examinees. An asterisk indicates that your performance band extends beyond the displayed portion of the scale. Small differences in the location of bands should not be over-interpreted. If two bands overlap, performance in the associated areas should be interpreted as similar. Because Step 1 is designed to be integrative, many items contribute to more than one content area. As a consequence, caution should be used when interpreting differences in performance across content areas.

This profile should not be compared to those from other Step 1 administrations.

Additional information concerning the topics covered in each content area can be found in the *USMLE Step 1 Content Description and Sample Test Materials*.

돈을 아끼느라 USMLEWORLD 결제를 너무 늦게 하고 문제풀이 시간이 부족했다는 점이 내내 아쉬움으로 남았다. 시험은 매우 깊은 기초의학 지식에 임상 상황을 결합해 나오기 때문에 단순 암기로 접근해서는 안 되는 거였다. 물론 생화학에 나오는 TCA 사이클의 매 단계 효소 같은 것들을 세세하게 외워야 하는 것은 말할 것도 없거니와 이를 응용해 임상적으로 어떤 질환과 연관되는지도 파악해야 했다. 그러니 단순 암기로는 절대로 풀 수 없는 문제들이었다. 만약 다시 그때로 돌아가 7개월이 주어진다면 최대한 빨리 2개월 정도에 암기 사항을 마무리하고, 나머지 5개월은 UW 문제를 풀면서 시험연습을 반복했을 것 같다. 실망스러운 성적을 받았지만 이대로 중단할 수는 없었다. Step 1 시험 직후 바로 Step 2CK 준비를 시작했다.

부끄럽지만 그때 느낀 감정을 usmlekorea.com에 후기로 남긴 것이 있어 소개한다.

10월 13일 후기입니다.

어제 성적표를 받았습니다. 10/13 여선생님 두 분이 같이 시험을 쳤는데 아래의 chloee님이 그중 한 분인 것 같네요. 고득점 축하드려요. 저는 점수가 너무 안 좋아 후기를 올릴 용기가 없지만 UK에서 받은 도움을 조금이나마 보답하는 길은 후기를 올리는 것이라 생각해서 용기를 내봅니다.

Step 1 준비하는 동안 거의 UK에 들어와 살았고, 앞서 간 여러 선생님들의 후기를 읽으면서 위로도 받고 스스로를 채찍질했습니다. 최근의 irene3201 선생님의 후기를 읽고 많은 감동을 받았고, irene 선생님 말씀처럼 제 인생을 한번 돌아보는 의미도 있을 것 같습니다.

저는 만 39세로 지방의대 소화기내과에 근무하고 있고, 내년에 부교수 승진을 앞둔 1인입니다. 1991년 의과대학에 진학 후 무난히 졸업했고, 모교에서 인턴, 레지던트를 마치고 공중보건의 3년을 마쳤습니다. 운이 좋아 펠로우 1년 반 만에 모교의 스텝이 되었으니까 남들이 보기에 대단한 성공을 하였지요. 교수가 되어서는 나름 논문도 열심히 썼고 임상 경험도 꽤 쌓았고, 학회도 열심히 참여했습니다. 저도 근무하는 병원이 평생직장이 될 줄 알았고, 때 되면 승진하고 나이가 들면 정년퇴임하는 남들과 똑같은 그렇고 그런 과정을 밟을 줄 알았습니다.

그런데 인생이 제 마음대로 되지는 않더군요. 병원 스텝이 되어서는 지금까지 쉽지 않은 생활을 했습니다. 하루도 마음 편한 날 없었고 행복하지 않았습니다. 병원을 관두고 싶었지만 그동안은 감히 말을 꺼낼 수 없는 레벨이었고 용기도 없었습니다. 더 이상 견딜 수 없는 지경에 이르니 용기가 생기더군요.

금년 3월에 많은 고민을 한 끝에 내년에 병원을 사직하기로 결심했습니다. 그리고 진로에 대하여 많은 고민을 했습니다. 답은 미국밖에 없더군요. 미국에서 무얼 할 것인가 생각을 했습니다. 리서치가 좋지만 리서치에 올인하는 것은 위험부담이 많겠더군요. 쟁쟁한 phD와 경쟁하는 것도 쉽지 않고요. USMLE에 대하여 UK에서 정보를 얻은 다음 3월 25일부터 공부를 시작했습니다. 8월 13일 시험을 쳤으니 딱 6개월 반을 공부한 셈이지요. 기간은 나름 길었지만 처음 한두 달은 공부 방향을 못 잡아 헤맸고, 하루 평균 2~3시간 공부한 것을 치면 공부한 절대 시간은 충분치 않았던 것 같습니다.

외래와 입원환자 진료, 내시경 검사, 학생 교육, 각종 위원회, 많은 모임의 총무와 간사, 학회 준비 등의 벅찬 일과에서 공부할 시간을 내는 것은 쉽지 않았습니다. UK에서 많은 후기를 읽고 결정한 것은 FA+UW를 집중하기로 했습니다. 강의를 듣거나 전체 리뷰를 하는 것은 불가능하다고 판단하고 우선 FA를 사서 독학을 했습니다. 어렵더군요. 진도 나가기 정말 힘들었습니다. 초기에는 평일엔 2~3시간 정도, 금요일, 토요일에는 밤샘을 하기도 했습니다. 일요일에도 공부를 했습니다. 휴가 때도 공부했습니다. 가족들과의 시간을 많이 갖지 못한 것이 안타깝습니다. FA를 공부하면서 암기노트를 만들어 틈틈이 외우고, 모르는 내용은 구글의 위키피디아를 검색했습니다.

USMLE를 준비하면서 첫 난관은 접수더군요. Eui-Haksa diploma, 학위증, form 186, 187, 344, 345 준비해서 보냈는데, 새로운 학장님 사인이 등록되어 있지 않아 리젝되는 좌절을 맛보았습니다. 행정실에 이야기하여 학장님 사인 등록 후 form 186을 다시 보내서 6월에 accept 되었으니까 접수에 3개월이 걸린 셈이지요. 접수의 난관이 커서 접수가 accept 되는 것만으로도 기뻤습니다. 6월에는 공부에 대한 대략적인 감을 잡은 상태였고, 계획했던 8월 말 시험은 불가능하다는 결론을 내렸습니다. 그래서 시험날짜를 10월 13일로 잡았습니다.

3/25~7월 말까지 FA 3독(저의 1독은 다른 사람의 1독과는 다릅니다. 저의 2독=다른 사람의 1독 정도로 건너뛰는 것도 많았습니다)했고, 중간에 Kaplan Q-book을 사서 1독했습니다(후회함). 7월 9일부터 온라인 UW 3개월 치를 결제하고 풀었는데, 2,080 문제를 다 푸는데 두 달 넘게 걸렸고, 10월 7일까지 겨우 2번 봤습니다. 정답률이 50% 정도 되었고, 기존에 풀었던 문제와 같이 풀면 70% 되었습니다. 내가 제대로 공부하는 것이 맞나 의심하면서도 자신을 믿고 꿋꿋하게 하면 된다고 말하는 많은 후기들에서 용기를 얻고 계속 했습니다. 참고하려고 샀던 리뷰 관련 책들은 결국 못 봤습니다.

시험 때까지 FA 4독, UW 2독, Kaplan Q-book 1독, UW Self-assessment 2nd set(5,6,7,8) (1은 에러나서 사용 못함), sample 문제 풀었습니다. 과목별 리뷰는 못했고, 사두었던 FA Q&A 못 봤고, NBME 못 풀었습니다.

시험 하루 전 서울로 올라갔습니다. 오전, 오후 full로 외래진료하고 회진 돌고 KTX 탔습니다. 몸이 부서질 듯하더군요. 공덕동 한미교육문화원 위치를 확인해 두고 롯데시티호텔로 갔습니다. 요금은 17만원이고 방이 없다더군요. 택시 타고 신촌 모텔에 갔습니다. 6만원이었는데 방도 깨끗하고 일회용품 주고 인터넷도 되고 좋았습니다. 도착해서 액티피드 반알 먹었습니다. 제가 수면제로 애용하는 약입니다.

텔레비전 보다가 12시쯤 잠들어 6시쯤 잠이 깼습니다. 7시까지 침대에 누워 있다가 준비해서 모텔을 나왔습니다. 편의점에서 삼각김밥을 하나 먹고 빵과 물을 챙겼습니다. 시험장 근처 김밥천국이 마침 문을 열길래 김밥 한 줄 샀습니다. 저 말고 젊은 여선생님 두 분이 Step 1을 치러 오셨더군요. 시험을 관리하는 여직원분이 친절하고 시험장 환경은 좋았습니다. 히터를 틀어서 그런지 약간 덥고 답답한 건 있었지만 전체적으로는 시험에 집중할 수 있는 편안한 환경이었습니다.

시험이 시작되었습니다. 문제가 정말 어렵더군요. 처음에는 보통 쉽다고들 했는데 저는 아니었습니다. 다른 선생님들은 어땠는지 모르겠지만 암튼 저는 정말 어렵게 느껴졌습니다. 7블록 중에 6블록이 어려웠고, 7번째 블록은 너무너무 어려웠습니다. 내가 제대로 공부한 것이 맞나 싶었습니다. 문제 복원은 원천적으로 불가능해 보였습니다. 왜냐하면 암기형 문제가 아니라 대부분 판단을 묻는 문제였습니다. 아주 쉬운 문제도 몇 개 있긴 했지만 대부분은 어렵게 느껴졌습니다. 시험시간도 매우 부족하고 쫓기듯 시험을 마쳤습니다. 46문제를 60분에 푸는데 겨우 2~3분 남으니 풀었던 문제 리뷰 할 시간은 없었습니다. 문장이 길고 생화학 실험 문제 같은 것은 아예 그냥 찍고 넘어갔습니다. 그래야 다른 문제에 더 집중할 수 있겠다 싶었습니다.

매 시간마다 화장실 가고 물을 마시면서 쉬었습니다. 계속 모니터 보고 집중하는 것이 힘들었습니다. 전날 잠을 푹 자고 컨디션 조절이 중요하겠더라구요. 평균 15~20개의 깃발을 꽂았던 것 같습니다. UW밖에 공부하지 않아서 비교하기 어렵지만 비슷한 난이도였던 것 같습니다. 제가 공부한 부분에서 본 것은 얼마 되지 않은 느낌이고, 그나마 FA에서 skip한 부분에서 여럿 나오고, 시험에 나오면 실수하지 말아야지 했던 것들도 많이 실수하면서 결과적으로 점수가 좋지 않았던 것 같습니다.

이틀 전 오아시스 트릭으로 확인해 보려고 하는데 접수가 되어 떨어진 줄 알고 마음고생이 심했습니다. 어젯밤 10시 20분에 성적이 올라왔습니다. 엄청 긴장하면서 PDF 파일을 열었는데 점수는 223/82. 좀 실망스러웠습니다. 그렇지만 돌이킬 수 없는 일이고 지금까지처럼 Step 2CK, CS 차근차근 해 나가려고 합니다.

후기를 쓰시는 많은 선생님들이 못해도 230점 이상씩 받으셨는데, 이는 Step 1이 그렇게 만만해서가 아니라 시험 잘 치신 선생님들이 주로 후기를 올렸기 때문이라고 생각합니다.
미국 및 캐나다 의대생 평균이 222점이라고 하니까 저는 딱 평균인 것 같습니다. IMG 평균 합격률이 70%라고 하니까 30%는 커트라인인 188점이 안 된다는 이야기겠죠. 훨씬 많은 선생님들이 저와 비슷하거나 혹은 Fail 하셔서 후기를 올리지 못했을 것으로 생각합니다. Step 1 준비하시는 많은 선생님들께서는 부디 좋은 점수 받으셔서 후기 많이 올리시길 바랍니다. Step 1 진짜 힘든 시험이었습니다.

12월에 Step 2CK를 치고, 내년 2월에 미국 캘리포니아 새크라멘토에 리서치하러 연수를 떠납니다. 3년 반 생각하고 있습니다. 그동안 영어공부 열심히 해서 2015년 매칭에 도전하려 합니다. 미국을 향한 머나먼 여정에서 이제 한걸음을 떼었습니다. 시험 준비하시는 여러분의 건승을 기원합니다.

USMLE
Step 2CK와 미국행

Step 1 성적이 나오기 전인 2011년 10월 21일, Step 2CK를 신청했다.

제목	Your USMLE(tm)/ECFMG(r) Identification Number is 0-825-176-1
보낸사람	주소록추가 OnlineServices@ecfmg.org 수신거부
보낸날짜	2011. 10. 21 오후 11:40:57
받는사람	dreun@ynu.ac.kr
참조	

Dear Doctor: We are pleased to confirm that the On-Line part of your USMLE Step 2 CK application (Application Identification Code 3-[ ]) has been received by ECFMG. Your USMLE/ECFMG Identification Number is listed in the Subject line of this message. You must use this number in all communications with ECFMG. Once your application has been reviewed, ECFMG will notify you of the outcome of your application. ECFMG typically processes USMLE applications within three weeks of receipt of the complete application. You may track the status of your application by using ECFMG's On-line Applicant Status and Information System (OASIS). Access OASIS on the ECFMG website at www.ecfmg.org. Please do not submit inquiries to this mailbox. Messages sent to this e-mail address will not receive responses. Sincerely, Registration and Credentials Services

10월 27일, 시험 일정 허가서scheduling permit를 받았다.

제목	Your Scheduling Permit is Available
보낸사람	주소록추가 onlineservices@ecfmg.org 수신거부
보낸날짜	2011. 10. 27 오후 2:31:21
받는사람	dreun@ynu.ac.kr
참조	

Name: Jong Ryeol Eun
USMLE ID: [ ]

Your STEP 2 CK SCHEDULING PERMIT IS NOW AVAILABLE on the ECFMG Interactive Web Applications (IWA) website.

YOU MUST PRINT YOUR SCHEDULING PERMIT AND BRING IT WITH YOU TO THE TEST CENTER ON YOUR SCHEDULED DATE. You will not be able to take the test if you do not bring your Scheduling Permit to the test center. Note: You will NOT receive an orange Scheduling Permit for this exam in the mail.

To access your Scheduling Permit, go to IWA at https://iwa2.ecfmg.org, login, and select "Print/Reprint your USMLE Step 2 CK Scheduling Permit." Your permit will open in a new browser window. Use your browser's "Print" function to print the permit.

If you have any questions, contact ECFMG Applicant Information Services at info@ecfmg.org or call (215) 386-5900.

Sincerely,

ECFMG

Step 2CK는 처음부터 UW 결제를 해 시험문제 풀이를 하면서 암기 사항들을 정리했다. 분량은 Step 1에 비해서는 매우 적었다. 암기용으로 정리한 파일도 몇 개 안 되었다.

UW Step 2CK(산부인과) 정리	2011-11-10 오후 8:29
UW Step 2CK (외과) 정리	2011-11-20 오전 2:39
UW Step 2CK(내과) 정리	2011-11-24 오후 7:50
UW Step 2CK (소아과) 정리	2011-11-24 오후 8:22
UW Step 2CK (정신과) 정리	2011-11-26 오전 2:25
또 틀린 문제 정리	2011-12-05 오후 10:08

제목 USMLEWORLD LLC Customer Receipt/Purchase Confirmation

보낸사람 주소록추가 USMLEWORLD Support<support@usmleworld.com> 수신거부

보낸날짜 2011. 10. 16 오전 10:18:30

받는사람 Jong Ryeol Eun<dreun@ynu.ac.kr>

This is www.usmleworld.com Payment receipt. This transaction will appear on your credit card statement as USMLEWorld, LLC.

Thank you for your order!

Order Information

Merchant:	USMLEWORLD LLC
Description:	STEP2 CK Qbank (60-days) Self-assessment Form 1 (2-weeks)
Customer ID:	354184

Billing Information
Jong Ryeol Eun
317-1 Daemyung-5dong, Namgu, Daegu
Daegu city, Daegu city 705-717
South Korea
dreun@ynu.ac.kr
82-53-620-3985

Shipping Information

Total: US $155.00

Visa

Date/Time:	15-Oct-2011 09:18:29 PM ET
Transaction ID:	3920037302

지금 UW 가격표를 보니 3개월에 439달러다.

과목마다 암기해야 할 내용들은 파일로 정리했다.

UW Step 2CK 내과 정리(I)

1. Patients with IM may develop autoimmune hemolytic anemia and thrombocytopenia up to 2-3 weeks after the onset of initial symptoms.
: RBC, platelet에 대한 autoantibodies (IgM cold-agglutinin antibodies)
= anti-i antibodies
=> complement-mediated destruction of red blood cells
(=usually Coombs'-test positive)
2. Tinea versicolor is characterized by pale, velvety pink or whitish, hypopigmented macules that not tan and do not appear scaly, but scale by scraping. Topical treatment with **selenium sulfide** lotion and **ketoconazole** shampoo is recommended.
3. CHF에서 leg edema의 기전
CHF -> effective blood volume 감소 -> renal hypoperfusion
-> RAA system activation -> Na reabsorption
4. 노인에서 hydration status를 반영하는 가장 민감한 지표? increased BUN/creatinine
5. Amaurosis fugax is defined as a painless loss of vision from emboli.
cholesterol particles에 의한 emboli = impending stroke의 warning sign
carotid bifurcation에서 emboli기원.
6. Senile purpura: 노인, extensor surfaces에 ecchymoses
이유: perivascular connective tissue atrophy
7. Lidocaine is not used prphylactically in patients with acute coronary syndrome. Although its use decreases the risk of ventricular fibrillation, it may increase the risk of asystole.
8. Sick euthyroid syndrome; acute, severe illness에서 TFT이상.
주로 T3감소, TSH, T4는 정상 ="low T3 syndrome"
9. First-generation H1-antihistamines have potent anticholineratic effects and may cause eye and oropharyngeal dryness as well as urinary retention, especially in order males who may have some underlying BPH urinary retention caused by anticholinergic agents results from **failure of detrusor contraction**. Detrusor activity is controlled by parasympathetic input from the pelvic splnachinic nerves.
10. **Erythema nodosum** is a condition of painful, subcutaneous, pretibial nodules. It can be a symptom of more serious disease processes including sarcoidosis, TB, histoplasmosis, recent streptococcal infection, and inflammatory bowel disease.

USMLE Step 2CK 외과학 정리

1. stress fracture: tarsal bone
   Plantar fascitis: worse with walking, runners with repeated microtrauma
   foot plantar aspect
   아침에 첫발을 내딛을때 통증
   Tarsal tunnel syndrome: ankle fracture -> tibial N. compression
   -> foot & toes의 distal plantar burining, numbness, aching
2. trauma -> EDH -> transtentorial (uncal) herniation
   : ipsilateral PCA, ipsilateral CN III, contralateral cerebral peduncle
3. **Tortus palatinus**: benign bony growth, midline hard palate
   genetic and environmental. younger pts. women, Asian
   <2cm, 커질수 있다. 치료가 필요없으나 증상있으면 수술
4. The risk factors for **DDH (Developmental dysplasia of the hip)** are Caucasian race, female, first-bone infants, breech position and a family history of DDH). The Barlow and Ortolani tests are used to assess for hip dislocatibility. Positive physical exam findings should attempt a radiologic diagnosis with ultrasound (<4 mo old) or radiographs (>4mo old). Treatment may involve use of a hip hardness or spica cast.
5. In evaluating a patient with a shoulder injury, a positive drop arm sign suggests **rotator cuff tear** (mc: supraspinatus).
6. Venous insufficiency (vascular incompetence) is the mc cause of lower extremity edema. 낮에 심하고, 자고나거나 누우면 덜하다.
7. Acute shoulder pain after forceful abduction and external rotation at the glenohumeral joint suggests an ant. shoulder dislocation, which may cause injury the **axillary nerve injury**.
   배구 블로킹할 때 어깨가 forceful abduction & ext. rotation -> ant. dislocation
   (ant. shoulder fullness on exam) -> axillary n. injury(humerus head 아래로 지나감)
   -> deltoid & teres minor paralysis, lateral upper arm sensation loss
8. Popping sensation후 knee pain & swelling (acute knee injury 당시 기억가능)
   = **meniscal injury** (hemarthrosis 때문에 rapid joint swelling)
   증상: tenderness, ROM감소, McMurray's test (+)

UW Step 2CK 산부인과 정리 (I)

1. Preterm labor: 20-37주 사이의 산통.
   24-34주 사이에는 systemic corticosteroid 투여(NRDS 예방)
   치료: tocolysis (분만억제) + bed rest (24-26주까지)
2. Infant born to patients with Graves' disease treated with surgery are at risk for thyrotoxicosis because of the pasaage of TSI across the placenta.
3. Patients with Mullerian agenesis have a blind ended vaginal pouch with little or no uterine tissue and a XX genotype.
4. IUFD (INtrauterine Fetal Demise) <20주 사망
   fibrinogen감소, plt감소는 DIC 의미
5. The mc cause of an abnormal MSAFP level is a gestational age error.
6. Women should be screened for group B streptococcus colonization with vaginal and rectal cultures obtained between 35-37 weeks gestation.
7. Gestational DM에서 ideal glucose control: 75-90 mg/dL
   치료) subcutaneous insulin (category B, placenta 통과안함)
8. Gestaional DM risk
   macrosomia, hypoglycemia, hypocalcemia, hyperviscosity due to polycythemia (<-fetal hypoxia, 혈당높으면 에너지 대사 높아져서 태아는 저산소증), respiratory difficulties, cardiomyopathy, CHF
9. 분만후에 미열 + leukocytosis + vaginal discharge (lochia) 는 정상소견이고 안심시켜주면 된다.
   normal lochia rubrra (-수일)
   lochia serosa (3-4일)
   lochia alba (이후, white or yellow)
   * foul smelling lochia = endometriosis 의심
   * lochia: bloody -> serous -> white or yellow
10. Early deceleration: uterine contraction전에 onset.
    fetal head compression (->vagal response)

UW Step 2CK 소아과 정리 (I)

1. Fetal alcohol syndrome: **irritability**, mental retardation, hypoplastic maxilla, **long philtrum, thin upper lip border**, and microcephaly
2. acute bacterial sinusitis
   S. pneumoniae (30%) - mc
   non-typable H. influenzae (20%), Moraxella catarrhalis (20%)
3. Nursemaid's elbow (=subluxed radial head)
4. Preseptal cellulitis vs. orbital cellulitis
   (eye movement↓, visual acuity↓, double vision, proptosis, fever, malaise, systemic sx)
5. The TORCH infections cause a syndrome characterized by **microcephaly**, hepatosplenomegaly, **deafness**, chorioretinitis, and thrombocytopenia.
   cf. TORCH: toxo, syphilis, rubella, CMV, HSV
6. Night terrors: non-REM sleep, 기억못함
   Nightmare: REM sleep, 악몽, 기억함, alert
   Somnambulism (sleep walking): 몽유병 non-REM
7. By the first birthday, a child should triple his birth weight and increase his height by 50%.
8. Friedreich ataxia is the mc type of spinocerebellar ataxias.
   DM, CMP, skeletal (scoliosis, hammer toes)
9. Neuroblastoma: 진단당시 70%에서 전이가 있음 (long bones, skull 등)
   VMA, HVA 증가, N-myc, **calcifications and hemorrhages**
10. 21-hydroxylase deficiency is the mc form of CAH. It presents with virilization, walt wasting, and increased 17α-hydroxyprogesterone levels.
11. -1yr: 2-3단어 말하기(mamma, dadda), reciprocal game
    2 yrs: 6개 블록쌓기, 계단오르기, 점프, 공던지기, 200단어 말하기, 2-word phrases
    2-step commands, 옷벗기
    3 yrs: 원 따라 그리기, 9블록쌓기, 번갈아가며 계단오르기, 세발자전거, 3단어문장, 손씻기, 그룹놀이

USMLE Step 2CK 정신과학 정리

1. Most antidepressant must be taken for 4-6 weeks before they provide symptomatic relief.
2. acute stress disorder(<1mo) vs. PTSD (>1mo)
3. Marijuana (Cannabis) abuse: **dry mouth**, tachycardia, **conjunctival injection**, increased appetite
4. Opioid overdose: respiratory depression, CNS depression, pinpoint pupil
   Opioid withdrawal: N/V, diarreha, sweating, pupil dilatation
5. Bipolar 1% risk
   부모중 한명이 Bipolar라면 10% risk
   부모 둘다 bipolar라면 60%
   monozygotic twin: 70%
6. "contracting herself" => vaginismus
7. Narcolepsy Tx: modafinil or methyphenidate
8. Childhood disintegrative disorder (male)
   : 2년간 정상발달하다가 퇴행 (자폐증세)
   Rett disorder (female only) 6개월째까지 정상발달하다가 퇴행
   Asperger syndrome: 인지, 언어발달은 정상, Autism의 milder form
9. Desmopressin is a first line medication treatment for enuresis that can be used if behavioral techniques fail. (2nd: imipramine)
10. Mania Tx: mood stabilizers (lithium, carbamazepine, valproic acid)
    * lithium: 신장으로 배설
11. Child abuse 의심시
    complete P/E -> radiographil skeletal survery (if necessary) -> coagulation profile (multiple bruises) -> report to Child Protection Service -> 입원 -> 정신과협진
12. ADHD Tx: methylphenidate (CNS stimulant)
    S/E: nervousness, decreased appetite, wt loss, insomnia, and abdominal pain
13. SSRI (citalopram 등) s/e: sexual dysfunction (impotence, delayed ejaculation, libido↓)

또 틀린 문제 정리

1. Osler-Weber-Rendu syndrome
   : diffuse telangiectasia, recurrent epistaxis,
   widespread AV malformation (Rt-to-Lt shunt)
2. Down syndrome
   감소: AFP, Estradiol (AE)　　증가: HCG, Inhibin-A (HIgh)
3. Septic shock
   : CO↑, PCWP↓, systemic vascular resistance↓, RA pr↓
   mixed venous oxygen concentration: normal
   cf. neurogenic shock, hypovolemic shock: MVO2↓(∵tissue hypoperfusion)
4. Ethylene glycol is associated with hypocalcemia and calcium oxalate deposition in the kidneys.
5. Heroin intoxication; 의식이상, 호흡억제, pinpoint pupil
   Cocaine, amphetamine intoxication; dilated pupil, hypertension, and tachycardia
   **** amphetamine = psychotic sx**
6. Trachoma presents with follicular conjunctivitis and **pannus (neovascularization)** formation in the **cornea**.　(코니아-트라코마)
   Tx. tocical TC or oral azithromycin
   cf. Herpes Simplex keratitis: **pain**, photophobia, decreased vision, **dendritic ulcer**
   cf. CMV - pain 없음.
7. Pronator drift is a relatively sensitive and specific physical exam finding for UMN damage affecting the upper extremities. In particular, many patients with stroks will demonstrate pronator drift.
8. Rotator cuff tendinitis caused by impingement is most common in middle-aged

2개월 정도 공부하고 12월 21일에 시험을 보았다. 2012년 1월 18일 Step 2CK 성적이 발표되었는데 251점으로 나쁘지 않았다. 성적표를 출력 보관하지 않아 성과performance가 어땠는지 기록이 없다. 합격하고 기뻤는지 usmlekorea.com에 후기를 올린 게 아직 남아 있다.

부끄럽지만 소개한다.

지난 10월 13일 Step 1을 쳤습니다. Step 1 후기에 소개했듯이 참 힘든 과정이었고 성적도 만족스럽지 못했습니다(223/82). 저의 스케줄상 12월 말부터는 많은 행사들이 잡혀서 도저히 공부할 시간도 없고 공부할 의지도 없을 것 같아 서 Step 2CK 공부 기간을 딱 두 달로 잡았습니다. Step 1의 실패를 거울삼아

이번에는 철저히 UW-based로 하기로 했습니다. 참고 교재로 Step-up to medicine, 4학년 국시 교재(KMLE) 등을 장만했으나 전혀 손도 못 댔습니다(시간부족 + 엄두가 안 남). UW만 하기에도 다소 벅찬 시간이었습니다.

2,000문제 이상을 내것으로 소화한다는 것이 결코 쉽지 않았습니다. 하루 44문제 풀기도 벅찼구요, 밤샘하면 100문제 풀 때도 있었습니다. 평균 하루 3시간 정도 x 50일 정도 공부했던 것 같습니다. 해설을 이해하려고 노력했고, 암기노트 만들어 포인트는 반복 암기했습니다. 2달 결제 기간 끝나고 UW Self assessment 풀었는데 예상 점수가 240점 정도 나왔던 것 같습니다. Step 1도 예상 점수가 240점 넘었는데 223점 나와서 이번에도 그러리라 예상했고 나름 목표를 230점 받으면 좋겠다고 생각했습니다. 시험은 정말 어려웠습니다. 하루 9시간을 시험 친다는 것이 보통 힘든 게 아니었습니다. 오후는 정말 고통의 시간이었습니다. 앉아서 모니터 보는 데 토할 것 같았습니다. 정신없이 풀어도 시간이 2~3분 남는 게 고작이었고, 약 광고, 저널 문제는 아예 시험 전에 포기하기로 하고 그냥 대충 찍었습니다. 다른 문제에 집중하는 게 낫겠다 싶어서요. 4주째 되는 어젯밤(1/18) 늦게 성적이 올라온 것 같습니다. 오늘 아침 결과를 확인했는데 251/85의 amazing한 점수가 나왔습니다.

Step 1이 더 중요하다지만 어쨌든 점수가 기대 이상으로 나와서 얼마간은 기쁠 것 같네요. 미국을 향한 작은 한걸음을 또 뗀 것 같습니다. 저는 다음 달 미국으로 출국합니다. 리서치 랩에서 3.5년 정도 보내고 2015년 매칭을 목표로 합니다. 금년에는 NIW 영주권을 받는 것과 Step 2CS 합격을 목표로 합니다. 미국을 꿈꾸시는 여러 선생님들의 행운을 기원하고, 그 꿈 꼭 이루시길 바랍니다.

드디어 미국연수를 떠날 시간이 왔다. 2월 28일 밤 비행기를 탔다. 집사람은 막내가 아직 아기라서 안고 가느라 착륙 때까지 한 번도 쉬지 못해 힘들었는데, 나는 옆자리가 비어 있어 편하게 누워 잘 자면서 가더라며 섭섭하다고 했다. 이 이야기를 기회 있을 때마다 한다.

지난했던 미국연수 준비 과정

외장하드에 저장된 파일들을 뒤져보니 '미국연수 준비일지'라는 이름의 파일이 눈에 들어온다. 열어보니 그때의 심정을 적은 일기였다. 당시 나의 마음이 지금 기억과는 좀 달라서 놀랍다.

2010년 7월 2일 금요일

2012년 2월에 연수를 가야겠다고 결심했다. 2006년 9월에 전임강사 임용 후 5년 6개월 되는 때다. 원래 계획보다 1년 늦었는데 셋째가 태어난 점, 연구재단의 3년 연구과제에 선정되어 2012년에 완료되는 점, ○○○ 선생님이 금년 9월 연수를 가게 된 것 등이 시기 결정에 복합적으로 작용하게 되었다. 최소 1~2년 전부터 준비를 해야 한다는 전임자들의 조언에 따라 준비를 시작한다. 일단 올해 9월까지 연수지를 정하기로 했다. 목적지를 정하는 것이 가장 중요한 부분이라고들 한다. 연수의 목적을 정해야 하는데 들은 바로는 1) 배움에 목적을 둘 것인지 2) 그동안 힘들게 살아왔으니 휴식을 택할 것인지 3) 아이들의 어학연수에 목적을 둘 것인지를 분명히 해야 한다고 했다. 모두를 다 얻기는 어려우니 목적을 분명히 하는 게 중요하다. 나는 배움에 목적을 두고자 한다. 리서치에 전념한다 하더라도 현재의 병원 생활보다는 힘들지 않을 것 같다. 무엇을 배울 것인가를 생각해 보았다. 간질환 분야에서 깊이 있는 연구를 해보고 싶다. 바이러스 간염, 알코올 간질환, 간경변, 간암 등 다양한 질환이 있다. 많은 전임 연수자들이 이 분야들에 대해 연수를 다녀왔다. 나는 '줄기세포'에 관심이 많다. 앞선 분야들이 완전히 해결되지는 않았으나 많은 진전이 있었고, 또한 많은 사람들이 연구에 매진하고 있다. 줄기세포는 아직 개척해야 할 부분이 많다고 생각한다. 5년 전에 비해 현재 괄목할 만한 발전이 있는 것도 아닌 것 같다. 현재는 줄기세포가 임상에 적용이 될 수 있을까 싶지만 10년, 20년 후에는 그럴 수도 있겠다는 생각이 든다. 줄기세포에 대해 PubMed 논문들을 검색해 보았다. 한국인이 있었다. 그것도 Cell에 논문을 낸 한국을 빛내는 과학자로 검색이 된다. 존스홉킨스에서 포닥을 하고 현재 존스홉킨스에서 assistant professor로 있다. 너무 반갑다. 일단 이메일을 보내 보기로 했다.

당시 줄기세포에 꽂혀 있었다. 줄기세포를 간부전이나 간경변 환자에 적용할 수 있다면 좋겠다는 생각을 하고 연수 주제도 줄기세포 쪽으로 알아보았다. 먼저 한국인으로 존스홉킨스에서 자리 잡은 모 교수에게 메일을 보냈다.

제목 Research Fellow Application
보낸사람 은종렬<dreun@ynu.ac.kr>
보낸날짜 2010 7 3 오후 6:01:05
받는사람 주소록추가 은종렬<dreun@ynu.ac.kr>

Dear [ ]

It's a great pleasure to have a chance to write to you.
I have come to know of you through your many worthy articles.
I am very happy and proud you are Korean.
I am writing this letter to inquire about research fellowship opportunity in Stem Cell Laboratory.

I am a 38-year-old physician in the Department of Gastroenterology and Hepatology, Yeungnam University Hospital, Daegu, South Korea, and also Assistant Professor in Yeungnam University College of Medicine.
I graudated from Yeungnam University College of Medicine in 1997, and finished residentship in 2002 and army sevice in 2005. I have been working here for 4 years as a faculty after finishing fellowship at Yeungnam University hospital.
Working as a clinician, I did not have enough chances to be involved in basic research works.
Thus, I decided to look for a further training position such as a research fellowship to broaden my medical experience and knowledge.

My major is hepatology including hepatitis, cirrhosis and liver cancer.
I am interested in the research fields of stem cell biology. If you have any research fellowship programs or any other opportunities for foreign medical doctors such as myself, would you please send me details.
Although my school usually provides a small part of the reauired stipend, it would be very convenient if you have any potential financial aids for me. I would like to accompany my wife, two daughters and one son.

Being well aware of your outstanding academic accomplishments, I would greatly appreciate if you provided me with an opportunity to work as a research fellow under your supervision. I intend to return to my present position in Korea after completing my fellowship. I can start working from Mar. 2012 or anytime thereafter for 1 or 2 years under your circumstances. Enclosed is my curriculum vitae for your close review.

Looking forward to hearing from you soon.
Thank you very much in participation for your consideration.

Sincerly yours,

Jong-Ryul Eun, M.D.
Assistant Professor
Division of Gastroenterology and Hepatology, Department of Internal Medicine
Yeungnam University College of Medicine
317-1 Daemyung-5dong, Namgu, Daegu 705-717, Korea
(E-mail) dreun@ynu.ac.kr
(TEL) (82) 53-620-3985

친절한 거절 메일을 받았다.

제목	RE: Research Fellow Application
보낸사람	주소록추가 [ ]@jhmi.edu> 수신거부
보낸날짜	2010. 7. 5 오전 7:11:23
받는사람	은종렬 <dreun@ynu.ac.kr>

Dear Dr. Eun,

We currently have many Korean fellows in my lab. I believe this may not be fair to other international fellow candidates. So I regret to say that I do not hire any more Koreans for the time being.
Good luck for your search.

[   ] M.D., Ph.D.
Assistant Professor of Oncology
Stem Cell Biology Laboratory
Sidney Kimmel Comprehensive Cancer Center
Johns Hopkins University School of Medicine
1550 Orleans Street, CRBII Room 552
Baltimore, MD 21231
Phone [   ]
Fax [   ]
[   ]@jhmi.edu

2010년 8월 4일 수요일

존스홉킨스의 ○○○ 교수에게는 거절 메일을 받았고, 이후 몇 군데 더 보냈는데 UC Davis medical center의 Mark Zern 교수에게서 오늘 수락 통보를 받았다. 기쁘다.

닥터 전[Dr. Zern]에게서 흔쾌히 오라는 답장을 받았다. 다만 월급은 못 주는데 괜찮겠냐는 말과 함께. 연수 가는데 월급까지 바라는 것은 염치없는 일이라고 생각하고 있던 터라 아무런 문제가 되지 않았다. 연수지는 캘리포니아 UC 데이비스[Davis]로 정했다. 그해 가을 미국간학회[AASLD]에서 한번 보자는 메일을 받았고 미국 학회장에서 만나서 근처 카페에서 차를 마셨는데, 영어가 전혀 안 되던 때이기도 하고 매우 긴장했던 기억이 난다.

제목	Re: Research Fellow Application
보낸사람	주소록추가 Mark Zern<mazern@ucdavis.edu> 수신거부
보낸날짜	2010. 7. 23 오전 9:29:09
받는사람	은종렬 <dreun@ynu.ac.kr>

Dear Dr. Eun,
Thank you for your kind note. Also, please excuse my delay in writing back to you. One reason for the delay is my attempt to determine whether I have any funding available for research positions. Unfortunately, I do not have funding available for additional positions. I have had several physicians from Korea work in my lab in the past, and they have been great additions to our work. They have used their time as a sabbatical, and have brought financial support from their universities. Will you be able to supply funds for your salary support while you are here? In the past I have provided health benefits for the visiting scholars and any family members that have come with them.
Again, I apologize for my delay in writing.
My best regards,
Mark Zern

2010년 8월 30일 월요일

지난주 휴가 중에 논문을 검색하다가 김태헌 선생님에 대해 알게 되었다. Dr. Zern 교수에게 연수를 했고 논문의 correspondence가 Mark Zern 교수여서 반가워 메일을 보냈는데 답장이 왔다. UC Davis는 연수하기 좋은 곳이고 Dr. Zern은 나이스한 분이란다. 그런데 한 가지 학문적으로는 아주 앞서 나가는 곳은 아니고, Dr. Zern이 stem cell에 관심은 있지만 여러 가지 연구를 한단다. 암튼 전체적으로는 매우 만족스럽고 희망적인 답을 들어서 기뻤다.

2010년 10월 3일 일요일

어제 가톨릭성모병원에서 〈8회 Catholic international stem cell symposium〉이 있었다. Stem cell에 대한 정보를 얻기도 힘들고 막연하던 참에 잘 됐다 싶어 토요일 이른 새벽에 일어나 길을 나섰다. 수백 명의 청중이 모인 대규모 심포지엄이었다. 들어도 거의 이해되지 않았지만 전체적인 분위기를 느낄 수 있었다. 학회장에서 원광대 조은영 선생님을 만났다. 나와 비슷하게 stem cell 분야에 관심이 있어서 연수를 이쪽으로 할 생각이 있으신가 보다.

2010년 12월 28일 화요일

그동안 많은 일이 있었다. UC Davis에 연수를 다녀오신 분들이 많다는 것을 알게 되었다. 원자력병원 박수철 선생님은 2011년 1월 25일부터 1년간 다녀올 예정으로, 귀국 시점에 내가 출국하게 될 것 같다. 집 문제가 해결될지도 모르겠다. 10월 말 AASLD에서 Zern 교수를 만나고 온 것이 큰 소득이었다.

닥터 전 랩lab에 연수를 가게 된 것은 내게 큰 행운이었다. 첫인상은 해리슨 포드를 보는 듯했고 인품이 너무 훌륭하신 분이었다. 연수 동안 세심하게 잘 챙겨주셨고 후일 레지던트 지원 및 영주권 추천서도 잘 써주셨다. 나와 가족은 캘리포니아 데이비스를 정말 좋아하게 되었다.

2011년 1월 17일 월요일

시간이 후딱 지나가는 것 같다. 어제 간지회 연수강좌를 마쳤고, 이번주 금요일 영남대 간연구회 심포지엄만 무사히 마치면 정말 큰일은 다 마친다. 물론 춘계간학회가 남아 있지만… 이제 연수가 1년 남았다. 연수 가겠다는 말을 어떻게 꺼낼지 걱정이다.

그동안의 일들을 모두 밝힐 수는 없지만 당시 내 심경에 많은 변화가 있었다. 병원 사직을 결심하게 된 것이다.

2011년 4월 6일 수요일

계획을 급선회하여 병원을 사직하고 장기 연수를 하기로 했다. 결심한 지 한 달이 아직 되지 않았는데 우선 USMLE Step 1과 Step 2CK를 보고 가야겠다고 결심했다. 오늘은 우체국에서 접수 원서를 ECFMG로 발송했다. 내년에 출국하여 약 3년간 연수를 할 생각이다. 그동안 영어공부를 하고 USMLE Step 2CS를 합격하고 논문을 쓴다. 그리고 추천서를 받아서 레지던트 지원을 한다. 모든 과정을 마치면 8년이 걸린다. 그때 내 나이 49세다.

만약 미국에서 레지던트 매치가 되었다면 정규 과정을 마치고 지금쯤은 자리를 잡기 시작할 시기일 것이다. 그러나 결국 쓰디쓴 좌절을 맛보고 돌아와 국내 대학병원에서 근무하고 있다.

2011년 4월 14일 목요일

하루하루가 너무 힘들다. 그중에서도 진료가 가장 힘들다. 외래 보는 것이 왜 이리 힘든지… 태어나서 이렇게 힘든 적이 있었던가 싶다. 쓰러질 듯 피곤하다.

돌이켜보니 그때 육체적 피로보다 우울증이 심했던 것 같다.

2011년 6월 2일 목요일

여전히 하루하루가 힘들다. Zern 교수에게 보낸 서류 요청 편지에 대한 답이 아직 오지 않아 걱정이다. 그리고 문제가 생긴 USMLE 원서에 대한 답이 오지 않은 것도 걱정이다. 이 둘이 빨리 해결되었으면 좋겠다. 다음주에 간 학회가 있다. 간 학회와 의국연수 강좌만 무사히 마치면 큰 산은 넘었다고 할 수 있겠는데 두렵다.

2011년 6월 4일 토요일

Zern 교수로부터 이메일이 왔다. 일단 한 가지는 해결된 듯하다. 오늘 답장을 보내야겠다.

2011년 6월부터는 연수와 관련한 실질적 서류 준비에 들어가게 되었고, 접촉할 실무자를 소개받았다. 이제 실무자와 서류를 주고받는 과정이 필요하다. 기본은 여권, 이력서, 비자 그리고 DS-2019이다. DS-2019가 있어야 미국비자를 받을 수 있다.

제목	RE: [RE]Re: [RE]Re: [RE]Re: Research Fellow Application
보낸사람	주소록추가 Mark Zern< @ucdavis.edu> 수신거부
보낸날짜	2011. 6. 4 오전 3:00:51
받는사람	은종렬 <dreun@ynu.ac.kr>
참조 +	@ucdmc.ucdavis.edu, @ucdmc.ucdavis.edu, @ucdavis.edu

Dear Dr. Eun,
Thank you for the note. Of course I remember our time together at AASLD. I look forward to your coming here in February. I will pass this on to Jonathon Dimitriadis and Maria Hayes who will help with the VISA issues. You should write to Dr. Park and have him give you progress reports on the work. I will also send this on to Yuyou Duan who can supply you with information about the project as the time gets closer to your coming.
My best regards,
Mark Zern

과거 인터넷이 없던 시절에는 일일이 서류를 국제우편으로 주고받았다고 한다. 서류가 한 번 가고 오는데 수개월씩 소요된 걸 어떻게 했나 모르겠다.

I sent a copy of my passport, CV and recent visa information in response of your request.
But you seem not check my e-mail.
So, I send e-mail again.
Could you please check the attaching files?
Thank you,
From Jong Ryeol Eun

-- [**Original Message**] --
Sender : < @ucdmc.ucdavis.edu >
To : 은종렬 < dreun@ynu.ac.kr >
Date : 2011-08-04 01:46:39
Subject : Re: Research Fellow Application: Reminder

Jong,

Hello, I will need a copy of you passport, CV, any old visa information if you have been to the US in the past 2 years.

That should be enough to get me started on your DS-2019 paperwork

Thank you,
Jon Dimitriadis
Administrative Assistant
Division of Gastroenterology/Hepatology
Department of Internal Medicine
4635 2nd Ave Suite 1001
Sacramento, CA 95817

@ucdmc.ucdavis.edu

2011년 8월 7일 일요일

3월 25일부터 USMLE를 준비하기 시작해 5개월째를 맞고 있다. 10월 13일 Step 1을 보고 가능하면 빨리 11월 말이나 12월 초에 Step 2CK를 마치고자 한다. 병원생활과 병행하면서 공부하기가 고통스럽다. 이제 영어공부를 시작하려 한다. 2014년 3월 매칭을 목표로 하면 3년이 못 되는 촉박한 시간이다. 어제 고수민 저 <뉴욕의사의 백신 영어>를 구입하여 읽었다. 요약하면 읽기, 듣기, 말하기, 쓰기를 골고루 열심히 해야 한다는 것이다. 당분간은 하루 한 시간씩이라도 꾸준히 하고 USMLE 시험이 끝나는 12월부터는 하루 3시간 이상으로 공부 양을 늘려야겠다.

간 학회-GSK 연수지원 프로그램에 제출할 초청장도 정식으로 받았다.

UNIVERSITY OF CALIFORNIA, DAVIS

BERKELEY • DAVIS • IRVINE • LOS ANGELES • MERCED • RIVERSIDE • SAN DIEGO • SAN FRANCISCO | SANTA BARBARA • SANTA CRUZ

SCHOOL OF MEDICINE
DEPARTMENT OF INTERNAL MEDICINE
TRANSPLANT RESEARCH PROGRAM
4635 Second Ave. Suite 1001
SACRAMENTO, CALIFORNIA 95817
Tel. (916) 734-8063
FAX: (916) 734-8097

UC DAVIS MEDICAL CENTER
2315 STOCKTON BOULEVARD
SACRAMENTO, CALIFORNIA 95817

September 26, 2011

Korean Association for the Study of the Liver

To whom it may concern:

I write this letter to formally invite Dr. Jong-Ryul Eun to join our lab at the University of California, Davis Medical Center, in the Division of Gastroenterology and Hepatology. He will arrive in February, 2012 and spend at least a year working in our laboratory to help differentiate human embryonic stem cells along a hepatocyte lineage. Our hope is to be able to employ the cells for cell transplantation into humans. He will actively work to optimize our differentiation protocol and to characterize the cells before their transplantation into animal model systems. In addition, he will help analyze a unique hepatic cancer stem cell line that we have developed. He has been an active clinical researcher in Korea and has the background and desire to contribute significantly to the above-mentioned research projects. We very much look forward to his joining our group.

Please contact me if I can be of further assistance in this matter.

Sincerely yours,

Mark Zern

Mark A. Zern, M.D.
Professor of Medicine
Fred and Pat Anderson Family Professor of Transplant Research
Director, Transplant Research Program

2011년 10월 6일 목요일

DS-2019 독촉 메일도 보냈다.

From: 은종렬 <dreun@ynu.ac.kr>
To: @ucdmc.ucdavis.edu
Date: 10/06/2011 02:00 AM
Subject: [RE]Re: [RE]Re: Research Fellow Application: Reminder

Jon Dimitriadis,
I am waiting DS-2019. Could you please send it? I heard from Dr. Park that he started the process November last year. But I'm a little nervous. I want to start the process a little earlier.
I hope your reply.
Sincerly,
From Eun

SISS Services for Inernational Students and Scholors에서 완료되는 대로 10월 말까지 보내주겠다고 했다.

제목	Re: [RE]Re: [RE]Re: Research Fellow Application: Reminder
보낸사람	주소록추가 @ucdmc.ucdavis.edu> 수신거부
보낸날짜	2011. 10. 7 오전 1:40:41
받는사람	은종렬 <dreun@ynu.ac.kr>

I should be sending your completed DS-2019 out to you by the end of this month I will let you know as soon as SISS has completed it

2011년 11월 2일 수요일

아내와 아이들 여권사본이 필요하다고 했다.

제목	Re: [RE]Re: [RE]Re: Research Fellow Application: Reminder
보낸사람	주소록추가 @ucdmc.ucdavis.edu> 수신거부
보낸날짜	2011. 11. 2 오전 1:42:40
받는사람	은종렬 <dreun@ynu.ac.kr>

I will need a copy of your wife and kids passport

비서가 이메일도 잘 확인 안 하는 것 같고, 진행도 더뎌서 속이 탔던 기억이 난다. 어쨌든 필요한 정보들을 알려주고, 마지막이라고 하지만 정말 마지막인지 믿음이 가지 않았다.

제목	Re: [RE]Re: [RE]Re: [RE]Re: Research Fellow Application: Reminder
보낸사람	주소록추가 @ucdmc.ucdavis.edu> 수신거부
보낸날짜	2011. 12. 9 오전 4:42:13
받는사람	은종렬 <dreun@ynu.ac.kr>

Dr. Eun,

The last thing I need is

Your wife's email address

your wife and kids city of birth, country of birth, country of citizenship, and country of permanent residence.

Thank you

Administrative Assistant
Division of Gastroenterology/Hepatology
Department of Internal Medicine
4635 2nd Ave Suite 1001
Sacramento, CA 95817
@ucdmc.ucdavis.edu

From: 은종렬 <dreun@ynu.ac.kr>
To: @ucdmc.ucdavis.edu
Date: 11/19/2011 09:46 AM
Subject: [RE]Re: [RE]Re: [RE]Re: Research Fellow Application: Reminder

---

I sent copies of my wife and kids passport last week.
You seem not to check my e-mail.
Please proceed the processing.
Eun

제목	DS-2019
보낸사람	주소록추가 @ucdmc.ucdavis.edu> 수신거부
보낸날짜	2011. 12. 23 오전 2:52:02
받는사람	은종렬 <dreun@ynu.ac.kr>

Please sign the attached forms and send back to me ASAP

Thank you,
Jon Dimitriadis
Administrative Assistant
Division of Gastroenterology/Hepatology
Department of Internal Medicine
4635 2nd Ave Suite 1001
Sacramento, CA 95817
(916)734-8056 vm
jonathon.dimitriadis@ucdmc.ucdavis.edu

· 첨부파일
일괄다운로드 scan0004.pdf (1.35MB) 다운로드

Revised 4/4/2011 Page 8 of 8

Attachment to Request for Form DS-2019 for J-1 Physician*

Section I **or** II below is to be completed by the J-1 physician's host department chair and supervisor and is to accurately reflect the type of patient contact that the physician will have. This form should be faxed to prospective J-1 physician for signature on Section III. Please attach this completed form to the *Request for Form DS-2019* and return it to SISS.

I. If the J-1 physician is coming to UCD to pursue a program that does not involve patient contact, the applicant's UCD sponsor must certify the following:

This certifies that the program in which Dr Eun is to be engaged is solely for the purpose of observation, consultation, teaching, or research and that no element of patient care services is involved.

Timothy Albertson, M.D.	[signature]	12/19/11
Print or type name of Department Chair	Signature of Department Chair	Date
Mark A. Zern, M.D.		
Print or type name of Faculty Sponsor	Signature of Faculty Sponsor	Date

II. If incidental patient contact is involved in the J-1 physician's duties, the UCD sponsor must certify the following five points:

1. The program in which Dr. ________ will participate is predominantly involved with observation, consultation, teaching, or research.
2. Any incidental patient contact involving the J-1 physician will be under the direct supervision of a physician who is a U.S. citizen or resident alien and who is licensed to practice medicine in the state of California.
3. The J-1 physician will not be given final responsibility for the diagnosis and treatment of patients.
4. Any activities of the J-1 physician will conform fully with state licensing requirements and regulations for medical and health care professionals in the state of California.
5. Any experience gained in this program will not be creditable toward any clinical requirements for medical specialty board certification.

Print or type name of Department Chair	Signature of Department Chair	Date
Print or type name of Faculty Sponsor	Signature of Faculty Sponsor	Date

III. To be completed by prospective J-1 Physician:

I understand and agree with the above statement(s) regarding the level of patient contact I will have during my proposed activity at UC Davis.

Jong Ryeol Eun		
Print or type name	Signature of Prospective J-1 Physician	Date

If the J-1 physician's program involves significant patient contact or otherwise does not conform with Section I or II above, the physician cannot be sponsored through the UCD J-1 Exchange Visitor Program.

Clinical training for J-1 physicians who are interns, residents or who hold other clinical positions involving patient contact can be authorized under a program sponsored by the Educational Commission for Foreign Medical Graduates (ECFMG). For further information regarding ECFMG sponsorship, contact the School of Medicine Office of the Dean: http://www.ucdmc.ucdavis.edu/dean/contactus/

*Note: If bringing a J-1 physician scholar in the J-1 specialist category, please consult with an international scholar advisor before completing this form.

Revised 4/4/2011 Page 5 of 8

This Health Insurance Memo of Understanding is to be signed by the prospective J-1 Exchange Visitor before a Form DS-2019 can be issued. Fax copies of the signed MOU are acceptable.

International Scholar Health Insurance Memo of Understanding

I understand that the Department of State requires all J-1 Exchange Visitors and their accompanying dependents to have health and accident insurance at the following minimum level of coverage:

- --medical benefits of at least $50,000 per accident or illness
- --repatriation of remains in the amount of $7,500
- --expenses associated with medical evacuation in the amount of $10,000
- --deductible not to exceed $500 per accident/illness

I understand that I am responsible for the purchase of health insurance that meets these requirements.
Some scholars who receive a UCD salary may be provided with University health insurance. If you will receive payment from UC Davis, please discuss health insurance coverage with your sponsoring department, including the option of coverage for your dependents, if applicable.

I understand the cost of this insurance.
Insurance information can be found on the SISS website at http://siss.ucdavis.edu/health_j1.cfm Please review this website for information on the cost of "premiums" (insurance payments) and health insurance companies in the US that offer insurance to J-1scholars. SISS also recommends that J-1 scholars purchase travel insurance coverage for the first month, to provide health coverage until a longer-term health insurance plan is selected and/or purchased.

The insurance corporation underwriting the policy must have one of the following ratings:

- --an A.M. Best rating of "A-" or above
- --an Insurance Solvency International, Ltd., (ISI) rating of "A-i" or above
- --a Standard & Poor's Claimspaying Ability rating of "A-" or above
- --a Weiss Research, Inc. rating of "B+" or above

Note: Insurance coverage backed by the full faith and credit of your home government meets these requirements.

I understand that U.S. government regulations require the University to notify the U.S. Department of State and to terminate my J-1 exchange visitor status if they determine that my family members or I willfully fail to comply with the insurance requirements.

I understand the health insurance requirements, the costs involved, and the need to maintain the insurance throughout my stay at the University of California, Davis.

Name: Eun (family (last)) Jong Ryeo (given (first)) ______ (middle)

Signature: ______ Date ______

Name of UCD Department: IM: GI/Hepatology

2011년 12월 23일 금요일

이제 서류가 급하다. 바쁜 와중에 2012년 1월 18일 Step 2CK 성적이 발표되었는데, Step 1 성적으로 우울했던 기분이 조금은 나아졌다.

2012년 1월 19일 목요일

DS-2019가 있어야 비자 인터뷰를 할 수 있어서 속이 타들어갔다.

제목	Re: [RE]DS-2019
보낸사람	주소록추가 Jonathon Dimitriadis<jonathon.dimitriadis@ucdmc.ucdavis.edu> 수신거부
보낸날짜	2012. 1. 19 오전 4:35:26
받는사람	은종렬<dreun@ynu.ac.kr>

Dear Dr. Eun.

SISS has work DS-2019 I talked with them this morning they are hoping to get the approval by the end of this week. as soon as I get it I will be send it off to you I will send you the tracking # once I send it off I hope this will be this Friday or early next week

2012년 2월 1일 수요일

UC 데이비스의 SISS로부터 반가운 이메일을 받았다.

제목	New J-1 scholar information
보낸사람	주소록추가 siss@ucdavis.edu 수신거부
보낸날짜	2012. 2. 1 오전 1:01:53
받는사람	dreun@ynu.ac.kr

Dear Jong Ryeol Eun,

As you prepare for arrival at UC Davis, you may find the below website resources helpful in addition to the pre-arrival information packet that you received with your DS-2019:

* UC Davis Campus Map: http://www.cevs.ucdavis.edu/map/
* Life in Davis: http://www.ucdavis.edu/about/davis_life.html
* Childcare: http://www.hr.ucdavis.edu/Work_Life/Life/childcare/childcare
* City of Davis: http://www.daviswiki.org/
* City of Sacramento: http://www.sacwiki.org/
* Health Insurance (if you do not receive benefits from UCD): http://siss.ucdavis.edu/health_j1.cfm
* UCD Postdoc Association: http://postdocs.ucdavis.edu/index.html
* U.S. Port of Entry: http://www.ice.gov/sevis/factsheet/100104ent_exchng_fs.htm
* J-1 visa: http://www.travel.state.gov/visa/temp/types/types_1267.html
* Driver License: http://www.dmv.ca.gov/dl/dl.htm
(International Driver License is not recognized in California)
* Housing: http://siss.ucdavis.edu/housing.cfm?id=scholar
http://siss.ucdavis.edu/listserv.cfm (SISS Bulletin)
http://cityofdavis.org/cs/fairhousing/

Have a safe trip! We are looking forward to meeting with you at SISS.

2012년 2월 2일 목요일

27일 출국이므로 25일 남았다. 아직 DS-2019를 받지 못해 매우 불안하다. SISS는 페이퍼웍을 마친 것 같다. 일단 비자 인터뷰 예약을 해야 하고 항공권 예매도 해야 한다. 영어공부한 지 6개월이 되었다. 영어가 느는지 모르겠다. 계속 하다보면 늘겠지. 병원에 내가 사직할 것이라는 소문이 돌고 있나 보다. 당황스럽다. 엎질러진 물을 주워 담을 수 없으므로 할 수 없다. DS-2019 제발 빨리 와라.

2012년 2월 8일 수요일

속이 타들어 가던 와중에 페덱스FedEx로 DS-2019을 보낸다는 이메일을 받았다.

제목	**Re: [RE]Re: [RE]DS-2019**
보낸사람	주소록추가 [ ]@ucdmc.ucdavis.edu> 수신거부
보낸날짜	2012. 2. 7 오전 5:46:43
받는사람	은종렬<dreun@ynu.ac.kr>

Dr. Eun,

Sorry for delay I was out of the office last week due to a death in my family, Your DS-2019 is done and I will be sending it to you tomorrow I will email you the tracking #

Thank you,
Jon Dimitriadis
Administrative Assistant
Division of Gastroenterology/Hepatology
Department of Internal Medicine
4635 2nd Ave Suite 1001
Sacramento, CA 95817
(916)734-8056 vm
(916)734-8097 fax
[ ]@ucdmc.ucdavis.edu

From: 은종렬 <dreun@ynu.ac.kr>
To: [ ]@ucdmc.ucdavis.edu
Date: 02/03/2012 04:34 PM
Subject: [RE]Re: [RE]DS-2019

Dear Jonathon,
I am looking forward to DS-2019. But I didn't receive it yet.
I am very nervous because I cannot proceed the interview for visa issue and reserve an airplane.
I'd appreciate if you check DS-2019 and send it ASAP.
Thank you.
Sincerely
From Eun

제목	**Re: [RE]DS-2019**
보낸사람	주소록추가 [ ]@ucdmc.ucdavis.edu> 수신거부
보낸날짜	2012. 2. 14 오전 8:02:02
받는사람	은종렬<dreun@ynu.ac.kr>

I am sending DS-2019 to SISS today and should have it approved by end of week

I will double check if we can make your first visit 2 years normally the J1 I apply for is good for 5 years but we have to renew it once a year to ensure you have funding ect.

인터뷰 예약일 직전에 극적으로 DS-2019를 받았다. J 비자를 받기 위해 가장 중요한 서류다. 이 한 장을 받기 위해 그렇게 고생하고 마음을 졸였다.

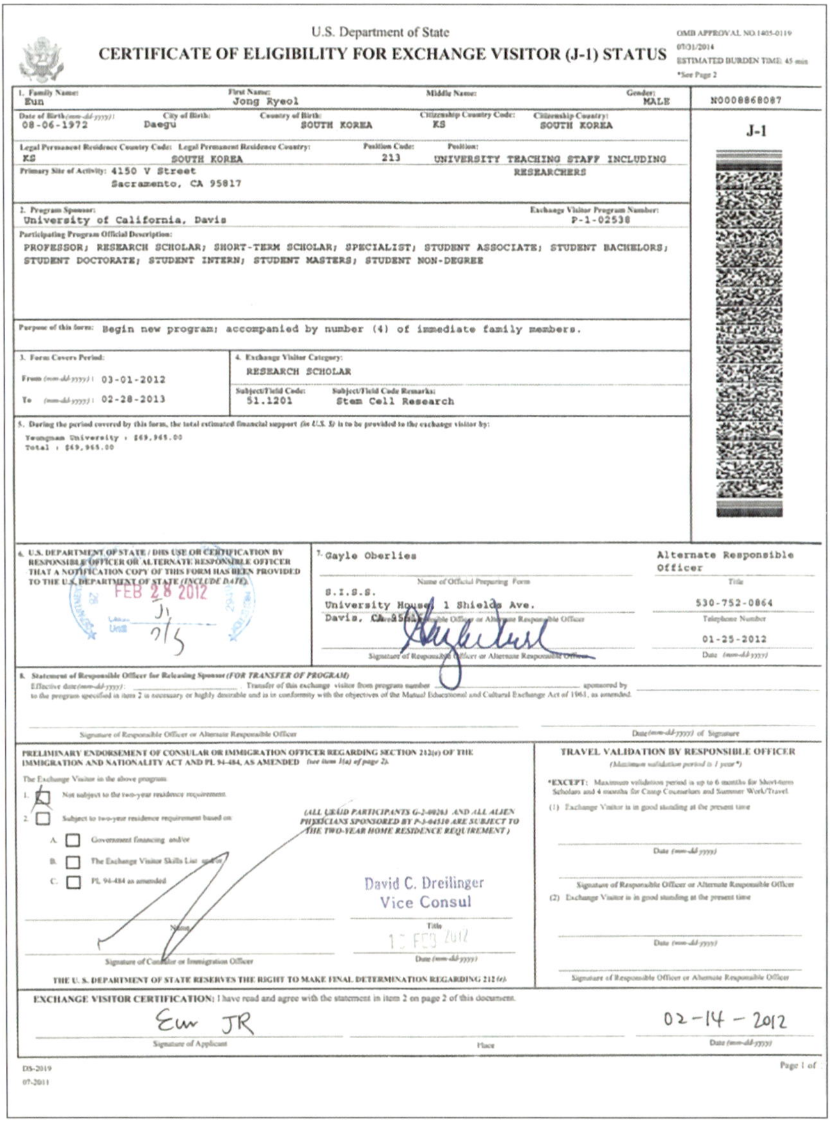

U.S. Department of State

CERTIFICATE OF ELIGIBILITY FOR EXCHANGE VISITOR (J-1) STATUS

OMB APPROVAL NO.1405-0119
07/31/2014
ESTIMATED BURDEN TIME: 45 min
*See Page 2

N0008868087

J-1

1. Family Name: Eun
First Name: Jong Ryeol
Middle Name:
Gender: MALE

Date of Birth (mm-dd-yyyy): 08-06-1972
City of Birth: Daegu
Country of Birth: SOUTH KOREA
Citizenship Country Code: KS
Citizenship Country: SOUTH KOREA

Legal Permanent Residence Country Code: KS
Legal Permanent Residence Country: SOUTH KOREA
Position Code: 213
Position: UNIVERSITY TEACHING STAFF INCLUDING RESEARCHERS

Primary Site of Activity: 4150 V Street
Sacramento, CA 95817

2. Program Sponsor: University of California, Davis
Exchange Visitor Program Number: P-1-02538

Participating Program Official Description:
PROFESSOR; RESEARCH SCHOLAR; SHORT-TERM SCHOLAR; SPECIALIST; STUDENT ASSOCIATE; STUDENT BACHELORS; STUDENT DOCTORATE; STUDENT INTERN; STUDENT MASTERS; STUDENT NON-DEGREE

Purpose of this form: Begin new program; accompanied by number (4) of immediate family members.

3. Form Covers Period:
From (mm-dd-yyyy): 03-01-2012
To (mm-dd-yyyy): 02-28-2013

4. Exchange Visitor Category: RESEARCH SCHOLAR
Subject/Field Code: 51.1201
Subject/Field Code Remarks: Stem Cell Research

5. During the period covered by this form, the total estimated financial support (in U.S. $) is to be provided to the exchange visitor by:
Yeungnam University : $69,965.00
Total : $69,965.00

6. U.S. DEPARTMENT OF STATE / DHS USE OR CERTIFICATION BY RESPONSIBLE OFFICER OR ALTERNATE RESPONSIBLE OFFICER THAT A NOTIFICATION COPY OF THIS FORM HAS BEEN PROVIDED TO THE U.S. DEPARTMENT OF STATE (INCLUDE DATE).
FEB 28 2012

7. Gayle Oberlies — Name of Official Preparing Form
Alternate Responsible Officer — Title
S.I.S.S.
University House, 1 Shields Ave.
Davis, CA 95616 — Address of Responsible Officer or Alternate Responsible Officer
530-752-0864 — Telephone Number
Signature of Responsible Officer or Alternate Responsible Officer
01-25-2012 — Date (mm-dd-yyyy)

8. Statement of Responsible Officer for Releasing Sponsor (FOR TRANSFER OF PROGRAM)
Effective date (mm-dd-yyyy): ______ Transfer of this exchange visitor from program number ______ sponsored by ______ to the program specified in item 2 is necessary or highly desirable and is in conformity with the objectives of the Mutual Educational and Cultural Exchange Act of 1961, as amended.
Signature of Responsible Officer or Alternate Responsible Officer — Date (mm-dd-yyyy) of Signature

PRELIMINARY ENDORSEMENT OF CONSULAR OR IMMIGRATION OFFICER REGARDING SECTION 212(e) OF THE IMMIGRATION AND NATIONALITY ACT AND PL 94-484, AS AMENDED (see item 3(a) of page 2).
The Exchange Visitor in the above program:
1. ☒ Not subject to the two-year residence requirement.
2. ☐ Subject to two-year residence requirement based on:
A. ☐ Government financing and/or
B. ☐ The Exchange Visitor Skills List and/or
C. ☐ PL 94-484 as amended
(ALL USAID PARTICIPANTS G-2-00263 AND ALL ALIEN PHYSICIANS SPONSORED BY P-3-04510 ARE SUBJECT TO THE TWO-YEAR HOME RESIDENCE REQUIREMENT)
Name — David C. Dreilinger, Vice Consul — Title
Signature of Consular or Immigration Officer — 10 FEB 2012 — Date (mm-dd-yyyy)
THE U.S. DEPARTMENT OF STATE RESERVES THE RIGHT TO MAKE FINAL DETERMINATION REGARDING 212(e).

TRAVEL VALIDATION BY RESPONSIBLE OFFICER
(Maximum validation period is 1 year*)
*EXCEPT: Maximum validation period is up to 6 months for Short-term Scholars and 4 months for Camp Counselors and Summer Work/Travel.
(1) Exchange Visitor is in good standing at the present time
Date (mm-dd-yyyy)
Signature of Responsible Officer or Alternate Responsible Officer
(2) Exchange Visitor is in good standing at the present time
Date (mm-dd-yyyy)
Signature of Responsible Officer or Alternate Responsible Officer

EXCHANGE VISITOR CERTIFICATION: I have read and agree with the statement in item 2 on page 2 of this document.
Eun JR — Signature of Applicant
Place
02-14-2012 — Date (mm-dd-yyyy)

DS-2019
07-2011
Page 1 of

2012년 2월 16일 목요일

추운 겨울 새벽에 서울로 상경해 미국대사관에서 비자 인터뷰를 했다. 항상 한 번에 제대로 하는 법이 없었는데 이번에도 역시 실수를 했다. DS-160을 내 것만 작성하고 가족들 것을 작성하지 않아 대사관 주변 PC방에서 서류를 작성하는 생쇼를 한 것이다. 어찌어찌 1층 서류접수를 겨우 통과하여 3층(?)에 있는 영사 인터뷰까지 가게 되었다. 미리 인터뷰 예상 질문을 연습했는데 의외로 우리 인터뷰 영사는 나이스했고 덕담을 해주었던 기억이 난다. 옆 창구에서는 비자가 거절되어 실망한 사람이 있었는데 계속 어필을 하는데도 잘 안 되는 것 같아 안타깝다는 생각을 했다.

2012년 2월 20일 월요일

나와 가족들 비자를 우편으로 받았다. 지난 목요일 인터뷰를 하러 서울에 갔다. 실수로 가족들 신청서application forms를 빼먹었다. 대사관 주변 PC방에 가서 다시 작성하느라 예약된 KTX를 놓쳤다. 어쨌든 인터뷰는 잘했고 비자를 받았다. J 비자 인터뷰에 필요한 서류는 다음과 같다.

1) DS-2019

2) DS-160 application forms : each for family members

3) others ; certificate for a job, 주민등록등본 또는 가족관계증명서, 소득금액증명원, 근로소득원천징수 영수증 1부, 여권, 사진1매(가로×세로 5cm), SEVIS fee 납부 영수증($180), 비자 Fee 납부 영수증($140), 인터뷰 예약증

2012년 2월 25일 금요일

오전 마지막 진료를 했다. 환영받지 못한 연수라 연수 전 휴가 부탁도 하지 못하고 꾸역꾸역 연수 직전까지 진료했다. 금요일 오후에 핸드폰을 해지하고 교수님들을 찾아다니면서 인사를 하느라 정신이 없었다.

다음날인 토요일, 짐을 정리하고 27일 일요일 아침 대구공항에서 출발했다. 인천공항에 내려 근처 호텔에서 하루를 묵었다. 대구 촌놈이라 바로 출국하면 힘들 것 같아서 인천에서 하루 묵은 것인데 결론적으로는 더 힘들었다. 28일 월요일 밤 비행기로 이륙했다. 드디어 미국연수의 험난한 여정이 시작되었다.

2011/06/24

영어와의 전쟁,
미국연수 1년차

미국에 도착하자마자 3월 1일부터 첫째와 둘째는 바로 등교했다. 집 근처 파이오니어 초등학교Pioneer Elementary school에 자리가 없어 조금 떨어진노스 데이비스 초등학교North Davis Elementary school에 입학했다. 오피스에 서류를 제출하고는 바로 교실로 들어갔다. 아이들은 정말 적응이 빠른 것 같다. 폴짝폴짝 뛰면서 교실로 들어가는 모습을 뒤로 하고 집으로 왔다.

아파트 오피스에서 리스 계약서를 작성했다. 순서상 리스계약서가 가장 우선이다. 주소가 적힌 아파트 계약서가 있어야 학교 입학 등의 모든 업무 처리가 가능하기 때문이다.

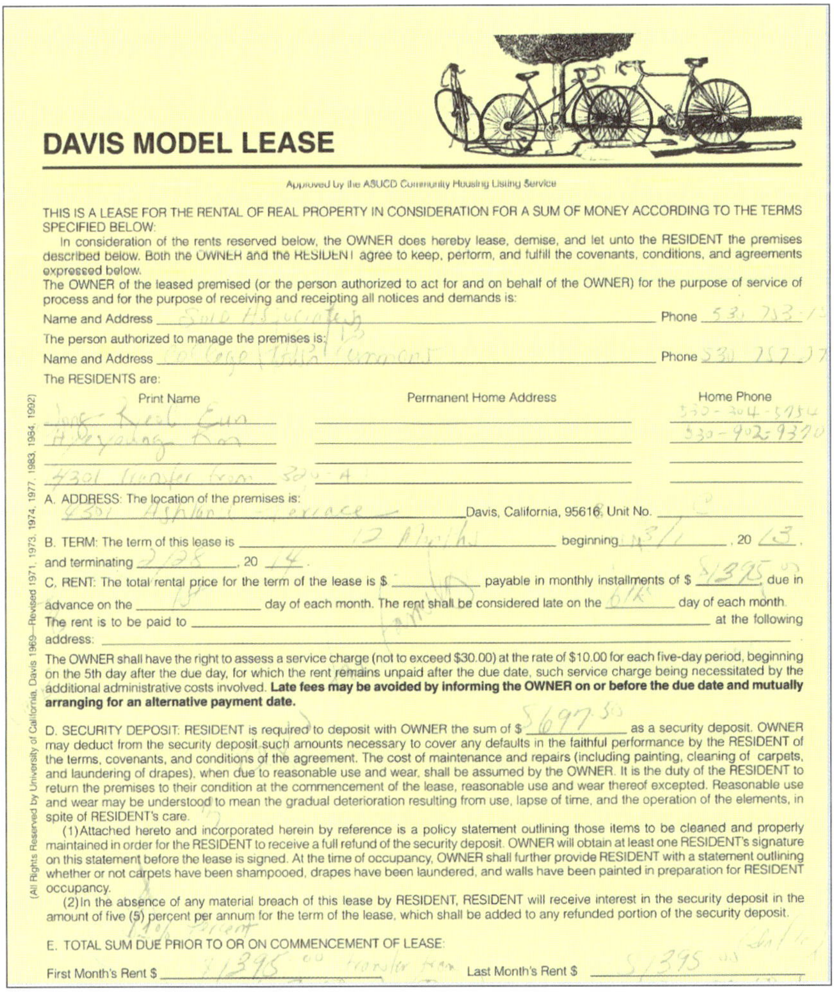

DAVIS MODEL LEASE

Approved by the ASUCD Community Housing Listing Service

THIS IS A LEASE FOR THE RENTAL OF REAL PROPERTY IN CONSIDERATION FOR A SUM OF MONEY ACCORDING TO THE TERMS SPECIFIED BELOW:

In consideration of the rents reserved below, the OWNER does hereby lease, demise, and let unto the RESIDENT the premises described below. Both the OWNER and the RESIDENT agree to keep, perform, and fulfill the covenants, conditions, and agreements expressed below.

The OWNER of the leased premised (or the person authorized to act for and on behalf of the OWNER) for the purpose of service of process and for the purpose of receiving and receipting all notices and demands is:

Name and Address ______ Phone ______

The person authorized to manage the premises is:

Name and Address ______ Phone ______

The RESIDENTS are:

Print Name	Permanent Home Address	Home Phone

A. ADDRESS: The location of the premises is: ______ Davis, California, 95616, Unit No. ______

B. TERM: The term of this lease is ______ beginning ______, 20 ______, and terminating ______, 20 ______.

C. RENT: The total rental price for the term of the lease is $ ______ payable in monthly installments of $ ______ due in advance on the ______ day of each month. The rent shall be considered late on the ______ day of each month. The rent is to be paid to ______ at the following address: ______

The OWNER shall have the right to assess a service charge (not to exceed $30.00) at the rate of $10.00 for each five-day period, beginning on the 5th day after the due day, for which the rent remains unpaid after the due date, such service charge being necessitated by the additional administrative costs involved. **Late fees may be avoided by informing the OWNER on or before the due date and mutually arranging for an alternative payment date.**

D. SECURITY DEPOSIT: RESIDENT is required to deposit with OWNER the sum of $ ______ as a security deposit. OWNER may deduct from the security deposit such amounts necessary to cover any defaults in the faithful performance by the RESIDENT of the terms, covenants, and conditions of the agreement. The cost of maintenance and repairs (including painting, cleaning of carpets, and laundering of drapes), when due to reasonable use and wear, shall be assumed by the OWNER. It is the duty of the RESIDENT to return the premises to their condition at the commencement of the lease, reasonable use and wear thereof excepted. Reasonable use and wear may be understood to mean the gradual deterioration resulting from use, lapse of time, and the operation of the elements, in spite of RESIDENT's care.

(1) Attached hereto and incorporated herein by reference is a policy statement outlining those items to be cleaned and properly maintained in order for the RESIDENT to receive a full refund of the security deposit. OWNER will obtain at least one RESIDENT's signature on this statement before the lease is signed. At the time of occupancy, OWNER shall further provide RESIDENT with a statement outlining whether or not carpets have been shampooed, drapes have been laundered, and walls have been painted in preparation for RESIDENT occupancy.

(2) In the absence of any material breach of this lease by RESIDENT, RESIDENT will receive interest in the security deposit in the amount of five (5) percent per annum for the term of the lease, which shall be added to any refunded portion of the security deposit.

E. TOTAL SUM DUE PRIOR TO OR ON COMMENCEMENT OF LEASE:

First Month's Rent $ ______ Last Month's Rent $ ______

이 책을 준비하면서 필요한 자료들을 찾기 위해 컴퓨터 파일을 뒤져보았는데 미국 연수기간 동안에 기록한 일기 파일이 보였다. 영어로 일기를 쓰면 영어 실력이 좀 늘지 않을까 싶어서 영어로 적었다. 대부분은 랩에서 실험했던 내용들로 중간 중간 나의 일상이 기록되어 있었다. 실험과 관련된 내용은 빼고 나의 일상에 대해 기록한 것들 위주로 소개한다.

2012년 3월 9일 금요일

랩에 첫 출근을 했다. 모든 것이 낯설어 긴장을 많이 했다. 다른 사람들의 말을 거의 알아들을 수 없어서 난감했다. 뭐, 점점 나아지겠지.

2012년 3월 12일 월요일

9시, 랩에 출근했는데 아무도 없었다. 10시까지 아무도 오지 않았다. 랩 미팅이 있어 모두 거기 갔나 싶어 걱정이 되었다. 10시 30분에 닥터 쳉Dr. Zeng에게서 전화가 와서 빌딩 문을 열어 달라고 했다. 닥터 유유Dr. Yuyou에게 가서 출입 카드키를 언제쯤 받을 수 있는지 물어보았다. 카드키를 아직 받지 못해서 건물 출입이 불편하다. 건강보험 문제, 카드키 문제 등 이것저것 걱정이 많다. 운전면허 시험보러 DMV에 가야 하고, 사회보장국social security office에도 가야 하고, 오후에는 TV 세팅도 신청하러 디시 네트워크에도 가야 한다. 영어 때문에 스트레스가 너무 심하다.

* 닥터 쳉은 중국에서 자연과학을 전공하는 교수로 나와 같은 시기에 1년 연수를 왔다. 나는 주로 쳉과 같이 지냈고, 점심도 함께 먹으며 랩에서 일어나는 일들을 전해 들었다.

* 닥터 유유는 랩을 관장하는 매니저로 연수기간 동안 많은 도움을 주었고, 덕분에 다수의 논문이 출간되었다. 또 liver cancer stem cells에 대해 관심을 갖게 해주었다.

2012년 3월 13일 화요일

비가 오고 있다. 데이비스에 온 지 2주가 지났다. 아직 랩 일을 시작하지 않았다. 다음주부터는 집사람이 아이들을 학교에 태워다 줄 수 있게 되어서 랩에 집중할 수 있을 것 같다.

2012년 3월 15일 목요일

구입한 버라이존 폰을 취소하고 반납했다. 비싼 요금이 감당이 안 될 것 같았다. 취소는 의외로 쉽게 되었다. 세이프웨이에 가서 선불 쿠폰prepaid coupon을 구입했다.

2012년 3월 16일 금요일

집사람이 처음으로 혼자서 운전했다. 오후 3시 12분 집사람이 흥분된 목소리로 전화를 했다. 주차하는데 옆줄 선을 물었다는 것이다. 정말 아무것도 아니지만 도움 없이 스스로 운전을 했다는 것이 중요하다.

* 사회 보장 카드 Social Security Card를 받았다.

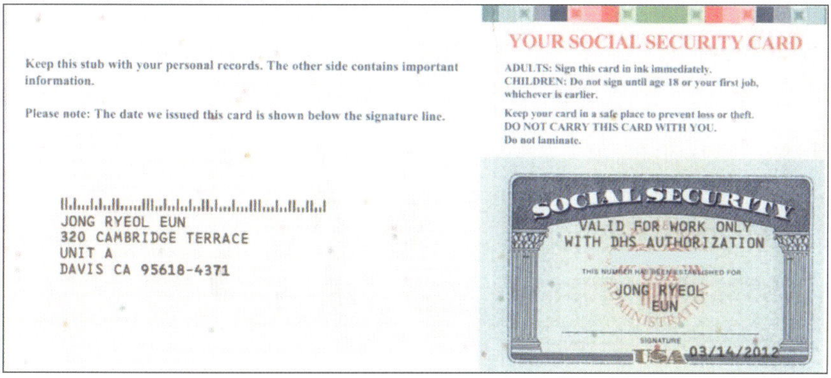

Keep this stub with your personal records. The other side contains important information.

Please note: The date we issued this card is shown below the signature line.

JONG RYEOL EUN
320 CAMBRIDGE TERRACE
UNIT A
DAVIS CA 95618-4371

YOUR SOCIAL SECURITY CARD

ADULTS: Sign this card in ink immediately.
CHILDREN: Do not sign until age 18 or your first job, whichever is earlier.

Keep your card in a safe place to prevent loss or theft.
DO NOT CARRY THIS CARD WITH YOU.
Do not laminate.

SOCIAL SECURITY
VALID FOR WORK ONLY
WITH DHS AUTHORIZATION
THIS NUMBER HAS BEEN ESTABLISHED FOR
JONG RYEOL
EUN
SIGNATURE
USA 03/14/2012

2012년 3월 26일 월요일

한 달이 지났다. 이제 시차로부터 자유롭다. 성공적으로 정착한 듯하다. 랩 미팅에서 돌아가면서 한 마디씩 보고하는데 아직 할 말이 없다.

2012년 3월 29일 목요일

DMV 가서 실기시험을 봤다. 첫 번째 시험에 떨어져서 긴장했지만 시험관이 매우 나이스해서 운이 좋았다. 실수했지만 결국 합격해서 너무 기뻤다. J1 장학생scholar을 위한 SISS 오리엔테이션을 받으러 UC 데이비스 캠퍼스를 방문했다. 오리엔테이션 파일들을 몇 번씩 읽어본 터라 새로운 내용은 없었다. 그래도 서류들을 모두 제출하고 와서 기분이 좋았다. 집에서 점심을 먹고 랩으로 다시 갔다. 오후에 유유와 나의 프로젝트에 대하여 의논했다. 내가 간암 줄기세포liver cancer stem cells를 하게 될 것이고, 준비 과정이 3~6개월 정도 소요될 것이라고 말했다. 잘 됐다고 생각했다. 내일은 세자르 차베스Cesar Chevas 국경일이다. 3일 연휴라 랩에 안 나와도 되어서 한결 가뿐한 마음이 들었다.

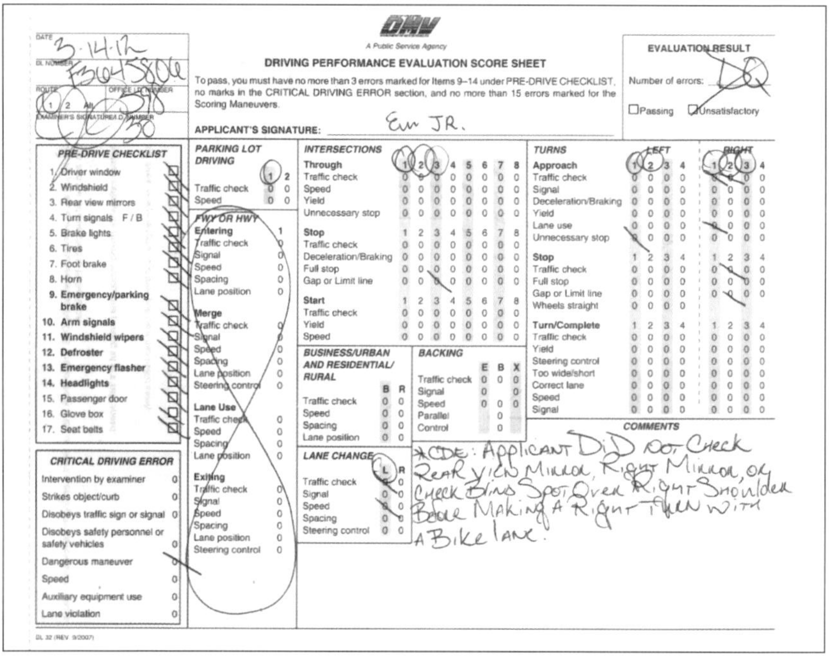

DMV
A Public Service Agency

DRIVING PERFORMANCE EVALUATION SCORE SHEET

DATE 3-14-12
DL NUMBER F3045806
ROUTE 1 2 Alt
OFFICE I.D. NUMBER
EXAMINER'S SIGNATURE/I.D. NUMBER

To pass, you must have no more than 3 errors marked for Items 9–14 under PRE-DRIVE CHECKLIST, no marks in the CRITICAL DRIVING ERROR section, and no more than 15 errors marked for the Scoring Maneuvers.

APPLICANT'S SIGNATURE: Eun JR.

EVALUATION RESULT
Number of errors: DQ
☐Passing ☒Unsatisfactory

PRE-DRIVE CHECKLIST
1. Driver window
2. Windshield
3. Rear view mirrors
4. Turn signals F / B
5. Brake lights
6. Tires
7. Foot brake
8. Horn
9. Emergency/parking brake
10. Arm signals
11. Windshield wipers
12. Defroster
13. Emergency flasher
14. Headlights
15. Passenger door
16. Glove box
17. Seat belts

CRITICAL DRIVING ERROR
Intervention by examiner 0
Strikes object/curb 0
Disobeys traffic sign or signal 0
Disobeys safety personnel or safety vehicles 0
Dangerous maneuver 0
Speed 0
Auxiliary equipment use 0
Lane violation 0

PARKING LOT DRIVING (1 2)
Traffic check 0 0
Speed 0 0

FWY OR HWY
Entering 1
Traffic check 0
Signal 0
Speed 0
Spacing 0
Lane position 0
Merge
Traffic check 0
Signal 0
Speed 0
Spacing 0
Lane position 0
Steering control 0
Lane Use
Traffic check 0
Speed 0
Spacing 0
Lane position 0
Exiting
Traffic check 0
Signal 0
Speed 0
Spacing 0
Lane position 0
Steering control 0

INTERSECTIONS
Through 1 2 3 4 5 6 7 8
Traffic check / Speed / Yield / Unnecessary stop
Stop 1 2 3 4 5 6 7 8
Traffic check / Deceleration/Braking / Full stop / Gap or Limit line
Start 1 2 3 4 5 6 7 8
Traffic check / Yield / Speed

BUSINESS/URBAN AND RESIDENTIAL/ RURAL (B R)
Traffic check 0 0
Speed 0 0
Spacing 0 0
Lane position 0 0

BACKING (E B X)
Traffic check 0 0 0
Signal 0
Speed 0 0 0
Parallel 0
Control 0

LANE CHANGE (L R)
Traffic check 0 0
Signal 0 0
Speed 0 0
Spacing 0 0
Steering control 0 0

TURNS (LEFT 1 2 3 4 / RIGHT 1 2 3 4)
Approach: Traffic check / Signal / Deceleration/Braking / Yield / Lane use / Unnecessary stop
Stop: Traffic check / Full stop / Gap or Limit line / Wheels straight
Turn/Complete: Traffic check / Yield / Steering control / Too wide/short / Correct lane / Speed / Signal

COMMENTS
*CDE: APPLICANT DID NOT CHECK REAR VIEW MIRROR, RIGHT MIRROR, OR CHECK BLIND SPOT OVER RIGHT SHOULDER BEFORE MAKING A RIGHT TURN WITH A BIKE LANE.

DL 32 (REV. 9/2007)

2012년 4월 2일 월요일

유유와 수요일에 서류 작업하러 오피스에 가기로 했다. 찰스가 배지 교체media change에 대해 가르쳐 주었다. 배아줄기세포Embryonic stem cells를 처음으로 보았다. 몬스터처럼 느껴졌다. 찰스가 아직 미성숙세포immature cells라고 말했다.

* 찰스는 20대로 의대를 준비하기 위해 스펙을 쌓는 중이라는 것 같았다.

2012년 4월 4일 수요일

유유와 15분 걸어 디파트먼트에 갔다. 서류에 필요한 사항들을 기입하고 사인했다. 미국 시스템은 매우 느린 것 같다.

2012년 4월 5일 목요일

서류 작업을 했으니 이제 일을 시작할 수 있게 되었다. 트위로부터 베이직 애니멀 트레이닝BAT을 배우게 되었다.

* 트위는 베트남계 미국인으로 20대 초반 정도의 여성이다. 정확한 신분은 모르겠지만 파트타임으로 테크니션 일을 하는 것 같다.

2012년 4월 6일 금요일

모두 랩 미팅에 들어가는데 나는 아무것도 모르고 있어 당황하고 있었다. 다행히 아흐마드Ahmad가 들어오라고 손짓해 주었다. 아흐마드는 이집트에서 연수 온 젊은 교수다. 역시 할 말이 없어 뻘쭘해 하고 있는데 닥터 전Dr. Zern은 지긋이 미소만 지었다. 유유가 아직 트레이닝 중이라고 말해 주었다. 랩 미팅 후 트위를 따라다녔다. 플로우 사이토메트리Flow cytometry를 위한 샘플을 준비하고 배지 교체media change를 매우 능숙하게 진행했다. 그녀에게 리서치 일한 지 얼마 되었는지 물어보았다. 1년 반이 되었다고 했다.

2012년 4월 9일 월요일

피곤하다. 주말에 바빴다. 금요일 저녁 우드랜드 코스트코에 갔다. 오는 길에 달이 떠오르고 있었다. 바로 앞에 떠 있는 것처럼 어마어마한 크기의 슈퍼 문이었다. 처음 보는 광경이었다. 토요일 이케아와 토이즈러스를 다녀와서 밤늦게까지 책장을 조립했다. 일요일에는 한인교회에 갔다. 마침 부활절이었다. 재미있었지만 사람들이 우리 가족에게 너무 관심을 보여 조금은 불편했다. 점심 식사 후 집에 오는 길에 달러트리에 들렀다. 오후에는 커뮤니티 파크Community park에 모여서 놀다가 오후 늦게 다른 가족들과 베트남 쌀국수집에 갔다. 사람들과 어울리는 것을 잘 못하는 나로서는 좀 불편했다. 저녁에는 토이즈러스에서 구입한 기차트랙을 조립했다.

2012년 4월 11일 수요일

비가 오고 있다. 어제는 따뜻하고 화창했다. 저녁을 먹은 후 타겟Target에 갔고, 다녀와서는 동네 드라이브를 했다. 쓰레기장에 조명스탠드가 버려져 있었다. 집사람이 주워 와서 전구를 교체했지만 작동하지 않았다. 어찌어찌 겨우 고치자 거실이 밝아졌다. 집사람이 좋아했다.

2012년 4월 16일 월요일

랩 미팅이 없어서 마음이 편안하다. 보고할 말이 없기 때문에 매번 뻘쭘하다. 여전히 유유와 트위를 따라다녔다. 지난주 금요일은 바빴다. 유유가 슬라이드를 보면서 흥분했다. 녹색은 HepPar1이고, 빨간색은 CK19인데, CD34+ double positive cells은 combined HCC-CC이고, CD34+ single postivie cells은 HCC or CC이고, CD34- cells은 only HCC라고 했다. 나에게 논문 초록abstract과 프로젝트 제안서project proposal를 주었다. 금요일까지는 비가 왔고 주말에는 화창하게 개었다. 우리 가족은 젤리빈 팩토리에 갔다. 킴스 마트에서 김밥을 사서 출발했다. 오후에는 이케아와 ACE 마트에 들러 정원용 흙과 토마토, 옥수수, 딸기 씨앗들을 구입했다.

* 이 결과는 좋은 저널에 발표되었고 나도 저자로 이름을 올리게 되었다

STEM CELLS AND DEVELOPMENT
Volume 24, Number 8, 2015
© Mary Ann Liebert, Inc.
DOI: 10.1089/scd.2014.0405

Identification of Cancer Stem Cell Subpopulations of CD34$^+$ PLC/PRF/5 That Result in Three Types of Human Liver Carcinomas

Su Cheol Park,[1–3,*] Ngoc Tue Nguyen,[1,2,*] Jong Ryeol Eun,[1,2,4,*] Yanling Zhang,[1,2,5] Yong Jin Jung,[1,2,6] Benjamin Tschudy-Seney,[1,2] Artem Trotsyuk,[1,2] Alexander Lam,[1,2] Rajendra Ramsamooj,[7] Yanghong Zhang,[7] Neil D. Theise,[8] Mark A. Zern,[1,2] and Yuyou Duan[1,2]

2012년 4월 19일 목요일

어제는 7시에 집에 돌아왔다. 집사람이 예린이와 지우의 수영 클럽 신청이 8시 마감이라고 해서 서둘러 저녁을 먹고 시빅 센터로 갔다. 신청서를 작성하여 제출하는데 문제가 생겼다. 보험이 없었다. 집으로 돌아와 SISS에 이메일을 보냈다. 스트레스다. 라이어빌리티Liability 하겠다고 하고 겨우 제출했다. 수업료는 두 명에 540달러다. 신청을 마치고 커뮤니티 파크로 갔다. 어제는 수요일로 파머스 마켓이 열리는 날이었다. 아이들에게 팝콘을 사주었고 점핑 벌룬에서 재밌게 놀았다.

* Liability는 사고가 생겼을 때 우리가 책임지겠다는 서약이다.

2012년 4월 20일 금요일

출근길 교통이 어마어마하게 막혔다. 꼼짝없이 갇혔다. 하이웨이는 차단되었다. 라디오 뉴스에서는 누군가 차를 강탈하고 총을 쐈다고 했다. 상공에는 헬리콥터가 호버링하고 있었다. 마침 방광이 터질 것 같고 기름도 바닥을 향해 가고 있었다. 2시간 갇혔다가 보이는 출구Exit로 나와 기름을 먼저 넣고 집으로 돌아왔다. 오전 10시 30분이었다. 새크라멘토 비 홈페이지에 들어가 보니 누군가 픽업트럭을 강탈하고 총을 쐈다고 했다. 경찰은 범인을 추적 중이고 하이웨이는 점심 이후에 다

시 오픈되었다. 2시에 다시 출근했다.

2012년 4월 23일 월요일

지난 주말은 매우 뜨거웠다. 금요일에는 코스트코에 가서 식료품을 샀다. 토요일에는 토이즈러스에 가서 온라인으로 주문한 자전거를 픽업하고, 아덴몰에 가서 내 백팩과 집사람 모자를 구입하고 근처 코리아나 마트에 가서 식료품도 구입했다. 집에 와서 자전거 조립을 하는데 브레이크가 없어서 당황했다. 반품해야 하나 생각하던 차에 인터넷 검색을 하니 코스터 브레이크 모델이었다. 코스터 브레이크는 손이 아니라 백 페달로 뒷바퀴가 서는 브레이크 방식이라고 했다. 일요일에는 교회에 가지 않고 GAP 매장에 가서 모자와 선글라스를 구입했는데 예린이가 지우 선글라스만 사줬다고 화를 냈다. 시빅 센터에 가기 전에 시간이 남아 달러트리에 들렀다. 시빅 센터에서는 지우 친구 생일파티가 있었다. 미국에서의 생일파티는 한국과는 많이 달랐다. 시빅 센터에 갔을 때 이미 많은 아이들이 짐에서 놀고 있었고 부모들은 관중석에서 지켜보고 있었다. 예린이와 준성이도 덩달아 함께 재밌게 놀았다. 매우 더운 날이었다. 한 시간 후 지우만 남겨두고 우리는 집으로 돌아왔다. 준성이는 이미 지쳐 있었다. 오후에 지우를 데려오는데 수영장에 준범이네 가족들이 보였다. 예린이와 지우가 엄마에게 수영장에 보내달라고 졸랐다. 2시간 동안 수영장에서 재밌게 놀았다. 저녁이 되니 쌀쌀해졌다.

2012년 4월 25일 수요일

나 빼고 모두 바쁜 것 같다. 아직 실험동물 취급 과정animal training course을 끝내지 못해서 동물실험을 시작할 수 없다. 어제 대학으로부터 이메일을 받았다. 부교수 승진에 관한 것이었다. 9월 1일 승진 예정이었다. 어젯밤 집사람과 장래에 대해 이야기했다. 집사람은 우리 미래에 대해 걱정했고 한국으로 돌아가자고 했다. 사실 나도 그러고 싶다. 그러나 아무 소득도 없이 돌아갈 수는 없다는 생각이 들었다. 우선 목표는 논문 2편을 쓰는 것이고, USMLE Step 2CS에 합격하고 영주권을 받는 것이다. 이후 미국 병원에서 레지던트 과정을 하고 싶다. 역시 영어가 문제다.

2012년 5월 1일 화요일

집에 오니 집사람이 도미노피자 무료 쿠폰에 당첨되었다고 했다. 웨스트 데이비스에 있는 도미노피자 가게에 가서 피자를 받아왔다.

2012년 5월 2일 수요일

호앙Hoang이 나에게 세포 분할cell splitting에 대해 가르쳐 주었다.

2012년 5월 3일 목요일

킴스마트에 갔다. 집사람이 만두를 쪄 주었다. 정말 맛있었다.

2012년 5월 7일 월요일

랜서를 타고 출근하던 길에 큰 사고가 났다. 하이웨이에 큰 타이어가 떨어져 있는 것을 피하지 못해 몇 바퀴 돌고 중앙분리대를 들이받고 말았다. 나는 별로 다치지 않았는데 차는 에어백이 터지고 크게 부서졌다. 누군가 와서 괜찮냐고 물었다. 잠시 후 하이웨이 순찰대가 도착했다. 갑자기 같은 랩에 있는 벤Ben이 나타났다. 출근길에 내 사고를 보았던 것이다. 기뻤다. 그가 대신 설명하고 해결해 주었다. 경찰에 진술서를 작성하고 보험회사에 연락했다. 트레일러가 와서 견인해 갔고 나도 따라 바디숍에 갔다. 보험약관에 사고 시 렌트카 제공이 되지 않는다는 것을 알았다. 에이전시에 전화해 추가 비용을 지불하고 토요다 코롤라를 렌트했다. 코롤라를 몰고 랩으로 출근했다. 이미 정오가 되었다. 유유와 닥터 전에게 사정을 이야기했다.

2012년 5월 9일 수요일

몸이 많이 안 좋고 오한이 든다. 어제 보험회사로부터 오는 무수한 전화를 받느라 매우 바빴다. 오늘은 파머스 에이전트로부터 전화를 받았다. 차를 폐차하는 것이 좋겠다고 했다. 동의할 수밖에 없었다. 3~5일 후 차량 가격을 산정하여 알려주기로 했다.

2012년 5월 10일 목요일

어제는 심한 두통과 오한이 있었다. 보험회사 조사관investigator으로부터 전화를 받았다. 결국 폐차가 결정되었다. 사고와 보험에 대해 더 생각하지 않기로 결심하고 나니 두통이 사라지고 몸이 점차 좋아지기 시작했다. 가족들은 집 근처 오토숍들을 둘러보았다. 나와 집사람은 크라이슬러 PT 크루저에 관심이 갔다.

FARMERS

Send all claims correspondence to:
Farmers Insurance Total Loss - COE
PO Box 108815
Oklahoma City OK 73101-8815
FAX: (877) 217-1389
Email: claimsdocuments@farmersinsurance.com

May 14, 2012

RE: Claim Number: 1021298657-1-1
Loss Date: 5/7/2012 12:00:00 AM
VIN: JA3AJ26E75U014167
Year/Make/Model: 2005 Mitsubishi Lancer Es

Dear Mr. Eun:

Your vehicle has been determined to be a total loss. The mileage, options, condition, and title history of your vehicle are taken into account when preparing your vehicle valuation and this information is utilized in order to establish the actual cash value of your vehicle.

The actual cash value of your total loss vehicle includes consideration for prior unrepaired damage and your vehicle title history. These considerations accounted for an adjustment of $0 in the value of your vehicle. The following is the breakdown of your settlement:

Actual Cash Value:	$8237.00
Sales Tax:	$638.36
License Fee Refund:	$102.00
Less: Deductible	- $750.00
Total Amount	$8227.36

Enclosed is a copy of the market appraisal used to determine the Actual Cash Value of your vehicle.

If within 35 days of receiving this settlement you cannot find a comparable vehicle for the gross settlement amount, you may notify us and we will re-open the claim for further evaluation.

Additionally, we urge you to contact your agent, if you have not already done so, to make further arrangements for your coverage needs. Please consult your policy for the exact terms and conditions of coverage.

2012년 5월 14일 월요일

오늘 랩 미팅의 주제는 풀파티였다. 보스인 닥터 전의 집에서 주말에 파티를 하자는 것이었다. 집에 와서 집사람과 무엇을 가져갈지 상의했다. 우리는 스파이시 누들을 준비해 가기로 했다. 딜러숍에서 새 중고차를 샀다. 크라이슬러 PT 크루저를 조금 깎아서 택스tax 포함 6,300달러에 샀다.

2012년 5월 15일 화요일

지난 토요일, 시에나 앞 유리에 금이 간 것을 발견했다. 오토숍을 검색해서 갔더니 수리는 안 되고 교체를 해야 하는데 450달러를 달라고 했다. 우선 ACE 하드웨어에서 앞 유리 수리 키트windshield repair kit를 구입해서 시도해 봤지만 잘 되지 않았다. 결국 파머스에 전화해서 보험으로 교체하기로 했다.

2012년 5월 17일 목요일

어제 우드랜드에 있는 마샬에 가서 아이들 장난감 몇 개와 집사람 옷들을 샀다. 오늘은 벤과 호앙을 따라 다니며 RT-PCR에 대해 배웠다. RNA 추출extraction, cDNA 생성generation 하는 것을 보았다.

2012년 5월 24일 목요일

오전은 예린이와 지우 여름 캠프를, 그 다음에는 준성이 프리케이pre-kindergarten에 등록하러 여기저기 돌아다녔다. 먼저 예린이와 지우를 학교에 태워준 다음 대학 교회University church에 준성이 신청서를 제출하러 갔다. 그다음 욜로 카운티 오피스

에 여름캠프를 등록하러 갔다. 그런데 클래스가 이미 마감되었다. 할 수 없이 다른 캠프 클래스를 찾아보아야 했다. 짐네스틱은 여유가 있어 거기 신청했다. ESL 클래스 수업 후에는 파티가 있었다.

2012년 5월 29일 화요일

일요일엔 샌프란시스코에 골든 게이트 브릿지Golden Gate bridge를 보러 갔다. 오전 10시 46분쯤에 샌프란시스코에 들어서는데 하이웨이 차선이 복잡하고 헷갈렸다. 앗, 그런데 다른 차들이 하나도 없었다. 순간적인 판단으로 시에나가 카풀 대상으로 착각하고 카풀 차선으로 들어간 것이다. 경찰이 손짓으로 갓길에 세우라고 했다. 다른 차도 한 대 단속되어 뭔가 적고 있는 것이 보였다. 경찰이 다가오더니 '카풀차선 위반carpool lane violation' 이라며 벌금이 500달러라고 했다. 서투른 영어로 샌프란시스코에 처음 왔는데 골든 게이트 브릿지 보러 가는 길이었다고 설명했다. 경찰이 티켓은 끊지 않고 그냥 가라고 하면서 친절히 길을 손짓으로 안내해 주었다. 그는 하이웨이 101번을 타라고 알려주기까지 했다. 500달러를 아끼게 되어 너무 기뻤다. 금문교에 도착했지만 주차를 할 수 없어 그냥 통과하고 아카데미 오브 사이언스로 갔다. 1회 입장료나 패밀리 멤버십이나 비슷해서 패밀리 멤버십에 가입했다. 오늘 아침에는 준성이 어린이집pre-school에 등록하러 갔다.

2012년 5월 31일 목요일

어제는 힘든 하루를 보냈다. 세포 분류Cell sorting 전 과정을 혼자서 했다. 오늘은 집사람과 준성이와 함께 CDCcenter for day care에 가서 슈퍼바이저를 만나 필요한 서류에 대해 이야기했다.

2012년 6월 4일 월요일

지난 금요일에는 닥터 전의 별장에서 풀 파티가 있었다. 우리는 케이크와 베이글, 음료수를 준비해 갔다. 별장은 어마어마했다. 옛날 동화에 나오는 성 같았다.

우측에 서 있는 친구가 내가 교통사고를 당했을 때 해결해 주었던 벤이다.
진중하며 괜찮은 친구였고, 최근에 하버드로 이직한 것 같다.

뒤에 보이는 큰 집이 메인인데, 닥터 전은 큰 집은 비워두고
사진에 안 보이는 오두막에서 살고 있었다. 오두막도 아주 컸다.

(위 왼쪽) 할아버지처럼 보이지만 보스인 닥터 전이다.
(위 오른쪽) 우리 가족 뒤에서 웃고 있는 사람이 트위다.
(아래) 풀장에 뛰어드는 아이가 첫째 예린이. 누워 있는 남자가 닥터 전. 여자 분은 UC 데이비스 재생의학연구소 책임자이면서 줄기세포의 세계적 권위자인 닥터 놀타(Dr. Nolta)다.

2012년 6월 5일 화요일

이유 없이 피곤하다. 휴식이 필요하다. 그러나 지우를 데리고 수영 테스트에 가야 한다. 지난번 테스트에서 순간 힘이 빠지며 물에 빠져 죽을 뻔해서 테스트를 거부하고 있다. 설득해서 데리고 가야지. 오늘은 지우 생일이기도 해서 선물도 사줘야 한다.

2012년 6월 6일 수요일

어제 지우가 수영 테스트를 받았다. 잘하지 못해서 클럽에 참가할 수 없게 되자 조금 실망했다. 집에 오는 길에 예린이와 지우에게 테니스 라켓을 선물로 사주었다.

2012년 6월 11일 월요일

지난 주말에는 모처럼 안 싸우고 좋은 시간을 보냈다. 토요일은 달러트리, 스마일 한인마켓, 올드네이비로 쇼핑을 다녔고, 밤에는 타이타닉을 보았다. 집사람도 좋아하고 나도 좋아하는 영화다. 일요일에는 우드랜드에 있는 마샬, 타겟, 코스트코에 가서 쇼핑하고 오후에는 아파트 수영장에서 온 가족이 함께 놀았다.

2012년 6월 19일 화요일

이번 주부터 예린이를 테니스클럽에 데려다 줘야 해서 평소보다 일찍 일어나야 한다.

2012년 6월 20일 수요일

요즘 이유 없이 너무 피곤하다. 어제는 잠도 많이 잤는데 피곤이 풀리지 않는다.

2012년 6월 22일 금요일

유유와 몇 가지 마커에 대한 면역 염색immunostaining을 했다. 지난 수요일에는 날이 너무 더워서 예린, 지우와 수영장에 갔고, 어제는 날이 춥고 바람이 불어 집에서 예린이와 지우에게 수학을 가르쳐 주었다.

2012년 6월 25일 월요일

몹시 우울하다. 몇 분 전 전화 한 통을 받았다. 준성이 어린이집에서 온 전화였는데 거의 못 알아들었다. 인터뷰에 대한 내용이었다. 선생님은 대화가 되지 않으니까 한국인 통역을 찾았는데 마침 통역사가 없었다. 불가피하게 통역 없이 어찌어찌 대화를 마쳤다. 최근 영어가 조금 느는 것 같았는데 착각이었나 보다.

지난 주말에는 날씨가 환상적으로 좋았다. 새크라멘토 주의사당에 갔다. 주차가 힘들어서 길가에 겨우 주차했는데 한 시간 제한이었다. 동전을 넣고 주차하는 시스템이었는데 처음 해보았다. 일요일에는 로우스에 가서 아이들의 만들기 프로그램도 하고, 이케아에 가서 예린이와 지우가 놀이공간에서 노는 동안에 집사람은 로스에 가서 옷을 샀다. 즐거운 주말이었다.

2012년 6월 26일 화요일

점심시간에 찰스와 트위Tue의 송별회가 있었다. 찰스는 더 큰 기관으로 간다고 하고, 트위는 아직 새로운 일을 구하지 못했다고 했다. 트위가 아직 새 일을 구하지 못해 유감인 상태로 작별했다. 그동안 트위가 하던 일을 내가 맡게 되었다.

2012년 6월 28일 목요일

USMLE Step 2CS 준비를 시작하기로 했다. 영어공부와 병행해야 하기 때문에 좀 더 열심히 해야 할 것 같다. 준성이 CDC로부터 전화가 왔다. 프린시플Principle이라고 소개한 그녀는 지난 월요일에 통화한 바로 그녀였다. 지난번보다는 대화가 다소 수월했지만 여전히 알아듣기 힘들어 스트레스를 받았다.

2012년 6월 29일 금요일

힘든 하루였다. 바빠서 영어를 공부할 시간이 없었다. 실수로 Huh7 셀에 배양액을 잘못 주었다. DMEM containing supplements를 주었어야 했는데 DMEM만

주었다. 그래서 Huh7 셀이 건강하지 않게 되었다. 모두 버리고 유유가 준 레시피로 미디움을 새로 만들었다. 6시 44분이다. 집에 가야겠다. 어제는 또 이유 없이 집사람이 화를 내서 나도 같이 화냈다.

2012년 7월 2일 월요일

지난 주말 집사람과는 냉전이었다. 서로 말하지 않았다. 예린이와 지우랑만 놀았다. 집에 가기 싫다.

2012년 7월 5일 목요일

지난 화요일에는 닥터 쳉이 카메라를 산다고 해서 새크라멘토 프라이스까지 태워주었다. 유유의 네비게이션을 빌려서 달고 플라이스Fry's로 갔다. 하이웨이 운전은 항상 두렵고 위험하다. 어제는 미국 독립기념일이었는데 우리 가족은 초저녁에 커뮤니티 파크에 가서 스카이다이버들이 낙하산으로 내려오는 것을 구경했다. 집에 와서 짜파게티를 끓여 먹고 9시 넘어서는 불꽃놀이를 보러 다시 커뮤니티 파크로 나갔다. 가는 길에 불꽃이 펑펑 터지는 소리가 났다. 아트센터에 주차하는데 바로 눈앞에서 엄청난 장관이 펼쳐졌다. 집에 오는 길에 타겟에 들러 준성이 피자를 샀다.

2012년 7월 6일 금요일

일찍 일어났다. 5시 40분에 일어나서 USMLE 스크립트를 읽었다.

2012년 7월 10일 화요일

지난 토요일, 집사람이 엄청 화를 냈다. 아침 일찍 샌프란시스코 동물원에 가고 싶었는데 모두 늦게 일어나서 틀어졌기 때문이다. 예린이와 지우를 데리고 욜로 도서관으로 탈출했다. 예린이와 지우는 공부를 하고 나는 2시간 동안 책을 읽었다. 아이들이 밖에서 놀자고 했는데 밖이 너무 뜨거워서 집으로 데리고 왔다.

다음날인 일요일 아침, 우리 가족은 샌프란시스코 동물원에 갔다. 동물들이 많아서 좋았다. 1년 가족회원권을 끊었다. 동물들에게 직접 먹이를 줄 수 있어서 재미있었다. 동물원을 나왔는데 집사람이 산호세 한인식당에 가서 저녁을 먹자고 해서 남쪽으로 방향을 틀었다. 네비게이션이 안내하는 대로 갔는데 산타클라라였고 네비게이션에 적힌 식당 위치에는 아무것도 없었다. 허탕을 치고 집으로 돌아올 수밖에 없었다. 배가 너무 고팠다. 집사람이 인앤아웃 버거에 가자고 해서 그곳에서 저녁을 먹었다.

2012년 7월 11일 수요일

본격적으로 USMLE Step 2CS 준비를 시작했다. 영남대 후배인 안준홍 선생님과 삼성의료원의 이 선생님으로부터 정보를 얻었다. 혼자서 스크립트를 만들고 있는 중이다. 이렇게 하는 게 맞는지 모르겠다. 짙은 안개 속에 서 있는 것 같다. 그러나 "Slow and steady will win the race(느리고 꾸준한 사람이 승리한다)"라는 말을 믿는다. Step 1을 처음 시작할 때를 기억한다. 그 당시 무엇을 어떻게 해야 할지 전혀 몰랐다. 서류 접수에만도 많은 난관이 있었다. 결국은 Step 1과 2CK에 합격했다. 이제 미국의사 도전 여정의 중간쯤을 향해 가는 것 같다. 힘들다.

2012년 7월 12일 목요일

유유와 PLC 셀에서의 EGM과 MEM 컨디션의 차이를 비교했다. 몇 가지 마커에 대한 면역 염색immunostaining을 했다. 어떤 마커는 어떤 조건에서만 염색이 되었다. 우리는 아직 어떤 컨디션이 더 나은지를 결정하지 못했다. 반복 실험을 하기로 했다. 나는 플로우 사이토메트리flow cytometry용 샘플을 준비하기로 했다.

2012년 7월 13일 금요일

어젯밤 실험이 늦게 끝나서 9시에 귀가했다. 뭔가 잘못된 것 같다. 세포 내 단백질 유세포 분석Intracellular protein flow cytometry용 샘플에서 셀이 보이지 않았다. 유유는 스피닝Spinning 하여 셀을 분리해 보자고 했다. 나도 동의했다.

2012년 7월 16일 월요일

지난 토요일 리노Reno에 가서 너겟Nugget 호텔에서 1박을 하고 왔다. 금요일 밤 인터넷에 핫딜이 떠서 바로 찍었다. 52달러였다. 가는 길에 레이크 타호Lake Tahoe에 들르기로 했다. 10시쯤 일어나 10시 50분에 집을 나섰다. 타호 가는 길에 스마일 마켓에 들러 식료품들을 구입했다. 타호는 장관이었다. 타호에 도착해서 해변으로 갔다. 우리 가족 5명 입장료가 25달러였다. 물은 차갑고 상쾌했다. 예린이와 지우는 수영을 하고 싶어 했는데 집사람이 안 된다고 했다. 결국 아이들은 옷을 입은 채로 물속에 들어갔다. 아이들이 정말 좋아했다. 잠깐 휴식시간을 가진 다음에 다시 리노로 향했다. 주 경계를 넘어 네바다로 들어섰다. 사막의 공기를 느낄 수 있었다. 호텔은 멋지고 좋았다. 호텔 로비는 카지노였다. 체크인을 하고 존슨클럽 부스에 가서 50% 할인 식사권을 받았는데 카지노 게임을 해야 포인트로 할인을 받을 수 있는 카드였다. 어쩔 수 없이 우리는 정상 가격으로 뷔페를 먹었다. 팁 10달러 포함해 88달러에 저녁을 먹었다. 뷔페 음식은 맛있고 훌륭해서 집사람과 아이들 모두 만족스러워했다. 저녁을 먹고 지하에 있는 기프트숍에 들러 기념품도 구입했다. 집사람은 어디 갈 때마다 마그네틱 기념품들을 모으고 있다. 5층에 있는 수영장으로 갔다. 요금은 7달러고 마감이 9시 50분이라고 했다. 그때 시간이 9시, 시간이 별로 없었다. 어떤 아주머니가 아이들에게 좀 이상하게 대해서 9시 30분에 나올 수밖에 없었다. 밤에 갑자기 심한 두통이 찾아왔다. 전신 근육통도 심해졌다. 다음날 오전 11시에 체크아웃하고 호텔을 떠났다. 한 시간 정도 리노 시내를 여기

너겟 호텔 창문으로 바라본 리노 전경

저기 차로 돌아다녔다. 심한 두통과 근육통에 시달리면서 겨우겨우 오후 3시쯤 집에 도착했다. 집에 오자마자 쓰러져 잠이 들었다. 저녁 6시쯤 준성이가 깨워서 일어났는데 몸이 가볍고 상쾌했다. 저녁에는 세차를 했다. 오늘부터 2주간은 짐네스틱 캠프 주간이다. 예린이와 지우를 시빅 센터에 데려다 주었다. 시빅 센터 문 앞 접수대에 있는 웨이버Waiver를 작성했다. 응급 시에 연락할 수 있는 이웃 전화번호가 필요해서 집사람에게 전화했는데 연결이 되지 않아 화가 났다. 할 수 없이 예린이와 지우를 남겨두고 집으로 돌아왔다. 집사람이 전화 못 받아서 미안하다고 사과했다. 금방 기분이 풀렸다.

2012년 7월 19일 목요일

닥터 전에게 영주권 추천서를 부탁했다. 어렵고 민망할 수 있는 부탁이라 긴장했는데 흔쾌히 써주겠다고 하셔서 너무 감사하고 기뻤다.

2012년 7월 23일 월요일

지난 금요일에는 콜로라도 덴버에 있는 극장에서 총기난사 사건이 있었다. 그래서 지금 미국 전역은 충격에 빠져 있다. 용의자는 24세 남자로 의대를 그만두었다고 한다.

2012년 7월 24일 화요일

어제는 준성이 세 번째 생일이었다. 일이 7시쯤 늦게 끝났다. 급하게 베스킨라빈스에 가서 아이스크림 케이크를 샀다. 옆집 준범이네 것도 하나 더 샀다. 집에 와서 준성이 생일축하 노래를 불렀다.

2012년 7월 27일 금요일

아침에 랩 미팅이 있었다. 미팅 후 호앙과 이야기를 나누었다. 그는 내가 일을 잘한다고 칭찬해 주었다. 나도 그가 좋다. 그는 랩을 떠나 8월 중순 UC 어바인Irvine에 석사 공부를 하러 간다고 한다. 2~3년 석사과정을 마치고 제약 회사나 리서치 회사로 갈 계획이라고 했다. 나도 내 계획을 이야기했다. 이메일로라도 연락을 계속하고 싶다는 생각이 들었다.

2012년 7월 31일 화요일

할 일이 없어 일찍 3시 40분에 퇴근했다. 예린이를 수영캠프에 데려다 주었다. 지난 토요일에는 핸리스 딜러숍에 시에나를 고치러 갔다. 단지 점검만 하는데 148달러라고 해서 놀랐다. 타이어에 공기 넣고 3열 좌석 고정이 안 돼서 고쳤다. 오일 교환도 권유했지만 거절했다.

* 미국에 있는 동안 집 근처 핸리스 딜러숍에서 눈탱이 맞은 게 엄청나다. 전부 사기 치려고 작정하고 덤비는 것 같았다. 결국 베트남계가 하는 허름한 정비소를 소개받아서 그곳에서 해결했다.

2012년 8월 3일 금요일

이번 주는 힘들고 피곤했다. 어제는 예린이 수영 챔피언십에 참가해야 해서 일찍 집으로 돌아왔다. 날씨는 뜨겁고 도착했을 때 이미 많은 사람들이 있었다. 먼저 벽에 붙은 리스트를 확인했는데, 예린이는 레드팀이었고 25 킥kick, 50 프리free에 참가 예정이었다. 25 야드킥에서 예린이는 21명 중 5등을 했다. 수고한 예린이에게 스낵과 아이스주스를 사 주었다. 잠시 후 50야드 프리스타일에 또 참가했다. 이번에는 3명 중 2등을 했다. 메달을 받을 줄 알았는데 아쉽게도 종합성적은 27명 중 15등이었다. 그래도 대단하다고 격려해 주었다.

2012년 8월 6일 월요일

지난 토요일에는 예린이 수영대회 3일차였다. 체크인 후에 우리 가족은 잔디에 앉았다. 관중석에 준범이네 가족이 보였다. 인사하고 우리 자리로 돌아왔다. 예린이는 25 평형breaststroke과 25 자유형free style 둘 다 6등을 했다. 오후에는 새크라멘토에 있는 한국인이 운영하는 중국집에 가서 짜장면과 짬뽕을 먹었다.

2012년 8월 8일 수요일

요즘 우울하고 마음을 잡기 힘들다. 집사람과도 자주 다툰다. 몇 가지 목표를 다시 정리해 본다. 먼저 리서치 테크닉과 지식을 쌓아야 한다. USMLE Step 2CS도 합격해야 하고, 영주권도 받아야 한다. 그래서 닥터 전에게 지난달 영주권 추천서를 부탁해 두었다. 영어 공부도 많이 해야 하고, 가족과도 함께 해야 한다. 쉽지 않다.

2012년 8월 9일 목요일

어제 드디어 카드키를 받았다. 나만 왜 이렇게 늦게 처리되었는지 모르겠다. 오늘은 드디어 다른 사람 도움 없이 건물에 출입할 수 있었다. 어제는 데이비스 커뮤니티 클리닉에 준성이 신체검진medical examination을 받으러 갔다. 예약을 하지 않아서 의사를 만나지 못했다. 다음주 월요일 아침 8시 30분으로 예약만 하고 왔다. 다음주 월요일은 검진기록 제출 마감일이다.

2012년 8월 14일 화요일

어제는 데이비스 커뮤니티 클리닉에 준성이 검진을 받으러 갔다. 이번 학기부터 데이비스 어린이 센터에 다니기 위해 필요한 서류다. 아침 8시에 예린이와 지우도 함께 갔다. 지난주에도 가봤기 때문에 클리닉을 찾는 데는 어렵지 않았다. 줄을 서서 접수하고 잠시 기다렸다가 검진실에서 여자 의사를 만났다. 빠르게 신체검사를 했다. 의사는 준성이가 97퍼센타일Percentile로 빅보이라고 하며 증명서를 건네주었다. 어린이 센터에 가서 서류를 제출했다. 다음주 화요일 10시에 학부모 오리엔테이션이 예정되어 있고, 수요일에 첫 등원이다. 오늘과 내일 파이오니어 초등학교Pioneer elementary school에서 예린이와 지우 ESL 테스트가 예정되어 있다. 오늘 랩에는 CIRMCalifornia Institute for Regenerative Medicine에서 중요한 사람들이 방문한다. 닥터 전이 매우 긴장하고 있다. 오후 1~4시 사이에 프레젠테이션을 하는데 보조금을 따느냐를 결정하는 매우 중요한 발표다.

2012년 8월 20일 월요일

호앙을 위한 송별회가 있었다. 영어가 유창했다면 계속 친구로 잘 지낼 텐데 아쉽다. 만랙과 애나는 데이비드 고등학교Davis senior high school 12학년이 되는 학생들인데 똑똑한 친구들이다. 그들이 내년에 좋은 대학에 들어갈 것임을 확신한다. 맥주를 마셨더니 어지럽다. 요즘 USMLE Step 2CS 준비로 매우 긴장된다. 영어 수준이 조악하고 발음은 끔찍한 수준이다. 스크립트는 몽땅 외우면 되는데 발음이 큰 문제다. 발음 연습에 딸들이 기꺼이 도와주어 다행이다.

2012년 8월 23일 목요일

닥터 전에게 영주권 추천서를 부탁한 지도 한 달이 넘었는데 아직 답이 없다. 편지를 써서 주어야겠다. 시간이 많지 않아서 마음이 조급하다. USMLE Step 2CS는 내 인생에서 가장 힘든 시험인 것 같다. 원고를 외우고 매일 반복해서 연습하고 있다. 시험 날짜는 12월 17일로 예약했다. 가능하면 10월 말로 당기고 싶다. 준비 기간이 길어지니 지친다.

2012년 8월 30일 목요일

드디어 보라매병원 정용진 선생님이 도착했다. 어제 샌프란시스코 공항에 정 선생님 가족을 픽업하러 나갔다. 비행기가 1시간 반 정도 연착되어 2시 30분이 되어서야 정 선생님 가족을 만날 수 있었다. 샌프란시스코 시내 교통체증은 정말 심각해서 빠져나오느라 힘들었다. 북쪽으로 방향을 틀어 골든게이트브리지를 통과해서 왔다. 아파트에 도착했을 때는 이미 5시 30분이 넘어 있었다.

봄에 첫째 예린이가 영재시험에 해당하는 STAR 프로그램 테스트에 합격해 새 학기에 영재반으로 배정되었다.

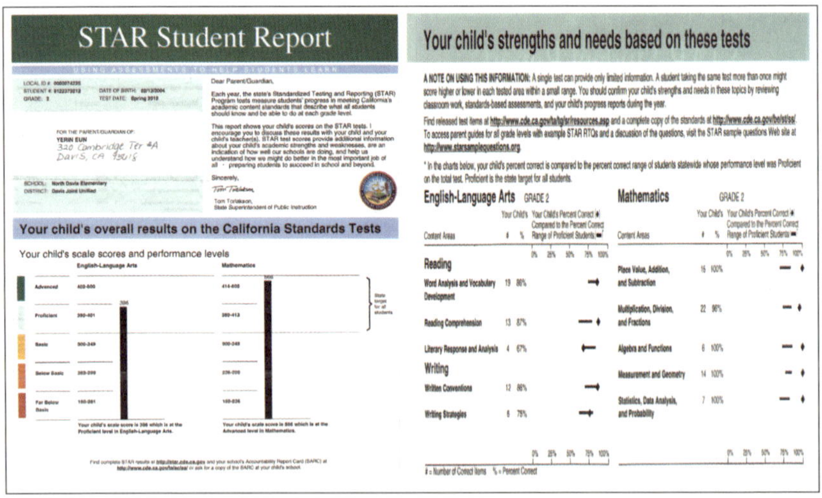

3년 후에는 성적이 더 향상되어 우수학생으로 뽑혔다. 미국에 계속 있었으면 어땠을까 하는 아쉬움이 남는다. 예린이는 2025년 현재, 카이스트 3학년에 재학 중이다.

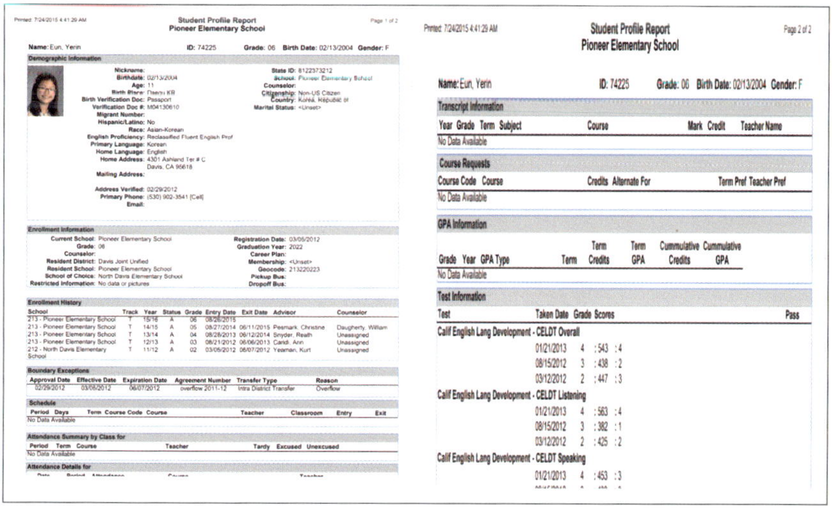

Printed: 7/24/2015 4:41:29 AM

Student Profile Report
Pioneer Elementary School

Page 1 of 2

Name: Eun, Yerin **ID:** 74225 **Grade:** 06 **Birth Date:** 02/13/2004 **Gender:** F

Demographic Information

Nickname:
Birthdate: 02/13/2004
Age: 11
Birth Place: Daegu KR
Birth Verification Doc: Passport
Verification Doc #: M04130610
Migrant Number:
Hispanic/Latino: No
Race: Asian-Korean
English Proficiency: Reclassified Fluent English Prof
Primary Language: Korean
Home Language: English
Home Address: 4301 Ashland Ter # C, Davis, CA 95618
Mailing Address:
Address Verified: 02/29/2012
Primary Phone: (530) 902-3541 [Cell]
Email:

State ID: 8122373212
School: Pioneer Elementary School
Counselor:
Citizenship: Non-US Citizen
Country: Korea, Republic of
Marital Status: <Unset>

Enrollment Information

Current School: Pioneer Elementary School
Grade: 06
Counselor:
Resident District: Davis Joint Unified
Resident School: Pioneer Elementary School
School of Choice: North Davis Elementary School
Restricted Information: No data or pictures

Registration Date: 03/05/2012
Graduation Year: 2022
Career Plan:
Membership: <Unset>
Geocode: 213220223
Pickup Bus:
Dropoff Bus:

Enrollment History

School	Track	Year	Status	Grade	Entry Date	Exit Date	Advisor	Counselor
213 - Pioneer Elementary School	T	15/16	A	06	08/26/2015			
213 - Pioneer Elementary School	T	14/15	A	05	08/27/2014	06/11/2015	Pesmark, Christine	Daugherty, William
213 - Pioneer Elementary School	T	13/14	A	04	08/28/2013	06/12/2014	Snyder, Reath	Unassigned
213 - Pioneer Elementary School	T	12/13	A	03	08/21/2012	06/06/2013	Caridi, Ann	Unassigned
212 - North Davis Elementary School	T	11/12	A	02	03/05/2012	06/07/2012	Yeoman, Kurt	Unassigned

Boundary Exceptions

Approval Date	Effective Date	Expiration Date	Agreement Number	Transfer Type	Reason
02/29/2012	03/05/2012	06/07/2012	overflow 2011-12	Intra District Transfer	Overflow

Schedule

Period	Days	Term	Course Code	Course	Teacher	Classroom	Entry	Exit

No Data Available

Attendance Summary by Class for

Period	Term	Course	Teacher	Tardy	Excused	Unexcused

No Data Available

Attendance Details for

Printed: 7/24/2015 4:41:29 AM

Student Profile Report
Pioneer Elementary School

Page 2 of 2

Name: Eun, Yerin **ID:** 74225 **Grade:** 06 **Birth Date:** 02/13/2004 **Gender:** F

Transcript Information

Year	Grade	Term	Subject	Course	Mark	Credit	Teacher Name

No Data Available

Course Requests

Course Code	Course	Credits	Alternate For	Term Pref	Teacher Pref

No Data Available

GPA Information

Grade	Year	GPA Type	Term	Term Credits	Term GPA	Cummulative Credits	Cummulative GPA

No Data Available

Test Information

Test	Taken Date	Grade	Scores	Pass
Calif English Lang Development - CELDT Overall				
	01/21/2013	4	:543 :4	
	08/15/2012	3	:438 :2	
	03/12/2012	2	:447 :3	
Calif English Lang Development - CELDT Listening				
	01/21/2013	4	:563 :4	
	08/15/2012	3	:382 :1	
	03/12/2012	2	:425 :2	
Calif English Lang Development - CELDT Speaking				
	01/21/2013	4	:453 :3	

2012년 9월 5일 수요일

닥터 전이 강의를 나가서 랩 미팅은 없었고, 정 선생님도 전을 만나지 못했다. 집으로 오는 길에 정 선생님 PG&E 계좌를 개설하러 갔는데 임대 계약서를 가지고 오지 않아서 집에 들렀다가 다시 갔다. PG&E 청구서를 가지고 파이오니어에 갔더니 불행히도 4학년 자리가 없었다. 오피스에서는 웨스트 데이비스에 있는 윌넷 초등학교Willet elementary school를 소개시켜 주었다. 정 선생님은 선택의 여지가 없었다. 다행히 나중에 정 선생님은 윌넷에 매우 만족했다.

2012년 9월 6일 목요일

정 선생님과 나는 간암 줄기세포liver cancer stem cells에 관한 프로젝트를 같이 하게 될 것이다.

2012년 9월 7일 금요일

랩 미팅 후 정 선생님과 SSAsocial security administration에 갔다. 정 선생님을 태워드리고 나는 다시 랩으로 돌아왔는데 조금 후에 벌써 인터뷰가 끝났다고 했다. 바로 다시 가야 한다.

2012년 9월 11일 화요일

시에나 앞 유리가 금간 것이 계속 커져서 고쳤다. 9시에 자동차 유리 회사Car glass company를 통해 앞 유리를 통째로 교체했다. 800달러 정도 들었고, 자기 부담금deductible이 100달러였다. 교체하고 나니 새 차 같았다.

2012년 9월 13일 목요일

어제 김종연 교수님으로부터 이메일을 받았다. 실로스타졸 특허를 한국 중소 제약회사에서 사겠다는 것이다. 매년 대학에 3천만 원을 주고 특허권자에게는 8년간 매출의 3% 로열티를 준다는 내용이었다. 기꺼이 동의했다. 또 한 통의 이메일을 받았는데, 전임의 선생이었다. 내년에 사직할 건지 말 건지 입장을 분명히 하라는 매우 불쾌한 내용이었다. 내가 입장을 분명히 하지 않아서 자기에게 교수 TO를 내줄 수 없다고 했다는 것이다. 나는 내년 2월에 분명히 사직 의사를 밝히고 왔다고 말했고, TO를 내줄 수 없는 것은 네 문제가 아닌지 돌아보라고 했다.

2012년 9월 18일 화요일

저녁에 GAP 매장에 갔다. 빅딜에다 40% 추가 세일이었다. 집사람은 흥분했다. 오늘 아침 정 선생님은 운전면허 실기 1차에 떨어졌다. 다소 실망한 모습이었다. 내일 아침에 2차 예약을 했다고 했다.

2012년 9월 24일 월요일

지난 토요일 아침 8시에는 랩에 잠시 셀 밥을 주기 위해 다녀왔다. 다녀와서 로우스 이벤트에 참여해 트럭을 조립했다. 멋진 트럭이 완성되었다. 근처 굿윌에 들러 집사람은 선글라스를 사고 나는 기세트플레이어를 1.99달러에 샀다. 집사람은 새크라멘토 다운타운에 있는 GAP 매장에 가자고 했다. 네비게이션 주소를 잘못 입력해서 다른 굿윌로 갔다. 근처 스마일마켓에서 장이나 보고 오기로 계획을 바꾸었다.

2012년 9월 27일 목요일

시간이 쏜살같이 지나가는 것 같다. 미국에 온 지 벌써 7개월이 지났다. 내가 잘하고 있는 건지 모르겠다. 이번 주는 랩 일로 바빴다.

2012년 10월 2일 화요일

지난 토요일 정 선생님 가족과 우리 가족은 나파밸리 와이너리에 갔다. 케이블카를 타고 올라갔다. 요금은 어른이 20달러, 어린이는 10달러였다. 아이들은 즐거워했다. 몇 종류의 와인을 시음하고 투어 후에 케이블카를 타고 다시 내려왔다. 준비해 간 김치김밥으로 주차장에서 점심을 먹고, 2층에 있는 캐슬와이너리로 갔다. 입장료가 비싸서 들어가지는 않고 대신 성 앞에서 사진만 찍었다. 3층 와이너리를 대충 둘러보고 햄버거 가게로 자리를 옮겨 햄버거를 맛있게 먹었다. 그때부터 준성이가 피곤해 하고 아파 보였다. 별일 아닐 거라고 무시했는데 큰 실수였다. 다운타운을 둘러보는데 준성이가 갑자기 토를 해 바로 차로 돌아왔다. 운전 중에 집사람이 준성이가 이상하다고 소리를 질렀다. 뒤돌아보니 준성이가 경련을 하고 있었다. 급히 차를 길가에 댔다. 다행히 차 안에는 물 7병이 있었다. 뒷자리로 옮기고 옷을 벗기고 찬물을 쏟아 부었다. 몇 분 후 준성이가 울음을 터뜨렸다. 약 40분 후

완전히 회복되었다. 조금만 늦거나 차 안에 물이 없었다면 큰일 날 뻔했다. 생각만 해도 아찔했다. 급히 집으로 차를 몰고 왔다. 준성이는 좀 나아보였다. 그러나 밤에 고열이 나서 수건으로 계속 열을 내리느라 한숨도 자지 못했다. 다음날 아침에는 다행히 괜찮아 보여 안심이 되었다. 월요일 일찍 퇴근해서 보니 준성이는 잘 놀고 있었고, 집사람도 안심한 듯 보였다. 열사병의 무서움을 느꼈고 다음부터는 정말 조심해야겠다는 교훈을 얻었다.

* 그 일은 나에게 평생 트라우마로 남아 있다. 준성이는 정말 죽을 뻔했다.

2012년 10월 15일 월요일

지난 토요일에는 콘 메이즈Maze Corn에 갔다. 11시쯤 집을 나섰다. 중간에 지우의 바이올린을 고치러 워터멜론Watermelon에 들렀다. 바이올린 브릿지가 부러져 있었다. 주차하고 혼자 가게 안에 들어갔다. 집사람은 45달러 미만일 거라고 했다. 점원은 브릿지가 5달러고, 공임비labor fee가 40달러, 총 45달러라고 했다. 또한 크랙에 대해서 어떻게 할 건지도 물어보았는데 나는 고치겠다고 답했다. 그러니 총 60달러가 되었다. 체크를 적어 내고 차로 돌아와 집사람에게 이야기했더니 분명히 자기는 브릿지만 고치라고 했는데 왜 크랙까지 고쳤냐며 화를 냈다. 나도 갑자기 화가 났다. 자기는 나한테 시키기만 하고 일이 끝나면 뭐라고 지적하는 데 진저리가 났다. 조금 싸우다가 딕슨Dixon을 향해 떠났다. 입장료는 5세 미만은 10달러였다. 총 40달러를 내고 지도를 받았다. 어떻게 미로 길을 찾을지 생각했다. 미로를 다 빠져나오는데 3시간쯤 걸려서 오후 3시쯤이 되었다. 날이 너무 뜨거워서 쓰러질 듯 피곤했다. 펌킨파이와 레모네이드를 사 먹었다. 바카빌에 있는 코스트코에서 쇼핑을 하고 집으로 돌아왔다.

2012년 10월 18일 목요일

어제 전임의로부터 이메일을 받았다. 읽고는 화가 났다. 교원 신청 공고 마감이 어제였는데 의국에서 신청을 하지 않았다는 것이다. 그는 나 때문이라고 생각하는 것 같았다. 여선히 내가 교수 자리를 차지하고 있어서 TO 신청을 못했다는 것이다. 당장 담당 교수에게 연락해서 사직하겠다는 의사를 분명히 하라는 것이었다. 뭐 이런 경우가 다 있나 싶었다. 처음 경험해 보는 무례함이었다. 예전에 병원에서 보았을 때는 성실하고 괜찮은 후배라고 생각했는데 본인의 이해관계가 얽힌 상황에서 하는 행동을 보니 무서운 사람이라는 생각이 들었다.

2012년 10월 23일 화요일

지난 금요일 오후 준범이네 가족과 레드우드에 놀러 갔다. 준범이네 아주머니와 집사람이 모든 준비를 했다. 준범이네가 앞서가고 내 차는 뒤따라갔다. 내 GPS가 항상 말썽이었다. 목적지가 제대로 표시되지 않아 뒤처졌다. 크레센트 시티를 지정했는데 375마일의 거리라고 표시되었다. 레딩에서 기름을 넣고 유레카로 향했다. 유레카로 가기 위해서는 100마일 정도 되는 숲속을 지나야 했다. 저녁 6시 30분인데 벌써 어두워졌고 비가 오기 시작하면서 심한 안개까지 끼었다. 때마침 앞유리 와이퍼도 작동하지 않았다. 운전은 더 힘들어졌다. 갑자기 차가 고장이 나면 어떡하나 생각하니 두려움이 몰려왔다. KOA 캐빈에 도착했을 때는 밤 11시가 다 되어 있었다. 거의 7시간이 걸린 것이다. 이불 등의 짐을 내리고 바로 잠자리에 들었다. 집사람이 전기패드를 가지고 와서 따뜻하게 푹 잘 수 있었다. 다음날 아침 일찍 일어났다. 준범이네가 준비해 둔 아침을 먹고, 10시쯤 크레센트 시티에 있는 인포메이션 센터로 갔다. 어린이 우드 레인저 배지Children's wood ranger's badges에 신청하고 숲Woods으로 갔다. 나무들이 엄청났다. 수백 년 된 나무들인데 나무 둘레와 높이가 어마어마했다. 사진을 찍고 캐빈으로 돌아와 내가 끓인 라면으로 점심을

해결하고, 다시 인포메이션 센터로 가서 배지를 받았다. 지우 것을 깜빡하고 못 받아서 지우가 주차장에서 엉엉 울었다. 지우 배지를 다시 신청해서 결국 모두 배지를 받았다. 곧 날이 어둑해지기 시작했다. 트리 오브 미스터리로 갔는데 4시 50분이었다. 4시에 문을 닫아서 못 들어가고 캐빈으로 돌아왔다. 돌아오는 길에 SAVE 마트에 들러 물과 라이터, 가스를 구입했다. 준범이네가 저녁을 준비했는데 준범이 아빠가 스테이크, 새우, 버섯을 그릴에 구웠다. 사실 나는 스테이크를 좋아하지 않는다. 양념 된 야채가 좋았다. 저녁을 먹은 후 10시쯤 자러 갔다. 다음날 아침 몹시 피곤했지만 잠이라도 잘 자서 다행이었다. 아침을 먹고 해안가 등대Lighthouse에 들러서 기념품 몇 개를 구입했다. 약간의 돈을 기부donation하니 담당자가 우리를

안내해 주었다. 침실, 거실, 가구 등이 멋졌다. 그리고 어제 못 갔던 트리 오브 미스터리로 갔다. 스카이 트레일까지 걷기는 다리도 아프고 피곤했다. 아이들은 스카이 트레일을 재미있어 했다. 투어를 마치는 데 2시간이 걸렸다. 집으로 돌아오는 길에 날씨가 좋았지만 길은 꾸불꾸불하고 험했다. 웨버빌에 있는 햄버거 가게에서 햄버거를 테이크아웃해 먹으면서 운전했다. 꾸불꾸불한 길을 운전하느라 우리 가족 모두는 머리가 아팠다. 마침내 레딩에 도착했다. 기름을 넣고 화장실에 들렀는데 지우가 토를 했다. 다행히 숲을 빠져나와 하이웨이로 접어들면서부터는 편하게 운전할 수 있었다. 집에 도착하니 밤 9시였다.

2012년 11월 6일 화요일

USMLE Step 2CS 스크립트를 모두 만들었다. 지금부터는 외우고 반복 또 반복 연습해야 한다. 영어가 별로 나아진 것 같지 않아 여전히 우울하고 스트레스를 받는다. 티아와 아흐마드에게 조언을 구했다. 그들은 내 발음이 괜찮다고 했지만 듣고 말하는 데 모두 어려움이 있다. 티아는 이번 달 말까지만 랩에 있을 거라고 했다. 닥터 전이 고용해 주면 좀 더 있을 수 있겠지만 그건 알 수 없는 일이었다. 티아는 있는 동안 내 영어를 도와주겠다고 했다. 내일은 벤과 티아가 웨스턴 블롯Western blot을 하기로 되어 있는데, 그 방법을 가르쳐 주기로 했다.

2012년 11월 15일 목요일

지난 주말에는 몬트레이와 카멜에 다녀오고, 토요일 밤에는 KOA에서 잤다. 이번 주 월요일에는 참전용사의 날Veteran's day이라 휴일이었다. 쉬는 날이었지만 출근해서 세포 계대 배양cell culture passage을 하고 SK 세포 한 바이알cells one vial을 리커버리 시켰다.

2012년 11월 29일 목요일

오랫동안 일기를 쓰지 않은 것 같다. Step 2CS가 18일 남았다. 몹시 불안하다. 우리 가족은 추수감사절을 맞아 쇼핑하러 여기저기 돌아다녔다.

2012년 12월 13일 목요일

그동안 두 가지 문제로 매우 불안한 날들을 보냈다. NIW와 CS 시험. 둘 다 미국으로 온 이유 중 가장 중요한 일들이다. 다행히 NIW 신청서petition가 승인되었다. 매일 USCIS 사이트에 들어가서 진행 상황을 살펴보았다. 처음 상태는 초기 검토Initial Review였는데, 오늘 아침 11시에 들어가 보니 결정Decision으로 바뀌어 있었다. 결과는 승인Approved이었다. 잠시 가슴이 터질 듯 흥분이 되어서 자리에 앉아 있을 수가 없었다.

다음주 월요일은 Step 2CS 시험이 있는 날이다. 너무 떨린다. 그렇지만 지금까지 최선을 다했으니까 합격할 거라고 믿는다. 시험을 준비하는 데 6개월이 걸렸다. 미국 학생들은 1~2주 정도 준비하고, 외국 학생들이 보통 2개월 준비하는 시험이다. 나는 영어가 안 되어서 준비 기간이 많이 걸렸다. 일단 새크라멘토 공항에서 비행기를 타고 LA로 갈 예정이다. 내일 정 선생님이 공항까지 태워주고 월요일 밤에 픽업하러 와 주시기로 했다. 고마운 일이다.

2012년 12월 18일 목요일

USMLE Step 2CS 시험을 드디어 끝냈다. 악몽 같은 6개월의 시간이 주마등처럼 지나갔다. 내게는 힘든 시간이었다. 오랜 기간 준비했지만 직접 스카이프Skype로 연습은 한 번도 못했다. 닥터 유진Dr. Eugene과 안준홍 선생님으로부터 7월에 정보를 얻어 공부를 시작할 수 있었다. 11월 초에 나의 스크립트를 완성해 암기하고 혼자 몰래 건물 밖에 나가서 아무도 없는 데서 큰 소리로 연습했다. 잠꼬대로도 나올 정도로 외우고 또 외웠다. 공부 방법이 적절했는지는 의문이지만 열심히 했다. 12월 즈음에는 지치기도 했다.

마침내 16일 일요일, LA로 갔다. 정 선생님이 고맙게도 공항까지 태워주셨고, 오후에 LA 공항에서 셔틀을 타고 하시엔다 호텔Hacienda hotel에 내렸다. 5시 셔틀을 놓쳐서 5시 30분에 겨우 탈 수 있었다. 시험장 건물인 블루 오브 캘리포니아로 가 보았다. 호텔로 돌아오는 길에 해빗Habbit 버거에 들러 햄버거 2개와 콜라를 사 와서 먹었다. 월요일 아침에는 6시 30분에 눈이 떠졌다. 집사람이 준비해 준 밥을 먹고 테스트 센터로 향했다. 엘리베이터에서 모의 환자로 보이는 2명을 만났다. 시험을 보러 온 학생들도 보였다. 모두 24명 정도인데, 그중 나를 빼고 2명만 외국인 같았다. 나와 중국인과 대만인. 시험은 정각 9시에 시작되었다. 첫 환자는 17세 남자 흉통 환자chest pain였다. 너무 긴장해서 진찰을 제대로 하지 못하고 시간도 맞추지 못했다. 다음 4 케이스는 다행히 심플해서 준비한 대로 할 수 있었다. 또 다음은 열이 나는 소아과 환자였다. 익숙한 환자였지만 갑자기 머리가 하얗게 되면서 블랙아웃 상태가 되고 말았다. 아무 말도 떠오르지 않았다. 한마디도 못하고 몇 분 만에 케이스를 종료하고 방을 나왔다. 우울했다. 환자 노트Patient note만 열심히 작성했다. 세 번째 케이스는 단순했다. 사실 모든 케이스가 내게는 쉽지 않았다. 끝날 때까지 계속 긴장 상태였다. 역시 영어가 문제였다. 발음에서 많이 실수한 것 같다. SEPspoken English proficiency가 걱정이다. 최선을 다했고 결과가 나올 때까지 기다리는 수밖에 없었다. 3시 30분에 시험장을 나왔다. 여기저기 돌아다니고 싶었지만 가방이 너무 무거워서 셔틀을 타고 호텔로 돌아왔다. 공항에서 비행기를 6시간 기다렸다. 지루하고 힘들었다. 10시 비행기를 타고 새크라멘토에 도착하니까 11시 20분이었다. 정 선생님이 데리러 와주셔서 정말 감사했다.

2012년 12월 19일 수요일

시험이 끝나면 여유가 있을 줄 알았는데 여전히 바쁘다. 영주권을 받기 위해 백신 접종vaccination을 포함한 서류들을 준비해야 한다. 오늘 아침 예린이와 지우 겨울 짐 수업winter gym class과 미술 수업art class을 신청하기 위해 커뮤니티 서비스에 갔다. 어제 전화로 신청했지만 나이가 안 되어서 직접 신청하려고 다시 가 보았다. 담당자Receptionist를 만났는데, 일단 그녀는 강사instructor가 결정해 줘야 할 문제라며 기다려 보라고 했다.

2013년 1월 2일 수요일

해피 뉴 이어! 2013년이다. 새해가 왔는지도 모를 정도로 정신이 없었다. 한참 동안 일기를 쓰지 않았는데, 그동안 많은 일들이 있었다. 먼저 우리 가족은 레고랜드와 유니버셜 스튜디오로 휴가를 다녀왔다. 크리스마스 전날인 12월 23일에 10시간을 운전해서 샌디에고와 LA 중간쯤에 있는 하얏트 호텔에 도착했다. 가는 길에 저녁을 먹으러 LA에 들렀다. 마트 푸드코트에서 저녁을 먹고 100마일을 운전해서 호텔로 돌아왔다. 하얏트 호텔은 깨끗하고 좋았다. 출발하기 전 인터넷 딜로 싸게 나와서 좋아했는데 인터넷이 85달러, 주차비가 15달러 별도였다. 이런. 날이 어두워지면서 비가 내렸다. 24일 둘째 날은 아침을 컵라면으로 간단히 때우고 10시쯤 레고랜드로 떠났다. 날씨가 걱정이었는데 갑자기 비가 그치기 시작하더니 날씨가 점점 좋아졌다. 레고랜드에는 많은 놀거리들이 있었다. 아이들이 무척 좋아해서 나도 좋았다. 저녁 6시쯤 저녁을 먹으러 다시 LA로 갔다. 한인마트에 있는 작은 카페테리아에서 저녁을 먹기로 했다. 나는 준성이를 업고 있어서 주문을 할 수가 없었다. 그런데 집사람이 사람이 5명인데 왜 3인분만 주문했냐고 화를 냈다. 내가 주문한 것도 아닌데 내게 화를 내는게 화가 나서 아무 말도 하지 않았다.

웨스틴 호텔에 도착했다. 주차비가 하룻밤에 40달러였다. 처음에는 80달러라서 싸다고 좋아했는데 역시 주차비가 별도였다. 텍스 포함 총 140달러였다. 크리스마스인 3일째 날에는 유니버셜 스튜디오에 갔다. 아이들의 천국이었다. 영화 〈언더월드〉의 일부 장면을 재현한 '언더월드 쇼'를 관람했다. 그리고 유니버셜 스튜디오 버스 투어, 쥬라기 공원, 그 외 다양한 3D 체험 등을 했다. 모두 즐거워했다. 저녁은 한식당인 대호갈비에서 먹었다. 4일째 날은 파머스 마켓과 게티 박물관에 갔다. 파머스 마켓의 놀이 기차는 괜찮았지만 게티 박물관은 지루했다. 여행 내내 아침은 컵라면을 먹고 점심은 건너뛰었다. 그래서 항상 배가 고팠다. 저녁에는 첫날에 갔었던 갈레리아 마켓에서 저녁을 먹었다. 5일째, 집으로 출발했다. 오전 10시에 출발했는데 저녁 7시나 되어서 도착했다. 금요일에는 출근해서 배지 교체media change, MSC-L 세포 동결liver cells freezing, MSC-L 세포 계대 배양cells passages, CD34+ 세포 계대 배양cells passage을 했다. 토요일에는 크리스마스 이후의 세일 시즌이라 쇼핑하러 돌아다니고, 일요일에는 밀린 일을 하러 랩에 출근했다. 그리고 오늘은 1월 2일 수요일이다.

2013년 1월 8일 화요일

어제 오후 유유에게 J1 비자 연장에 대해 물어보았다. I-485 준비를 서두르면 굳이 J1 비자 연장이 필요 없지만 I-485가 늦어질 것에 대비해 일단 비자를 갱신하기로 했다. 닥터 전이 나를 불러 올해 계획을 물어보았다. 나는 솔직하게 미국 레지던트 프로그램에 지원할 것이고 랩에서 일한 것은 올해 논문을 쓰고 싶다고 대답했다. 그러자 그는 무엇을 도와주면 좋겠냐고 물었다. 고마웠다. 나는 내 계획을 허락해 주면 좋겠다고 답했다. 몇 가지 부탁을 이메일로 보냈다. 그의 얼굴이 밝아 보이지 않아서 조금 걱정이 된다. 아마 올해 월급을 달라고 요구하기가 어려울 것 같다. 기다려 보는 수밖에 없을 것 같다. 매니Manny는 랩에서 고용을 해주지 않아서 랩을 떠나게 될 것 같다. 이런 상황에서 월급을 달라고 하는 것은 더욱 불가능하다.

마리아가 앤링Yanling에게 줄 급여 체크를 갖고 왔다. 좀 슬프다.

2013년 1월 10일 목요일

예린이와 지우를 학교에 태워주고 데이비스 커뮤니티 클리닉에 닥터 카츠Dr. Kats를 만나러 갔다. 이민국에 제출할 건강진단서medical examination certificate를 받기 위해서였다. 접수대 직원이 집사람도 같이 와야 한다고 해서 급히 전화했다. 기다리는 동안 양식을 써내려갔다. 5개 신청서 양식을 완료하는데 2시간 이상이 걸렸다. 나와 집사람은 1월 22일로, 아이들은 2월 12일로 예약되었다. 수수료Fee가 한 명당 300달러씩 총 1,500달러라고 해서 놀랐다. 물론 엑스레이는 포함이 안 된 비용이니까 총 비용은 더 늘어날 것이다. 중간에 리뷰나 랩 테스트를 하러 가야 해서 4번 정도는 더 클리닉에 가야 한다. 랩에 출근하니 정오였다. 오늘은 세포 실험만 하면 된다. 요즘은 약간 불안하다. 아마도 Step 2CS의 결과를 기다리는 것과 월급 문제 때문인 것 같다. 전의 표정을 봐서는 올해 급여를 받기는 어려울 것 같다. 또 가능

* 결국 유유는 많은 논문에 나의 이름을 올려 주었고, 그때의 고마움을 잊지 못하고 항상 그립다. 최근 펍메드(PubMed)를 보니 중국에 교수로 간 것 같다.

STEM CELLS AND DEVELOPMENT
Volume 24, Number 13, 2015
© Mary Ann Liebert, Inc.
DOI: 10.1089/scd.2015.0022

CUTTING-EDGE COMMUNICATION

Clonogenically Culturing and Expanding CD34+ Liver Cancer Stem Cells in Vitro

Su Cheol Park,[1–3,*] Changjun Zeng,[1,2,4,*] Benjamin Tschudy-Seney,[1,2] Ngoc Tue Nguyen,[1,2] Jong Ryeol Eun,[1,2,5] Yanling Zhang,[1,2,6] Rajendra Ramsamooj,[7] Yanghong Zhang,[7] Min Zhao,[8] Neil D. Theise,[9] Huaijun Zhou,[10] Mark A. Zern,[1,2] and Yuyou Duan[1,2,8]

STEM CELLS AND DEVELOPMENT
Volume 24, Number 21, 2015
© Mary Ann Liebert, Inc.
DOI: 10.1089/scd.2015.0202

RAPID COMMUNICATION

CD34$^+$ Liver Cancer Stem Cells Were Formed by Fusion of Hepatobiliary Stem/Progenitor Cells with Hematopoietic Precursor-Derived Myeloid Intermediates

Changjun Zeng,[1–3,*] Yanling Zhang,[1,2,4,*] Su Cheol Park,[1,2,5] Jong Ryeol Eun,[1,2,6] Ngoc Tue Nguyen,[1,2] Benjamin Tschudy-Seney,[1,2] Yong Jin Jung,[1,2,7] Neil D. Theise,[8] Mark A. Zern,[1,2] and Yuyou Duan[1,2,9]

OPEN ACCESS Freely available online PLOS ONE

Hepatoma SK Hep-1 Cells Exhibit Characteristics of Oncogenic Mesenchymal Stem Cells with Highly Metastatic Capacity

Jong Ryeol Eun[1,2,4,9], Yong Jin Jung[1,2,5,9], Yanling Zhang[1,2,6], Yanhong Zhang[3], Benjamin Tschudy-Seney[1,2], Rajen Ramsamooj[3], Yu-Jui Yvonne Wan[3], Neil D. Theise[7], Mark A. Zern[1,2], Yuyou Duan[1,2*]

1 Department of Internal Medicine, University of California Davis Medical Center, Sacramento, California, United States of America, 2 Institute for Regenerative Cures, University of California Davis Medical Center, Sacramento, California, United States of America, 3 Department of Pathology and Laboratory Medicine, University of California Davis Medical Center, Sacramento, California, United States of America, 4 Department of Internal Medicine, Yeungnam University College Medicine, Daegu, Korea, 5 Department of Internal Medicine, SMG-SNU Boramae Medical Center, Seoul National University College of Medicine, Seoul, Korea, 6 School of Biotechnology, Southern Medical University, Guangzhou, China, 7 Department of Pathology and Medicine, Beth Israel Medical Center, Albert Einstein College of Medicine, New York, New York, United States of America

한 빨리 논문도 써야 한다. 그래서 실험도 계속하면서 데이터를 모아야 한다. 유유는 나에게 1저자를 주겠다고 약속했지만 진심인지는 모르겠다.

2013년 1월 17일 목요일

집사람과 나는 커뮤니티 클리닉에 갔다. INS 리뷰를 위해 파상풍 백신을 맞았고, 수두 항체검사와 성병 관련 소변검사를 했다. 다음주 화요일 아침에 또 가야 한다. 최근 유유와 많은 이야기를 했다. HLE & HLF 프로젝트는 연구비 문제로 많이 늦어질 것이라고 했다. 나중에 마당발인 닥터 쳉으로부터 들은 이야기는 누군가 한 달 가용 예산보다 훨씬 많은 돈을 써버렸다는 것이다. 그래서 일부 실험이 3개월 정도 정지당했다고 한다. 유유는 당분간 SK 세포 프로젝트에 집중하자고 했다. 그는 엄청난 데이터가 나왔다고 흥분했는데, 단 100개 미만의 세포로 암을 일으킨다는 내용이었다. 정말 놀라운 결과였다. 몇 달 내 논문을 쓸 수 있을 것 같았다. 이런 좋은 결과에도 불구하고 계속 불안하고 우울하다. Step 2CS에 떨어지면 어떡하나 걱정이 떠나지 않고, 올해 급여를 받을 수 없을 것 같은 생각이 든다. 매니와 티아는 이번 달 말까지 일하고 떠난다고 한다.

* 돌이켜 보니 랩에서 열심히 일했던 것 같다. 만약 대학을 떠나지 않았다면 귀국해서 줄기세포 연구를 계속했을 것 같다. 재미있었고 간암 줄기세포의 기원에 대해 연구해 보고 싶었다. 결국 이도저도 안 되었지만.

Immunostaining results

Cells	Culture condition	CD 68	CK 18	CK 19	CK7	Hep Par1	C/EBPα	CD 44	CD 45	CD 16	CD 14	OV6	Lyso zyme	Macro	SCL	Klf4	c-Myc	AFP	Alb	Epo R	AE1/ AE3	Date
514, CD34+CSCs	MEM	+		-												++						6-13-12
419, CD34+CSCs	EGM	+				+																6-12-12
562, CD34+CSCs	MEM			+			+		+													6-12-12
597L, CD34+ EpCAM+				+		+			+													6-12-12
581 CD34+CD90+	MEM			-		- cyto		+							+ cy, nu						++	7-17-12
581 CD34+CD90+	EGM			++																	++	
CD34+CSCs	On MEFs, HAM (6th 1st D10)						+		+	-					+					+		
CD34+CSCs	On MEFs, HAM (8th 2nd)	+/- (+)						++	+		+	?	+	-								10-30-12
CD34+CSCs	6th 2nd							++									+					
CD34+CSCs	6th 3rd		++						+						++			+				
CD34+OV6+	Matrigel						-			-												
562, CD34+OV6+				+					+													
CD34+CSCs	Matrigel								+	-					+							
PLC/PRF/5	MEM	+		++	+	-			-		-				+	+	+					6-13-12
PLC/PRF/5	EGM	+		+	+/-	+			+									+				6-13-12
PLC/PRF/5	EGM(p4)	+		++		+			+									++	-			6-28-12 7-2-12
Huh7	DMEM								-	-						+						6-27-12
SK-Hep-1									+													

중요한 것은 직접 자리에 찾아가기도 했지만 업무보고는 주로 이메일로 했다.

2013년 1월 21일

Hi Dr. Duan,

I'm here the lab now on Sunday morning.
I checked the cells.

1. MSC-ad (1/16 recovery) d4
70% in confluency, healthy
I think it's OK to just change DM media (4mL/well)

2. MSC-Liver (1/18 Friday p2 recovery) d2 *one well for transplantation by Ben
80-90% in confluency, healthy
I'm not sure which one is better between passage or just media change.

3. SK(DM) Px5 3rd diff day4
>90% in confluency, not healthy

4. SK(MEM) Px4 (1/16 recovery) d4
>90% in confluency

5. SK(MEM) Px8 d6
>100%, peripheral small area peeled-off

6. SK reseeding of floating cells in Px5 1st DM condition
1) in MEM : crowded but no floating or dead cells
2) in DM: crowded cells but not healthy and croweded floating materials

7. SK cell differentiation into adipose or osseous (Px5 1st) d14
1) in ADM not healthy and countless black tiny materials floating
2) in ODM materials floating but less than in ADM

8. SK(MEM) Px7 to Px8 (Px7 1st) MEM vs DM d6
1) in MEM >100% some dead cells floating
2) in DM >100% but not healthy, many dead cells and materials floating.

Enclosed are pictures.

Please tell me what I should do today.

Jong.

세포들이 자라는 사진과 염색 사진을 정기적으로 찍었다.

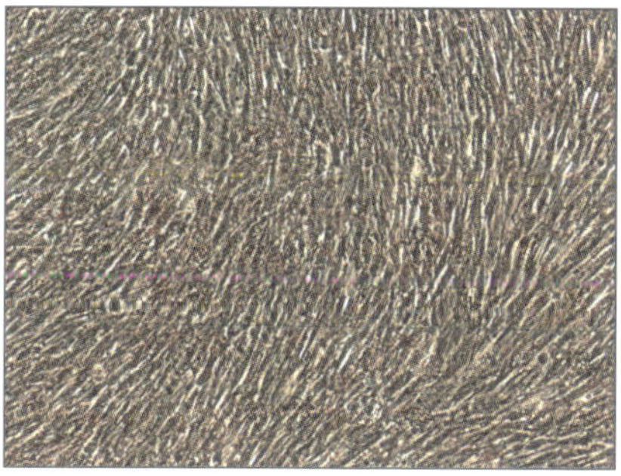

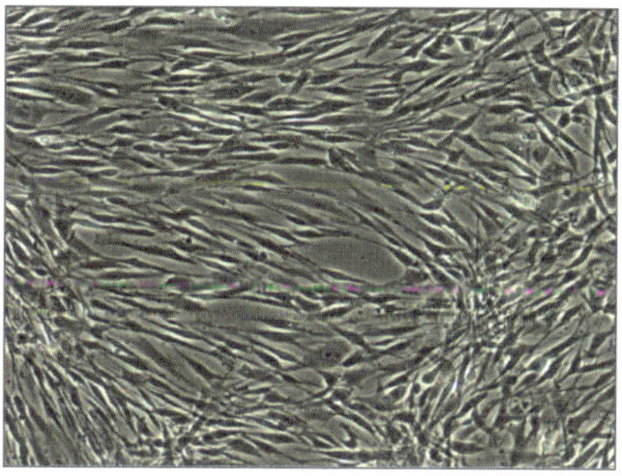

2013년 1월 23일 수요일

어제 아침 집사람과 함께 클리닉에 의사 진찰을 받으러 갔다. 나는 MMR 백신과 PPD 스킨 테스트를 받았다. 어제 주사 맞은 자리가 부어올랐다. 양성일지 몰라서 걱정이 된다. 내일 오전 10시에 다시 가서 팔을 보여주어야 한다. SK 셀 프로젝트는 성공적으로 잘 되어가고 있다. 논문을 쓸 수 있을 것 같다. 확실히 좋은 소식인데 이상하게 우울하다. 이유를 잘 모르겠다. 지난주 토요일에는 장인, 장모님이 오셨다. 샌프란시스코 공항으로 마중을 나갔다. 주말에는 쇼핑을 하고 집에서 바비큐를 구워 먹었다. 월요일은 마틴 루터킹 주니어의 날이었다. 오전에는 랩에 가서 일하고 오후에는 배커빌로 쇼핑을 갔다. 장인어른과 장모님이 나이키 매장에서 스니커즈 몇 개를 샀다.

2013년 1월 24일 목요일

집사람과 함께 PPD 스킨 테스트를 보여주러 클리닉에 갔다. 나는 양성이라 퀀티페론Quantiferon 혈액검사를 받게 되었다. 혈액검사를 위해 다시 예약을 해야 했다. 이런 시스템을 이해할 수가 없지만 어쩔 수 없는 일이었다. 2월 12일 오후로 혈액검사 예약을 잡았다. SK with differentiation에서 red oil O와 Alizarin red S 염색에 양성을 보였다. 흥분된다. 매일매일 놀라운 결과들이 나온다. 내일은 티아와 매니의 페어웰 파티(송별회)가 있다. 중국에서 온 창준이도 떠난다. 나도 랩에 1년 더 있고 싶지만 회의적이다. 전에게 전공의 지원 추천서를 부탁해야 한다.

* 매니는 인도계 미국인이다. 책을 준비하는 동안 링크드인(Linkedin)이라는 사이트에서 1촌을 맺으라는 광고 이메일이 왔는데 열어 보니 매니였다. 티아는 2013년 후반에 옆 랩에 새로 자리를 구해 일하는 것을 보고 반갑게 인사했던 기억이 난다. 매니는 이후 보지 못했다. 신경과의사가 되어 스탠포드에서 펠로를 하고 있다는 소개글을 보았다. 너무 반갑다.

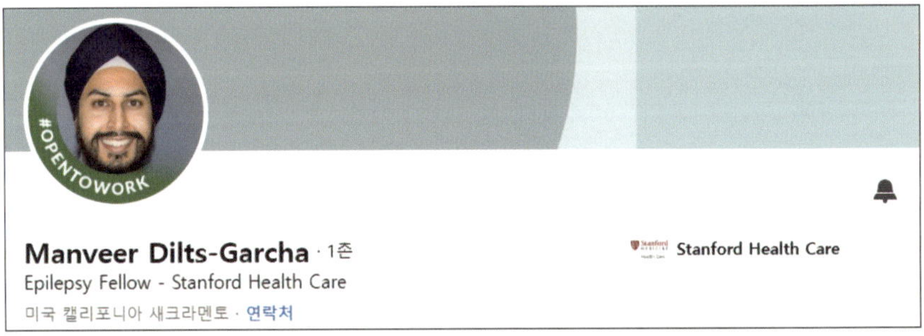

2013년 1월 28일 월요일

지난 12월에 보았던 USMLE Step 2CS 결과를 기다리는 중이다. 이번 주 수요일이 발표 날이다. 기다리기가 무척 힘들다.

2013년 1월 31일 목요일

와우, 합격했다. 최근 오아시스에 계속 들어가 보았는데 작동하지 않았다. 매일 불면증으로 액티피드를 반 알씩 먹고 잤다. 아침에 일어나자마자 컴퓨터를 켜고 오아시스에 들어갔는데, 어제 아침에는 PDF 채점표scoring report 파일이 있었다. 심장이 쿵쾅거렸다. 파일을 여는데 'PASS'라는 글자가 눈에 들어왔다. 성적을 보니 보더라인이라 거의 떨어질 뻔했다. 어쨌든 합격했고 흥분을 가라앉힐 수 없었다. USMLEKOREA에 포스팅하고 축하를 많이 받았다. 이제부터 매칭 준비를 해야 하므로 바빠질 것 같다. 먼저 Step 3 시험을 보고 캘리포니아 레터를 신청하고, 대학은 사직서를 제출하고 영어공부에 매진해야겠다.

2013년 2월 2일 토요일

뮤어 국립공원에 가족들과 함께 놀러 갔다.

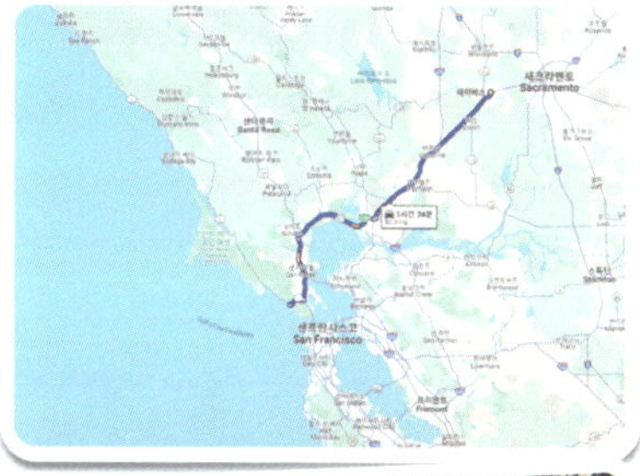

2013년 2월 3일 일요일

장인, 장모님과 새크라멘토 주의사당 구경을 갔다.

2013년 2월 7일 목요일

Step 2CS 합격했을 때 정말 떨리고 행복했다. 그런데 그 행복은 단 하루뿐이었다. 나는 다시 우울해졌다. 준비해야 할 서류들이 산더미다. 지금은 캘리포니아 레터와 Step 3 서류를 준비하고 있다. 우리 가족은 영주권 신체검사를 받으러 데이비스 클리닉에 다니느라 바쁘다. 이제 거의 다 끝나간다. 두 번만 더 가면 될 것 같다. 다행히도 아이들은 PPD 음성이었다. 자동차 보험과 여행자 보험을 갱신해야 하고, 오늘은 같은 아파트 안에서 이사를 하기로 했다. 조금 더 비싸지만 2베드는 너무 작아서 포기했다. 어제는 Step 3와 캘리포니아 레터를 공증하기 위해 UPS 오피스에 다녀왔다.

2013년 2월 28일 목요일

마침내 대학을 사직했다. 기분이 좀 이상하다. 슬픈 건지 아닌지 잘 모르겠다. 아무튼 사막에 떨어진 느낌이다. 교수님들에게 이메일을 써야겠다. 어제는 SISS에 DS-2019를 픽업하러 갔다. 그때 나와 집사람은 DMV에 운전면허를 신청하러 갔다. 집사람은 이미 합격했고 나는 갱신해야 했다.

이렇게 미국에서의 1년이 지나가고 있다.

2013/02/03

USMLE Step 2CS 합격기

2012년 7월 11일, 미국에 온 지 5개월이 되었다. 어느 정도 안정되어 계획한 대로 Step 2CS 준비를 시작했다. 안준홍 선생님과 여러 인맥을 동원해서 자료들을 얻고 UK에서 후기들을 읽어보았다. 자료들을 토대로 나의 스크립트를 만들기 시작했다. 7월 13일, Step 2CS 시험을 접수하고 7월 26일, 시험 일정을 잡을 수 있다는 연락이 왔다. 어떻게 준비해야 할지 막막했다. 11월 6일, 4개월 만에 대본을 모두 완성했다.

12. Nausea and vomiting F/23. Ms. Lincoln

Hi. How are you? Are you Ms. Lincoln? I'm Dr. Jong Ryeol Eun, the physician on duty today. Nice to meet you. (shake hands) Did I pronounce your name correctly? Thank you. I'd like to ask you some questions and examine you today. OK? OK. Before we start, let me make you more comfortable. Don't you mind if I sit down and take some notes? Thank you.

OK. Ms. Lincoln. How can I help you today? (I feel nauseated and vomited) Oh, I'm sorry. It must be tough on you. When did it start? (Nausea started 2 weeks ago and when vomiting 3-4 times a day for 3 days now) How many times did you throw up? (3-4 times a day) What color is it? Yellowish? Greenish? Any blood in it? (No blood) Did it start suddenly or gradually? Is it all the time or on and off? Is it getting worse? Is there any event you think related with your symptoms? (It started after I came back from the family gathering 2 weeks ago and I saw a sick kid throwing up there)

Does anything make it worse? Does anything make it better? Do you have any other symptoms? Fever, chills, nightsweats, headache, dizziness, chest pain, cough, palpitation, shortness of breath, belly pain, nausea, vomiting, diarrhea, constipation, any swelling in your body? Do you have any change in you body weight? Do you have any change in your appetite? **Any change on your breasts? Like pain or tenderness?**

Have you ever had similar symptoms before? Do you have any other major health problems? Like high blood pressure, high blood sugar, what about high cholesterol? Do you have any allergies? Are you taking any medications? Have you ever been hospitalized before? Any surgeries? Any accidents or injuries? **Do you have any urinary problems? (polyuria, nocturia, polydipsia)** How about your sleep? Have you traveled recently?

Is there anybody in your family having similar problems? What do you do for a living? (A student and a clerk at school bookstore) Is it stressful? I'm sorry. When was your last menstrual period? (6-7 weeks ago) Was it regular before? (No. It's kinda irregular) Is it possible that you are pregnant? Did you get a pregnancy test?

(CQ) Do you think I'm pregnant? I hope not. Oh no.. This is not a good time. I shouldn't have a baby. It can't be.
This is one of the possibilities. It's hard to say for sure right now. I need more information to be able to talk to you better about it. OK?By the way, pregnancy is a bad thing for you? (Yes) I understand your situation. Let's talk about that more specifically after we get the result.

Alright. Going back to the questions.

Do you smoke? Do you drink alcohol? Do you drink coffee or coke a lot? Do you use illicit drug? Do you exercise regularly? What is your diet like?

Now I'm going to ask you some questions about your sexual life. They are routine questions. Whatever you tell me will be kept confidential. Is this OK with you? OK. Are you married? Are you sexually active? How many partners have you had in the past year? What's your sexual preference? Male, female or the both? And are you using anything for protection from sexually transmitted infections or for contraception? (Condom) Every time? Have you had a sexually transmitted disease? Have you ever been tested for HIV?
(Sexually active with only her boyfriend, usually use condom, irregularly)

Thank you for answering all these questions. Is there anything that I missed out? Or anything else that you think I'd better know?

OK. I'm going to examine you now. Is it OK with you?

Excuse me for a moment. Let me wash my hands. Do you have any questions so far?

OK. Now I'd like to perform a quick general examination and look at your chest. Let's start with your eyes. Could you look up for me please? Thank you. I need to check the inside of your mouth and throat. Could you open your mouth? Thank you. I'll touch your neck. Is it OK? Thank you.

Now I'm going to examine your chest and lungs. May I untie your gown? Thank you. I need to listen to your lungs. Can you take a deep breath for me? Breathe in, out, x 6. Thank you. Now I'm going to tap on your back. Please tell me if you feel any pain. Thank you.

Now I need to listen to your heart. Breathe normally. Thank you. Let me tie your gown.

I'm going to take a quick look at your arms and legs. No swelling, no rashes, nothing abnormal. Thank you.

Now I'd like to examine your belly. Could you lie down for me? Let me help you. (pull the extension). I'll listen to your belly first. Just be comfortable. I'll tap on your belly. Tell me if you feel any pain. I'll press on your belly. Tell me if you feel any pain. Thank you.

Thank you for your cooperation. You can sit up now. Let me help you.

Ms. Lincoln. On the basis of information you gave me and physical examination, there are a couple of possibilities like pregnancy, the infection in your stomach, and electrolyte imbalance. So we'll have to run some tests to make more correct diagnosis. These may include pregnancy test, blood works and breast and pelvic exam if needed. Once I get the result of these tests, I'll be able to talk to you about the diagnosis. And I recommend you to use condom every time when you have intercourse in order to prevent sexually transmitted disease or to avoid unwanted pregnancy.

Do you have any questions for me? OK. I look forward to seeing you again. It was nice to meet you.

반복해서 외우고 또 외워서 꿈속에서도 대사가 떠오를 정도로 달달 외웠다. 랩 동료들에게 발음 교정을 부탁했지만, 파트너를 두고 연습하지는 못했다. 닥터 유진과 안준홍 선생님으로부터 7월에 자료를 얻어서 11월 초에 스크립트를 완성했다. 그때부터 반복하면서 외웠다. 마침내 12월 16일 일요일, LA로 갔다. 시험 당일의 내용은 2012년 12월 18일 일기에 적어두었다. 시험을 다 끝내고 나니 시험을 잘 마쳤다는 안내장을 주었다.

NBME ®

CSEC
Clinical Skills Evaluation Collaboration

CSEC Center – Los Angeles
Pacific Corporate Towers
100 North Sepulveda Blvd., 13th Floor
El Segundo, CA 90245
(310)322-2102 Fax

ECFMG ®

December 17, 2012

To Whom It May Concern:

This letter is to certify that the following examinee was present at the Clinical Skills Evaluation Center at Los Angeles, California on the following date for the express purpose of taking the USMLE™ Step 2 Clinical Skills (Step 2 CS) examination.

Examinee name: Jong Ryeol Eun

Examination date: December 17, 2012

Sincerely,

Peter O'Colmain
Center Manager
Clinical Skills Evaluation Center - Los Angeles

2013년 1월 30일, 성적이 발표되었다. 합격이었다. 아침마다 일어나자마자 컴퓨터를 켜고 오아시스에 들어갔는데 아침에 PDF 성적 파일이 있었다. 정말 긴장하면서 파일을 열었는데 'PASS'라는 글자가 눈에 들어왔다. 겨우 합격했다. 성적표를 스캔해 놓지 않아서 보관된 것이 보이지 않았다. 어쨌든 합격해서 너무 기쁘고 다행이라는 생각이 들었다. 1월 31일 ECFMG 자격증certificate이 발송되었다.

US·MLE
United States
Medical
Licensing
Examination®

United States Medical Licensing Examination® (USMLE®)
Certified Transcript of Scores

This document was prepared by the
Federation of State Medical Boards of the United States, Inc.
Federation Place, 400 Fuller Wiser Road, Suite 300, Euless, TX 76039-3856 – Telephone (817) 868-4000

Date : 09/12/2013

Recipient:

Jong Ryeol Eun
4301 Ashland Terrace Apt C
Davis, CA 95618

Examinee ID#: 0-825-176-1
Examinee: Eun, Jong Ryeol **Date of Birth:** 08/06/1972
Alt Name(s):

Results for Steps taken by this examinee (and for which results have been reported to date) are shown below. For Steps that span more than one day, the test date reflects the day on which the examination began. Where numeric scores are reported, the recommended minimum passing score ("MP") is shown in parentheses. Pass/fail outcomes are based upon the minimum passing level in place at the time of test administration and are not altered by subsequent revisions to the minimum passing level. Effective April 1, 2013, test results are reported on a three-digit scale only; two-digit scores reported for prior administrations will no longer be reported. Test results reported as passing represent an exam score of 75 or higher on a two-digit scoring scale.

USMLE STEP 1

	Test Date	Pass/Fail	Total	MP	Comments
	10/13/2011	Pass	223	(188)	

USMLE STEP 2

Clinical Knowledge (CK)

	Test Date	Pass/Fail	Total	MP	Comments
	12/21/2011	Pass	251	(189)	

Clinical Skills (CS)*

	Test Date	Pass/Fail	Total	MP	Comments
	12/17/2012	Pass			

USMLE STEP 3

	Test Date	Pass/Fail	Total	MP	Comments
CALIFORNIA	04/21/2013	Pass	216	(190)	

Educational Commission for Foreign Medical Graduates

The ECFMG® certifies that

Jong Ryeol Eun

has successfully passed the required examinations, satisfied all the requirements of the Commission, and has been awarded this Certificate.

Steven E. Minnick MD
Chair, Board of Trustees

Emmanuel Cassimatis M.D.
President and Chief Executive Officer

Certificate Number	0-825-176-1
Medical Science	
USMLE Step 1	October 13, 2011
USMLE Step 2 CK	December 21, 2011
Clinical Skills	
USMLE Step 2 CS	December 17, 2012

Date Issued January 31, 2013

매칭 준비를 해야 해서 바빠질 것 같았다. 먼저 Step 3 시험을 보고 캘리포니아 레터를 신청해야했다.

NIW 영주권,
준비부터 발급까지

2011년 4월은 USMLE를 보겠다고 결심하고 준비를 시작하던 때다. 미국연수와 미국 레지던트 지원, 궁극적으로는 미국 이민을 생각했다. 미국 이민을 위해서는 영주권이 필요하다고 결론지었다. 또 레지던트 지원에 영주권이 도움이 될 것이라고 생각했다. 영주권을 생각하고 있던 차에 영주권을 취급하는 법무법인으로부터 다음과 같은 광고 이메일을 받았다.

> Date : 2011-04-18 08:49:38
> **Subject** : 미국으로 안식년(교환교수)을 준비하시는 교수님을 위한 TIP
>
> **"이제는 미국 영주권, 비자도 신뢰와 믿음으로 안전한 法務法人에서" !!**
> **"미국으로 안식년(교환교수)을 준비하신다면 엄청난 혜택인 미국 영주권으로 떠나세요"**
> **"2001年 부터 오랜 경험으로 신뢰받는 미국 변호사와 함께 하세요"**
>
> 안녕하세요~
> **미국 NIW 취득 전문 法務法人**[   ]에서, 미국 영주권을 필요로 하시고, 자녀를 미국에 유학 보내시거나, 미국으로 안식년을 준비하시는 대학교 교수님들에게 **"미국 고학력자 독립이민"** (NIW) 이라는 교수님만의 스펙으로 **"가장 빠르고, 안전하고 저렴한" 미국 영주권 취득 방법에 대한 안내**를 드립니다.
> 가지고 계신 프리스타일의 이력서(CV)를 보내 주시면 법무법인 해승의 미국변호사와 NIW 전문 미국로펌의 사전 자격 평가를 **無料**로 해 드리도록 하겠습니다.
> 교수님들께서 많이 바쁘시겠지만, 시간을 할애해 주시면 방문을 드리거나 저희 법무법인 (서울 서초구 서초동)으로 방문 하여 주시면 자세한 상담 드리도록 하겠습니다.
>
> 저희 법무법인 "[   ] **미국변호사** 소개" "안식년 관련 안내" 및 "NIW 안내" 첨부하여 드립니다. 참고하시기 바랍니다.
>
> 감사합니다

다음과 같이 문의 메일을 보냈다.

보낸사람: 은종렬 <dreun@ynu.ac.kr>
받는사람 : ☐@hanmail.net
날짜: 2011년 4월 20일 수요일, 20시 07분 58초 +0900
제목: [RE]미국으로 연식년(교환교수)을 준비하시는 교수님을 위한 TIP

안녕하세요?
보내신 메일에 관심이 있어 답장드립니다.

저는 대구 영남대학교병원 소화기내과에 근무하는
은종렬이라고 합니다.
현재 조교수이고, 2012년 2월에 미국 캘리포니아로 연수를 떠납니다.
(연수후 병원은 사직하고, 미국에 장기간 있을 생각입니다)

원래의 계획은 J1 비자로 연수를 떠나고,
2-3년정도 연수기관의 실험실에서 근무한 후
연구원생활을 연장하거나 또는 추천서를 받아 내과 레지던트를 다시 할 계획입니다.
그런데 비자를 변경하고, 영주권이 문제가 될 것 같아서 도움을 주실수 있는지 여쭙니다.

현재 제 스펙은
1) 영남대학교병원 조교수
2) 내과전문의 및 소화기내과 분과전문의
3) 석사학위(+), 박사3학기째
4) 국내특허출원 1건, 국제특허는 현재 출원준비중
5) 저서는 번역서 1권
6) 논문 수십편
7) 연구비수혜: 한국과학재단 일반연구자 지원사업(신진연구자부문) (1억5천만원)
기타 교내, 의료원 연구비 다수
8) 신문출연기사 다수
9) 학술지 논문심사 다수
10) 위촉장 등
입니다..

NIW 가능한지와 NIW과 관련하여 드는 비용(수임료)이
대략 어느정도인지 여쭙니다.

대구에서
은종렬 드림

NIW와 영주권에 대한 간단한 설명과 함께 비용에 대한 회신을 받았다.

안녕하세요? 은 교수님~

미국 고학력 독립이민(NIW-National Interest Waiver)을 통한 미국 영주권 취득 전문 법무법인 00 수석컨설턴트/이사 ○○○입니다. 우선 무례한 이메일에 대한 관심을 가져 주시어 감사드립니다.

NIW는 단지 교수님의 스펙만으로 취득하는 미국 취업이민 2순위에 해당됩니다. 10여 년 전부터 시행을 해왔지만 그동안 인도, 중국 학자들이 주로 해당이 되었지요. 우리나라도 근래 이공계 분야 크레딧이 향상되어 2~3년 전부터 많이 신청하고 있습니다. 영주권을 취득하시고 난 후에는 개인적으로 영주권을 유지하는 것입니다. 교수님께서 포기를 하시더라도, 배우자나 자녀는 그대로 유지가 가능합니다.

미국 밖에서 12개월 이상 거주하신다면 미국 이민법상 영주권이 취소될 수 있습니다. 통상 6~12개월 사이에 한 번(미국본토)이라도 미국 입국 사실이 있으면 영주권 유지는 가능합니다. 그리고 NIW를 통하여 영주권을 취득하신 분들은 주로 본인은 국내에서 거주 및 경제활동을 하시고 배우자와 자녀들만 미국에 거주하므로, 사전에 영주권자로서 재입국허가서(Re-entry permit)를 발급받으신다면 2년/2년/1년(연장가능)까지 미국 밖에서 거주하실 수 있으며 이는 갱신이 가능하십니다. 또한, 만일 교수님이 영주권을 취소하더라도, 배우자나 자녀들이 영주권자로서 신분을 유지하셨다면 배우자와 자녀들의 영주권은 유효합니다. 그리고 5년 후에 (2년 6개월 이상 미국 체류) 미국 시민권을 취득하실 수 있습니다.

우선 궁금해 하시는 사항 먼저 답변드리겠습니다.

비용 부분은 보내드린 메일에도 언급했지만, 일반 업체의 2/3 수준입니다. 총 00,000달러이며, 계약금 00,000달러, 성공사례비(영주권청원서 승인 시) 0000달러입니다.

메일로 언급하신 경력으로 가능성이 있어 보입니다만은, 성공률을 높이기 위해서는 미국변호사의 면밀한 검토가 필요합니다. 가지고 계신 프리스타일의 이력서(CV)를 업데이트 하시어 보내주시면 법무법인 00의 미국변호사와 NIW 전문 미국로펌의 사전평가를 무료로 해 드리도록 하겠습니다. 간단한 이력으로는 면밀한 판단을 하기가 어렵습니다. 처음 메일 NIW 소개 부분에 있는 구비서류 리스트 입각하시어 모든 이력을 보내주셔야 성공률을 높일 수 있습니다.

교수님들께서 많이 바쁘시겠지만 시간을 할애해 주시면 방문을 드리거나 저희 법무법인(서울 서초구 서초동)으로 방문하여 주시면 자세한 상담을 드리도록 하겠습니다.

언제든지 궁금하신 사항은 연락 바랍니다. 메일이나 전화 모두 가능합니다. 자세한 안내 드리겠습니다.

감사합니다.

2011년 4~9월까지는 USMLE와 연수를 준비하느라 바쁘게 보냈다. 드디어 영주권 신청을 결심하고 법무법인에 이메일을 보냈다.

날짜: 2011년 9월 16일 금요일, 16시 44분 37초 +0900
제목: [RE]미국영주권 NIW 신청기준 완화 발표 <중앙일보>

안녕하세요?
메일 받고 답장이 늦었습니다.

영주권에 관심이 있고, 취득할려고 합니다.
그리고, 그냥 취득이 아니라 이민을 생각하고 있고, 미국에서 레지던트 다시 할 생각입니다.
현재의 제 상황이 지금 바로 진행하기에는 힘들것 같고 시간도 촉박한것 같습니다.

제 일정 한번 봐 주시면 감사하겠습니다.

2012년 2월: 출국 (Research fellow 2012-2015년 계획, J1-visa)
2012년 영주권 준비 (NIW 취급 법무법인 섭외) 및 진행
2014년까지 영주권 취득
2014년 9월 - 2015년 8월: 병원 레지던트 지원 및 인터뷰
2015년 9월 - 2018년 8월: 레지던트 수료 및 Fellow 준비

개략적인 제 계획이었습니다.
영주권이 있으면 레지던트 지원이 쉬울것 같습니다.
지금 영주권 준비를 시작하기에는 시간이 촉박할것 같고,
J1 visa interview때 미국이민 의향에 대한 질문에 대해 답하는데 문제가 생길것 같기도 합니다.
우선 도미하여 미국에 거주하면서 영주권 준비를 하려고 합니다.

영주권 취득 스케쥴에 대한 조언 부탁드립니다.

은종렬 드림

보낸날짜 2011. 9. 20 오전 9:47:14
받는사람 은종렬 <dreun@ynu.ac.kr>

안녕하세요~ 은 교수님~

교수님의 CV를 저희 미국변호사가 검토하고, 미국 NIW 전문로펌 으로 부터도 좋은 결과가 생각보다 빨리 와서 메일 전문을 먼저 보내 드립니다.
축하 드립니다.

Dr. Eun, Jong-Ryeol can certainly file for NIW.

"은 교수님의 NIW 진행이 가능하다는 판단 입니다"

어필 할 방향은
-전공하시는 의료 분야가 미국 국익에 상당한 도움이 되며
-특허
-저서
-GRANT 사항
-기사, 논문 심사
-과거 보다는 현재의 연구 실적이 중요합니다. 이점이 교수님은 유리 합니다
-보내주신 논문의 피인용 횟수는 60회로 파악 되었습니다(이는 NIW 승인 케이스 피인용 횟수 40여회 보다 상회하는 숫자 입니다)
-미국경력 부족한 부분은 외국인(1-2명) 추천서 로 어필하여 커버 가능 합니다
-미국 관련 학회의 가입도 효과가 배가 됩니다

상기와 같은 방향으로 컨설팅을 드립니다
후속 진행 여부를 알려 주시면 안내 드리도록 하겠습니다

법무법인과 이메일을 여러 번 주고받았고 정식 계약을 했다.

날짜: 2011년 9월 20일 화요일, 20시 50분 59초 +0900
제목: [RE]RE: [RE]RE:_[RE]미국영주권_NIW_사전 자격 판정 결과

먼저 감사드립니다.

NIW에 대해 생각은 하고 있었지만, 어디에 맡길지는 고민이 있었고
인터넷 검색에 안좋은 글들도 올라와 있고 해서 아직 불안한 마음은 있습니다.
그렇지만 영주권이 꼭 필요하고, 이렇게 알게 된것도 인연으로 생각합니다.

이제부터 말씀하시는데로, 시키는데로 믿고 따르겠습니다.
먼저 계약하고 다음 절차는 시키시는데로 따르겠습니다.
꼭 영주권을 취득할 수 있도록 도와주십시오.

꼭 서초동 사무실로 가야 한다면 토요일 시간을 내야 할 것 같구요..
혹시 대구 와주실수 있으면 감사하겠습니다.

은종렬 드림

Date : 2011-09-20 21:34:41
Subject : RE: [RE]RE: [RE]RE:_[RE]미국영주권 NIW 상담

안녕하세요~은 교수님

빠른 회신 감사드립니다

저희 법무법인 과 □ 미국변호사를 믿고 진행을 하시기로 하셨다니 감사드립니다
의대 교수님 케이스를 많이 다루어 보았고 승인도 받았으니 잘 되리라 믿습니다^^
우선, 교수님께서 중요한 계약서 검토가 순서 이신것 같습니다.
NIW 계약서 보내드리오니 충분히 검토하시고, 계약금을 입금 하시기를 바랍니다

제가 대구로 내려가도 무방하오나, 교수님께서 저희 법무법인도 한번보실겸 해서
토요일에 내방하시는것이 어떠 하실런지요~ 그날 저희도 계약서에 날인하고, 추가 상담을 해 드리도록 하겠습니다
원래 휴무일이오나, 저는 사무실과 가깝게 사니, 오신다면 출근을 하도록 하겠습니다
편하신 시간을 알려 주시기 바랍니다
(위치는 지하철 2호선 서초역, 대법원 대각선 건물)

P.S 입금계좌-국민은행 □ 예금주-□ 미국변호사
환율은 전일 매매기준율 (계약금-USD 10,000)

날짜: 2011년 9월 20일 화요일, 23시 16분 28초 +0900
제목: [RE]RE: [RE]RE: [RE]RE:_[RE]미국영주권 NIW 상담

10월 13일(목요일)에 USMLE 1차 시험이 있어
전날 오후에 올라갑니다.

그때 (10/12. 수) 가도 괜찮을런지요?
도착하면 시간이 좀 늦어서 초저녁이 될 수도 있을것 같은데요..
그전에는 시간내기가 쉽지 않네요..
계약금 입금은 그 전에 하도록 하겠습니다.
달러로 만불 입금하면 되는건가요?
제가 달러를 가지고 있어서 달러로 결재하는 것이 편할것 같습니다.

그때부터 서류준비하면 대략 시간이 얼마쯤 걸릴까요?
12월 전에 마칠수 있을까요?

은종렬 드림

2011년 9월 22일, NIW 영주권신청 계약을 완료했다.

보낸날짜 2011. 9. 22 오후 3:57:57
받는사람 은종렬 <dreun@ynu.ac.kr>
참조 □@apollo2.com<□@apollo2.com>, □@apollo2.com

안녕하세요~온 종열 교수님

입금 확인 하였습니다. 계약 하여 주시어 감사 드립니다.

날자와 시간을 정해주시면 제가 대구로 찾아뵙고 계약서 전달과 추가 상담 드리도록 하겠습니다

열과 성의를 다 하여 교수님의 미국 영주권 취득을 홍영규 미국변호사와 함께 원하시는 시기에 반드시 취득 하실수 있도록 노력 하겠습니다

앞으로는 NIW 서류담당 실무책임자인 이영미 실장이 교수님과 컨택을 할 것입니다. 곧 이영미 실장이 별도로 연락을 드릴겁니다. 앞으로 자주 연락 주고 받으셔야 진행이 빠릅니다^^ 혹시나 궁금 하신 사항이나 문의 사항 있으시면 언제든지 연락 주시기 바랍니다

말씀드린대로 인제부터는 교수님께서 서류준비를 얼마나 잘 준비 하시고 철저히 하시냐가 관건 입니다. 바쁘시더라도 서류 준비에 만전을 기해 주시기 바랍니다

저희가 도울 부분이 있으면 언제든지 말씀 해 주시기 바랍니다
다시한번 감사 드리며 또 연락 드리도록 하겠습니다

다음은 서류준비 단계다.

제목 은교수님, NIW 서류 안내 드립니다.

보낸사람 주소록추가 violet<　　@apollo2.com> 수신거부

보낸날짜 2011. 9. 26 오전 11:41:25

받는사람 은종렬 <dreun@ynu.ac.kr>

참조 + 　　<yumst@hanmail.net>, 홍영규　　@apollo2.com>

안녕하세요 은종열 교수님,

앞으로 교수님 수속을 담당할 　　 실장 입니다.

계획하신데로 접수하도록 하고, 수속이 진행되는 동안 최선의 노력을 다하겠습니다.

첨부한 파일은 NIW 접수를 위해 필요한 서류리스트 입니다. 살펴보시고, 궁금한 점 있으시면 연락 주시기 바랍니다.

추천서 준비에 필요한 내용 질문지도 첨부해서 보내드리니 작성하여 보내주세요.

미국 활동 계획서는 첨부한 샘플 참고하셔서 3페이지 정도로 작성하여 주시면 됩니다. (국문 or 영문) -교수님의 연구내용과 관련해서 미국에서의 연구활동 계획을 적어주시면 됩니다.

PDF 파일로 보내드리는 신청서에는 서명해서 보내주시면 됩니다.

(i-140: Part 8 에 서명하시고, G-28은 Part 1에 서명해서 보내주세요. 서명하신 페이지만 각 2부씩 보내주시기 바랍니다.)

교수님께서 첨부한 서류리스트의 서류들을 보내주시면, 저희가 서류 검토 후 번역 작업 및 커버레터 작성에 들어가게 됩니다. 보통 추천서 작성 및 받는데 시간이 소요되기 때문에, 추천서 받으시는 동안 저희는 교수님의 이력 서류들을 취합 정리하고, 보완이 필요할 경우 요청드릴 것이고, 서류 번역 및 신청서 준비하여 접수하게 됩니다.

향후 프로세스에 대해서는 진행 추이에 따라 다시 안내해드리도록 하겠습니다.

이외에도 이민 및 비자 관련 궁금하신 점 있으시면 언제든지 연락 주시기 바랍니다. 성심 성의껏 상담하여 드리겠습니다.

감사합니다.

· 첨부파일 일괄다운로드

- Plan(의대).docx (34.53KB) 다운로드
- 추천서 작성을 위해 필요한 information.docx (17.29KB) 다운로드
- NIW 구비서류.docx (25.23KB) 다운로드
- g-28.pdf (118.53KB) 다운로드
- i-140.pdf (406.29KB) 다운로드

답장 전체답장 전달 원문전달 삭제 원문저장 인쇄 이동 · 계속이동 ·

목록 · 윗글 · 아랫글

준비한 서류 목록 리스트는 다음과 같다.

NIW 준비된 서류들

1. 5인가족들 각각의 여권사본, 은종렬 본인의 비자(B1/B2) 사본
2. 가족관계증명서
3. 재직증명서
4. 이력서
5. 학위증명서, 성적증명서
6. 참가한 컨퍼런스 등 리스트 및 근거자료
7. 장래계획 본인설명 레터 (Future Plan)
8. 자격증(회원증)
9. 임명장(위촉장)
10. 논문별책
11. 논문 인용 인덱스 사본
12. 국제 컨퍼런스에 제출한 연구, 세미나 강연 등의 증거 => 6번 미국 및 국내컨퍼런스 참석 및 초록
13. 추천서: 국내 4명 초안작성 (미완성)
14. 학회 수상 및 연구비 수혜 + 일반상장 및 감사장
15. 석사 논문 리뷰 2건
16. 학회지 논문 심사 리뷰
17. 특허증 1건
18. 저서 1권 표지사본 (번역서) 복부초음파 14일 완성 (공역자: 김일봉)
19. 언론보도 및 기사
20. 논문추가인쇄요청서 2건
21. 강의, 원고 청탁
22. 히로시마대학 연수 (초청서, 연수 Certificate)
23. 기타 Certificate
24. I-48, G28 사인 페이지

파일별로 자료를 준비했다.

- I-140, G28
- 강의(원고)요청
- 기타Certificate
- 논문목록
- 논문심사의뢰
- 발표
- 보도자료
- 석사논문리뷰
- 신분증
- 언론보도 및 기사
- 연구비및수상내역
- 이력서
- 임명장(위촉장)
- 자격증사본
- 저서 및 출판물
- 참가한컨퍼런스목록
- 초청장증명서
- 추천서,장래계획소개
- 추천서_장래계획
- 특허증사본
- 현상할 사진
- 휴지통

초록	2015-11-10 오후 11:27
KJH(2011)	2011-09-26 오후 8:39
SJG(2011)	2011-09-26 오후 8:41
GNL(2010)	2011-09-26 오후 8:43
JHepatology(2010)	2011-09-26 오후 8:45
SJG(2009)	2011-09-26 오후 8:47
KJG(2009)	2011-09-26 오후 8:52
KJG(2009)(case)	2011-09-26 오후 9:05
KJH(2009)	2011-09-26 오후 9:06
Oncology(2009)	2011-09-26 오후 9:08
KJH(2008)	2011-09-26 오후 9:13
KJH(2008)(GSD type IIIa)	2011-09-26 오후 9:14
KJG(2008)(Original)	2011-09-26 오후 9:19
KJH(2006)(case)	2011-09-26 오후 9:22
알코올간질환의예후모델(춘계간학회)(2...	2011-09-26 오후 9:42
식도박리(내과학회지)(2009)	2011-09-26 오후 9:44
CMV식도염(내과학회지)(2009)	2011-09-26 오후 9:45
위림프상피종양(내과학회지)(2009)	2011-09-26 오후 9:51
담낭암(내과학회지)(2009)	2011-09-26 오후 9:53
단발신경섬유종(내시경학회)(2008)	2011-09-26 오후 9:54
순간탄성측정법(내과학회지)(2008)	2011-09-26 오후 9:56
하부위장관출혈고찰(내시경)(2008)	2011-09-26 오후 9:58
C형간염재발위험인자(2008)	2011-09-26 오후 9:59
C형간염분야(2008)(간학회지)	2011-09-26 오후 10:00
C형간염분야(2007)(간학회지)	2011-09-26 오후 10:03
톱니샘종(내시경)(2007)	2011-09-26 오후 10:07
CBD web(내과)(2007)	2011-09-26 오후 10:08
당원병1형(2006)(내과)	2011-09-26 오후 10:11
담즙유출(내시경)(2006)	2011-09-26 오후 10:11
위누공(내시경)(2006)	2011-09-26 오후 10:14
내시경지혈효과(내시경)(2006)	2011-09-26 오후 10:15
B형간염분야(2006)	2011-09-26 오후 10:16
바터팽대부출혈(내시경))(2006)	2011-09-26 오후 10:17
악성흑색종(내과)(2001)	2011-09-26 오후 10:23
혈관확장증내시경치료(내시경)(2000)	2011-09-26 오후 10:27
인터페론단기효과(간학회)(1999)	2011-09-26 오후 10:30
라미부딘(1999)	2011-09-26 오후 10:31
작은융종(영남의대)(2000)	2011-09-27 오전 8:14
폐쇄성황달(영남의대)(2008)	2011-09-27 오전 8:17
캡슐내시경(영남의대)(2006)	2011-09-27 오전 8:17
베체결장암(영남의대)(2006)	2011-09-27 오전 8:23
A형간염(영남의대)(2007)	2011-09-27 오후 4:49
엔테카비어(영남의대)(2008)	2011-09-27 오후 4:51

퓨처 플랜을 작성해야 하는데 기본 양식은 받았지만 결국 내 계획을 내가 적어야 했기 때문에 일천한 영어 실력으로 힘들게 작성했다. 아래는 어설픈 영어로 작성한 나의 미래 계획서다.

My Medical Expertise and Future Plan

I am applying to be considered as a National Interest as I do believe I possess unique and comprehensive research knowledge in liver diseases, specializing in chronic hepatitis B, alcoholic liver diseases and liver cancer, coupled with practical approach by treating patients with liver diseases in our university hospital. In this letter, I would like to describe my expertise and future plans in the United States if US permanent resident status is obtained.

Educational and Research Background

I have graduated from Yeungnam University, Daegu, South Korea in 1997. From 1997 - 2002, I completed my intern and resident course at the same university hospital. During this particular period, in 1999-2001, I completed the master degree at the same university. After 3 years of army service I completed fellowship in the Gastroenterology and Hepatology department from 2005 - 2006 then became a faculty at my alma mater. Based on the rich fellowship experience, I have gained the certificate for the gastrointestinal endoscopy specialist. During the fellowship and a faculty, I got many clinical experiences. For example, I performed at least 10,000 upper gastrointestinal endoscopy cases, 2,000 colonoscopy cases, 1,000 endoscopic retrograde cholangiopancreatography (ERCP), and 500 therapeutic endoscopy cases for esophageal and gastric variceal hemorrhage, and nonvariceal gastrointestinal hemorrhage. In addition, I treated thousands of patients with chronic hepatitis B and liver cancers, particularly advanced liver cancers. Based on these experiences, I published many clinical papers as well as basic research papers.

From 2006 - 2011, I was an instructor and assistant professor at Yeungnam University Hospital, S. Korea. At February 2012, I came to the University of California Davis Medical Center, Sacramento, CA, for concentrating further research. UC Davis medical center is a world known center in the United States led by a professor Mark A. Zern who is a greatly respected stem cell researcher and specialist. He is the editor of two books and the author of more 120 publications. He has received continuous funding from NIH since 1979. He is a nationally and internationally recognized authority in the areas of liver fibrosis, liver gene therapy and liver stem cell biology. He has been the chair of Gastroenterology and Hepatology at two institutions, chaired an NIH study section, the Grants Review Committee of the American Liver Foundation, and the Liver Task Force of the Alpha-1 Foundation. He is presently the President of the International Study Group for Stem Cell Therapy.

Many doctors wish to have a chance to work at the Zern's laboratory but not many are qualified.
I am also wanted to work here and applied then I had the honour of working here.

Research Findings and Contributions

1. While I was doing the course of master degree and fellowship in 1999-2001 and 2005-2006 at
   the Yeungnam University, I have accomplished the followings:
   - Epidemiology of hepatocellular carcinoma in Daegu, South Korea
   - Radiotherapy for hepatocellular carcinoma
   - Antiviral therapy for chronic hepatitis B

   Through these research findings, I could emphasize the importance the surveillance for early diagnosis for liver cancers.

2. Since a faculty in Sep 2006, while working as a full-time lecturer and an assistant professor at Yeungnam University Hospital, Daegu, S. Korea, I have continued my study in liver diseases and have accomplished the followings:

   - Importance of antiviral therapy to prevent liver cancer in patients with chronic hepatitis B
   - Chemotherapy for advanced liver cancers and good therapeutic results
   - Determining prognosis of intrahepatic cholangiocellular carcinoma
   - Cured cases of advanced liver cancer by chemotherapy
   - Long-term results of antiviral therapy in chronic hepatitis B
   - Role of hepatocyte growth factor for invasiveness in human hepatocellular carcinoma
   - Results of interferon therapy for chronic hepatitis C in Korean patients
   - Development of new drug for the treatment of alcoholic liver diseases

3. I have been treating patients while doing my fellowship and working as an assistant professor in Internal Medicine, and Gastroenterology and Hepatology at Yeungnam University Hospital since 2005. My research background has always been strength in treating my patients and vise versa.

National Concern on Chronic hepatitis B and Liver Cancers

Hepatitis B virus (HBV) infection, a main cause of liver cancer, and liver cancers are common disease and major medical concern in Asian countries; However; in the United States, many American hepatology doctors are focusing in hepatitis C virus (HCV) infection and fatty liver diseases. In the US, there are many Asians and patients who suffer from hepatitis B and the number is increasing due to an increased number of immigrants. Tremendous dollars will be spent in managing and treating these patients within the national health care system. Hepatitis B is not just a personal medical issue but it is a social and economical problem. In understanding hepatitis B, it is pivotal to know there is a significant relationship with liver cancers.

I have been investigating this relationship closely in the past 7 years and the details of this finding have been shared through numerous articles and conferences. It is a fundamental step to prevent and treat early hepatitis B in the prevention of liver cancers. In addition, specialists to treat liver cancers are needed. This is exactly what I have been focusing my research for last 10 years of my career.

Still now, no one knows how much decrease the risk of liver cancers by antiviral therapy in chronic hepatitis B. However, it is proven in my researches and cases that strict antiviral therapy tends to result in substantial reduction of the risk of liver cancers. Therefore, it is critical to continuously focus on this specific area to understand the HBV and liver cancers.

There are not many researchers and doctors who can do this research and I must say I am the right candidate in make headway in this research field. This is because I have been converging my last 10 years of research, focusing on liver diseases, particularly chronic hepatitis B and liver cancers, knowledge on virus and liver cancers through applying clinical research method and utilizing molecular biology techniques, and have produced great results from them. Bearing my acquired skills and produced results, I would like to contribute greatly in studying the relationship between HBV and liver cancer development. Based on these future researches, a treatment for hepatitis B and liver cancers can be found. This would provide a great relief to National Heath Care as well as a reduction in National Health Care spending.

National Concern on Alcoholic Liver Diseases

In the US, 16 millions of people suffer from alcohol abuse or alcoholism. Thirty five percent of them have alcoholic hepatitis during their life time. The only treatment of alcoholic liver disease is abstinence, and the effective treatments for alcoholic liver diseases are limited. Therefore, the development of new therapy with high efficacy is urgently needed. I and my colleagues investigated the effect of new drug, cilastazol, on the alcohol-induced liver injury mice. We found the good effect of cilostazol on the alcohol-injured liver injury mice. As the result, we got the certificate of patent of the drug by the Korean Intellectual Property Office (No. 10-1094934). Now it is under PCT (Patent Cooperation Treaty). If the favorable effect of cilostazol will be proven at the clinical trial in the future, many patients with alcoholic liver diseases, particularly alcoholic hepatitis will save their lives.

In Conclusion

If I obtain NIW with US permanent resident status, I am confident that I will be of great value to the American medical society by playing a key role in treating chronic hepatitis B and liver cancers through my many years of real life clinical experience and dedication to research.

Thanks you for this opportunity and hope to hear from you soon.

Regards,

Jong Ryeol Eun, M.D.
2012-03-29

지금은 챗GPT의 도움을 받을 수 있어서 영어로 번역하거나 교정에 문제없겠지만 그때는 되도 않는 실력으로 작성하느라 힘들었던 기억이 난다.

ETA750b1 (법무법인에서 작성해 주었던 것 같다)

U.S. DEPARTMENT OF LABOR
EMPLOYMENT AND TRAINING ADMINISTRATION
APPLICATION FOR ALIEN EMPLOYMENT CERTIFICATION

OMB Approval No. 1205-0015 Expires: 04/30/2014

PART B. STATEMENT OF QUALIFICATIONS OF ALIEN

FOR ADVICE CONCERNING REQUIREMENTS FOR ALIEN EMPLOYMENT CERTIFICATION: If the alien is in the U.S., contact nearest office of the United States Citizenship and Immigration Service. If the alien is outside the U.S., contact nearest U.S. Consulate.

IMPORTANT: READ ATTACHED INSTRUCTIONS BEFORE COMPLETING THIS FORM.

Print legibly in ink or use a typewriter. If you need more space to fully answer any questions on this form, use a separate sheet. Identify each answer with the number of the corresponding question. Sign and date each sheet.

1. Name of Alien (Family name in capital letters): EUN — First name: JONG RYEOL — Middle name: — Maiden name:

2. Present Address (No., Street, City and Town, State or Province and ZIP code): 102-2303 Raemian APT. 2030 Buhuh Dong. Susung Gu. Daegu — Country: Korea

3. Type of Visa (If in U.S.):

4. Alien's Birth date (Month, Day, Year):

5. Birthplace (City or Town, State or Province): — Country: Korea

6. Present Nationality or Citizenship (Country): Korea

7. Address in the United States Where Alien Will Reside: Undetermined

8. Name and Address of Prospective Employer if Alien has job offer in U.S.: N/A

9. Occupation in which Alien is Seeking Work: Medical Researcher

10. "X" the appropriate box below and furnish the information required for the box marked

a. ☒ Alien will apply for a visa abroad at the American Consulate in → City in Foreign Country: Seoul — Foreign Country: Korea

b. ☐ Alien is in the United States and will apply for adjustment of status to that of a lawful permanent resident in the office of the United States Citizenship and Immigration Service at → City: — State:

11. Names and Addresses of Schools, Colleges and Universities Attended (include trade or vocational training facilities)	Field of Study	FROM Month	FROM Year	TO Month	TO Year	Degrees or Certificates Received
Yeungnam Univ., Daegu	Medicine	March	1991	February	1997	B.A.
Yeungnam Univ., Daegu	Medicine	March	1999	February	2002	M.A.
Kyungpook Univ., Daegu	Medicine	March	2010	Present		

SPECIAL QUALIFICATIONS AND SKILLS

12. Additional Qualifications and Skills Alien Possesses and Proficiency in the use of Tools, Machines or Equipment Which Would Help Establish if Alien Meets Requirements for Occupation in Item 9.

See attached resume

13. List Licenses (Professional, journeymen, etc.)

Medical Doctor. Internal Medicine Specialist

14. List Documents Attached Which are Submitted as Evidence that Alien Possesses the Education, Training, Experience, and Abilities Represented

Certificates of Graduation. Transcripts. Employment. Letters of Recommendation. Books and other Publications

Endorsements — DATE REC. DOL — O.T. & C.

G-28

OMB No. 1615-0105; Expires 04/30/2012

G-28, Notice of Entry of Appearance as Attorney or Accredited Representative

Department of Homeland Security

Part 1. Notice of Appearance as Attorney or Accredited Representative

A. This appearance is in regard to immigration matters before:

☐ USCIS - List the form number(s). ______ ☐ CBP - List the specific matter in which appearance is entered:

☐ ICE - List the specific matter in which appearance is entered:

B. I hereby enter my appearance as attorney or accredited representative at the request of:

List Petitioner, Applicant, or Respondent. NOTE: Provide the mailing address of Petitioner, Applicant, or Respondent being represented, and not the address of the attorney or accredited representative, except when filed under VAWA.

Principal Petitioner, Applicant, or Respondent

Name: Last	First	Middle	A Number or Receipt Number, if any	☐ Petitioner ☐ Applicant ☐ Respondent
EUN	Jong Ryeol			

Address: Street Number and Street Name	Apt. No.	City	State	Zip Code
102-2303 Raemian Apt. 2030 Bumuhdong,Susunggu Daegu				

Pursuant to the Privacy Act of 1974 and DHS policy, I hereby consent to the disclosure to the named Attorney or Accredited Representative of any record pertaining to me that appears in any system of records of USCIS, USCBP, or USICE.

Signature of Petitioner, Applicant, or Respondent **Date**

Part 2. Information about Attorney or Accredited Representative *(Check applicable item(s) below)*

A. ☒ I am an attorney and a member in good standing of the bar of the highest court(s) of the following State(s), possession(s), territory(ies), commonwealth(s), or the District of Columbia: New York State, the Supreme Court of New York State

I am not ☒ or ☐ am subject to any order of any court or administrative agency disbarring, suspending, enjoining, restraining, or otherwise restricting me in the practice of law (If you are subject to any order(s), explain fully on reverse side).

B. ☐ I am an accredited representative of the following qualified non-profit religious, charitable, social service, or similar organization established in the United States, so recognized by the Department of Justice, Board of Immigration Appeals pursuant to 8 CFR 1292.2. Provide name of organization and expiration date of accreditation:

C. ☐ I am associated with ______.

The attorney or accredited representative of record previously filed Form G-28 in this case, and my appearance as an attorney or accredited representative is at his or her request *(If you check this item, also complete item A or B above in Part 2, whichever is appropriate)*.

Part 3. Name and Signature of Attorney or Accredited Representative

I have read and understand the regulations and conditions contained in 8 CFR 103.2 and 292 governing appearances and representation before the Department of Homeland Security. I declare under penalty of perjury under the laws of the United States that the information I have provided on this form is true and correct.

Name of Attorney or Accredited Representative	Attorney Bar Number(s), if any
Young Kyoo Hong	3021706
Signature of Attorney or Accredited Representative	Date

Complete Address of Attorney or Organization of Accredited Representative (Street Number and Street Name, Suite No., City, State, Zip Code)

Haeseung Law Group, 607 Dongil Highville Seocho Dong 1542-1 Seocho Gu, Seoul

Phone Number *(Include area code)*	Fax Number, if any *(Include area code)*	E-Mail Address, if any
(822) 566-8420	(822) 565-1545	ykhong@apollo2.com

Form G-28 (Rev. 04/22/09)N

미국연수하면서 2012년 7월 19일, 닥터 전에게 영주권 추천서를 부탁했다. 추천서를 받는 대로 법무법인에 보냈고 사무실에서 서류 박스를 이민국으로 보냈다.

I-797C (접수증)

Department of Homeland Security
U.S. Citizenship and Immigration Services

Form I-797C, Notice of Action

THIS NOTICE DOES NOT GRANT ANY IMMIGRATION STATUS OR BENEFIT.

NOTICE TYPE		NOTICE DATE
Receipt		October 19, 2012
CASE TYPE		USCIS ALIEN NUMBER
I-140, Immigrant Petition for Alien Worker		
RECEIPT NUMBER	RECEIVED DATE	PAGE
SRC1390023047	October 17, 2012	1 of 1
PRIORITY DATE	PREFERENCE CLASSIFICATION	DATE OF BIRTH
October 17, 2012	203 B2 NATL INTEREST WAIVER	August 06, 1972

JONG RYEOL EUN
C/O YOUNG KYOO HONG ESQ
607 DONGIL HIGHVILL 1542 1 SEOCHO
SEOUL, 137 872
KOREA

APPLICANT/PETITIONER NAME AND MAILING ADDRESS

PAYMENT INFORMATION:

Application/Petition Fee:	$580.00
Biometrics Fee:	$0.00
Total Amount Received:	$580.00
Total Balance Due:	$0.00

The I-140, Immigrant Petition for Alien Worker has been received by our office for the following beneficiaries and is in process:

Name	Date of Birth	Country of Birth	Class (If Applicable)
EUN, JONG RYEOL	8/6/1972	SOUTH KOREA	

Please verify your personal information listed above and immediately notify the USCIS National Customer Service Center at the phone number listed below if there are any changes.

Please note that if a priority date is printed on this notice, the priority does not reflect earlier retained priority dates.

If you have questions about possible immigration benefits and services, filing information, or USCIS forms, please call the USCIS National Customer Service Center (NCSC) at **1-800-375-5283**. If you are hearing impaired, please call the NCSC TDD at **1-800-767-1833**. Please also refer to the USCIS website: www.uscis.gov.

If you have any questions or comments regarding this notice or the status of your case, please contact our customer service number.

You will be notified separately about any other case you may have filed.

NIW 신청을 한 뒤에는 매일 USCIS 사이트에 들어가 진행 상황을 확인했다. 평균 4개월 정도의 시간이 걸린다고 알고 있었지만 조급한 마음이 들어서 매일 확인했던 것 같다. 2012년 12월 13일, 영주권 NIW 청원서petition가 승인되었다. 아침에는 초기 검토Initial review였는데 오전 11시쯤에 들어가 보니 결정DECISION으로 바뀌어 있었다. 결과는 승인APPROVED이었다. 파일을 접수하고 승인까지 55일이 걸렸다. I-485status adjustment를 준비해야 하지만 형식적인 절차로 I-140immigration petition에 비하면 아무것도 아니었다. 2012년 12월 19일에서 2013년 2월 7일까지 영주권을 받기 위한 백신접종vaccination 및 신체검사physical를 위해 보건소Davis community clinic에 여러 번 방문했다. 미국 병원에 레지던트 지원을 위해서는 7월까지 영주권이 필요했는데 하루하루 영주권이 나오길 기다리며 마음을 졸였다. 2013년 7월 25일, 영주권 최종 승인을 통보받았다.

Department of Homeland Security
U.S. Citizenship and Immigration Services

I-797, Notice of Action

THE UNITED STATES OF AMERICA

RECEIPT NUMBER		CASE TYPE
SRC-13-902-90772		I485 APPLICATION TO REGISTER PERMANENT RESIDENCE OR ADJUST STATUS
RECEIPT DATE May 21, 2013	PRIORITY DATE October 17, 2012	APPLICANT A204 820 933 EUN, JONG RYEOL
NOTICE DATE July 25, 2013	PAGE 1 of 1	

JONG RYEOL EUN
C/O EUN JONG RYEOL
4301 ASHLAND TERRACE APT C
DAVIS CA 95618

Notice Type: Welcome Notice
Section: Adjustment as direct beneficiary of immigrant petition
COA: E26

This courtesy notice is to advise you of action taken on this case. The official notice has been mailed to the authorized representative. Any relevant documentation included in the notice was also mailed as part of the official notice.

WELCOME TO THE UNITED STATES OF AMERICA

This is to notify you that your application for permanent residence has been approved. It is with great pleasure that we welcome you to permanent resident status in the United States.

At the top of this notice you will see a very important number. It is your USCIS A# (A-number). This is your permanent resident account and file number. This permanent account number is very important to you. You will need it whenever you contact us.

We will soon mail you a new *Permanent Resident Card*. You should receive it within the next 3 weeks. You can use it to show your new status. When you receive your card you must carry it with you at all times if you are 18 or older. It is the law.

Please call us at **(800) 375-5283** if any of the information about you shown above is incorrect, if you move before you receive your card, or if you don't receive your card within the next 3 weeks. If you call us, please have your A# and also the receipt number shown above available. The receipt number is a tracking number for your application.

Please read the notice that comes with your card. It will have important information about your card, about your status and responsibilities, and about permanent resident services available to you.

Your new card will expire in ten years. While card expiration will not directly affect your status, you will need to apply to renew your card several months before it expires. When the time comes and you need filing information, or an application, or if you ever have other questions about permanent resident services available to you, just call our *National Customer Service Center* at **1-800-375-5283** or visit the USCIS website at **www.uscis.gov**. (If you are hearing impaired, the NCSC's TDD number is **1-800-767-1833**.) The best days to call the NCSC are Tuesday through Friday.

Once again, welcome to the United States and congratulations on your permanent resident status.

This courtesy copy may not be used in lieu of official notification to demonstrate the filing or processing action taken on this case.

THIS FORM IS NOT A VISA NOR MAY IT BE USED IN PLACE OF A VISA.

NOTICE: Although this application/petition has been approved, USCIS and the U.S. Department of Homeland Security reserve the right to verify the information submitted in this application, petition and/or supporting documentation to ensure conformity with applicable laws, rules, regulations, and other authorities. Methods used for verifying information may include, but are not limited to, the review of public information and records, contact by correspondence, the internet, or telephone, and site inspections of businesses and residences. Information obtained during the course of verification will be used to determine whether revocation, rescission, and/or removal proceedings are appropriate. Applicants, petitioners, and representatives of record will be provided an opportunity to address derogatory information before any formal proceeding is initiated.

Please see the additional information on the back. You will be notified separately about any other cases you filed.
IMMIGRATION & NATURALIZATION SERVICE
TEXAS SERVICE CENTER
P O BOX 851488 - DEPT A
MESQUITE TX 75185-1488
Customer Service Telephone: (800) 375-5283

2013년 7월 26일, USCIS에 접속해 보니 그저께까지 승인acceptance으로 되어 있던 것이 'card production'으로 바뀌어 있었다. 드디어 영주권 카드를 받을 수 있게 되었다.

영주권에 대해서는 여러 가지 생각이 든다. 미국에는 불법 이민자도 많고 직장을 가지고 있지만 영주권이 없어서 신분이 불안정한 사람들도 많다. 이들에게 가장 절실한 것이 영주권이다. 한국의 젊은 의사들이 미국에 가서 레지던트를 하고 미국에 정착하는 데 영주권이 큰 관문이기도 하다. 나는 NIW로 비교적 쉽게 영주권을 받았지만 정작 중요한 레지던트 매칭에 실패해서 결국에는 영주권이 쓸모없게 되었다. 그러나 아예 쓸모없지는 않았던 이유는 가족들이 4년 6개월 정도 미국에 체류했기 때문이다. 이때 비자 갱신 없이 잘 지낼 수 있었다. 다만 무인도에서 보석이 쓸데없는 것처럼 일 없이 영주권만 있는 것은 아무 소용이 없었다. 2014년 10월, 나만 한국으로 돌아오고 집사람과 아이들은 미국에 남는 기러기도 생활도 생각했지만 집사람이 가족은 함께 있어야 한다며 한국으로 돌아오겠다고 했다.

우리 가족은 2016년 8월에 모두 한국으로 돌아왔다. 귀국 후 재입국허가서Reentry permit로 영주권을 유지하는 것이 힘든 일이기도 하고, 미국 이민을 포기했기 때문에 영주권이 필요가 없게 된 것이다. 나중에 대사관에 영주권을 반납했다. 결국 모든 과정이 해프닝으로 끝났다. 지금 생각하면 영주권을 계속 가지고 있었으면 아이들 유학에 도움이 되었을 거라는 생각도 든다. 또 아이들에게 시민권을 받게 했으면 어땠을까 하는 아쉬움도 있지만 이미 지나간 일이다. 지금도 이 모든 과정에 있었던 일들을 생각하면 가슴이 아려오고 눈물이 날 것만 같다.

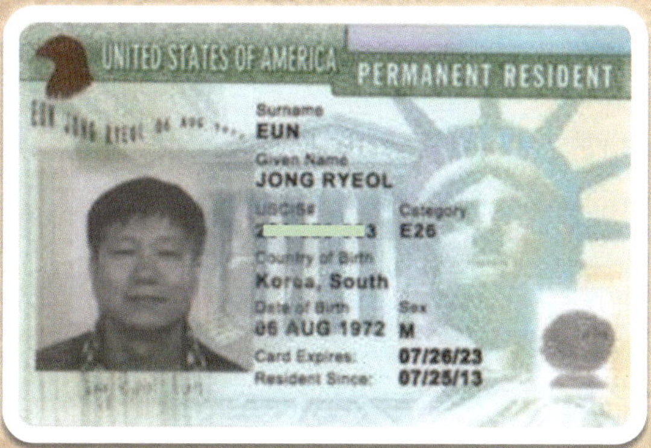
UNITED STATES OF AMERICA
PERMANENT RESIDENT
Surname
EUN
Given Name
JONG RYEOL
USCIS#
Category
E26
Country of Birth
Korea, South
Date of Birth
06 AUG 1972
Sex
M
Card Expires:
07/26/23
Resident Since:
07/25/13

정착과 방황 사이,
미국연수 2년차

2013년 3월 1일 금요일

같은 아파트에서 조금 더 좋은 곳으로 이사했다.

4301호 오른쪽이 우리집

2013년 3월 19일 화요일

레지던트 매치 결과가 발표되었다. UK 게시판에 매치 후기들이 올라왔다. 축하 인사를 건네고 싶다. 실패로 좌절하고 있는 사람도 많겠지만, 성공한 사람들이 지금 내게는 가장 부러운 사람들이다. 레지던트 매칭을 준비해야 하는데 너무 두렵다. 영어가 가장 큰 문제인데 작년보다 나아졌는지도 모르겠다. 어쨌든 조금씩 좋아질 거라고 생각하며 위안을 해본다. USMLE의 마지막 관문인 Step 3를 준비하고 있다. 이틀 동안 시험을 봐야 한다. 4월 21일과 24일로 예약했다. 내일 오후에는 INS 닥터노트를 받으러 데이비스 클리닉에 가야 한다. 어제는 예린이 결핵 혈액검사를 하고 3주 동안 연락이 없어서 다시 가야 했다. 결핵 혈액검사비는 환불되었으면 좋겠다.

* 클리닉에서는 무료, 사설 기관은 유료, 클리닉 사정으로 사설 기관에 의뢰하는 것은 무료라고 한다.

2013년 3월 22일 금요일

수요일에는 데이비스 클리닉에 INS 서류documents를 받으러 갔다. 예린이 혈액검사비가 환불되는지도 궁금했다. 데이비스 클리닉에 갈 때는 항상 긴장이 된다. 직원들이 그전 약속을 지키지 않는 경우가 많기 때문이다. 예를 들면, 예린이 혈액검사는 클리닉에서 할 수 없어서 퀘스트 다이아그노스틱Quest Diagnostics에 가서 받으라고 했는데, 매번 예약을 마음대로 취소하거나 연기해 버렸다. 그래서 신뢰가 가지 않았다. 이번에도 내 예감이 맞았다. 접수에서 닥터 카츠가 출근을 하지 않아서 서류에 사인이 안 되었다는 것이다. 사인이 되면 전화해 주겠다고 했다. 접수처에 있는 다른 직원에게 혈액검사 환불에 대해 물어보았는데, 매니저에게 전화해 보더니 매니저가 결정해 주면 알려주겠다고 했다. 이것도 역시 신뢰가 가지 않는다.

2013년 4월 8일 월요일

지난 토요일 식스플래그에 처음으로 갔다. 집 근처인데도 1년 동안 가볼 생각을 못하다가 시즌권을 끊었다. 어마어마한 놀이공원이었다. 매주 토요일마다 가기로 했다. 어제 쇼핑을 많이 다녀서 오늘 아침은 좀 피곤하다. 데이비스 클리닉으로부터 전화가 왔다. 너무 빨리 말해 알아들을 수가 없었다. 결론은 서류 리뷰가 끝나면 내일 오후에 다시 전화를 주겠다는 것이었다. 영어 때문에 또 한 번 절망했다. 이래서야 레지던트에 지원할 수 있을지 걱정이 된다.

2013년 4월 25일 목요일

지난주 일요일과 어제 이틀에 걸쳐 USMLE Step 3를 보았다. 첫날은 다소 어려웠고 어제는 조금 수월했다. 점수를 확신할 수는 없지만 큰 어려움은 없었던 것 같다. 이제부터는 정말 매칭 준비를 해야 한다. 영어가 가장 중요하다. 오늘 데이비스에 굿윌이 문을 열었다. 예린이와 지우를 학교에 데려다주고 집사람과 준성이와 함께 굿윌에 갔다. 오늘 오픈을 해서 괜찮은 것들이 많았다. 집사람은 신발 2켤레를, 나는 카세트플레이어를 샀다.

2013년 4월 30일 화요일

새 운전면허증을 받았다. 집사람 면허증은 오지 않았다. CCFS에 준성이 신청서와 100달러 체크를 냈다.

* CCFS(Center for Child and Family Studies)는 UC 데이비스에서 운영하는 어린이집 같은 곳으로 아이들을 돌보는 것뿐만 아니라 아이들의 행동을 연구하고 학생들이 실습할 수 있는 시설로, 비용이 저렴하고 제공하는 서비스가 우수하여 들어가기 위해 대기를 해야 한다.

2013년 5월 3일 금요일

어제 데이비스 클리닉으로부터 전화를 받았다. INS 서류가 완료되었다는 것이다. 바로 달려가 담당자를 기다렸다. 역시 기대를 저버리지 않았다. 내 것만 준비되었다. 실망해서 담당자에게 문의했더니 알아보겠다고 말했다. 오늘 오전 11시에 다시 전화가 왔다. 역시 불안하다. 7월까지는 영주권을 받아야 한다.

2013년 5월 21일 화요일

지우가 학교에서 공연을 했다.

2013년 5월 27일 월요일

오늘은 메모리얼 데이다. 지난 금요일에는 코스트코, 토요일 오전에는 노스트롬랙, 오후에는 수영장에서 보냈고, 저녁에는 판다익스프레스에서 외식을 했다. 그리고 일요일에는 한인교회에 갔다가 돌아오는 길에 굿윌에 들렀다. 저녁은 1+1 쿠폰이 있어서 KFC에서 4.99달러짜리 버거를 주문했다. 다음주에는 라스베이거스에 여행을 갈 예정이다.

어느 날 아파트 수영장에서

2013년 6월 11일 화요일

지난주에는 일주일 동안 라스베이거스 여행을 다녀왔다.

1일차(6/1, 토) 축구 클럽 신청 때문에 9시 50분에 집에서 출발했다. 지난번에는 여권을 가져오지 않아서 신청을 못했다. 어쨌든 출발은 좋았다. LA 근처 파나마에 있는 코스트코에 들러 점심을 먹었다. 저녁 7시에 라스베이거스에 있는 코트야드Coutyard 호텔에 도착했다.

2일차(6/2, 일) 6시 30분에 일어나 유타에 있는 자이언 캐년Zion canyon으로 떠났다. 7시 40분, 맥도날드에서 간단하게 아침을 먹었다. 캘리포니아와 유타는 1시간의 시차가 있었다. 오전 11시에 도착했는데 사람들과 차들이 너무 많아서 주차할 수가 없었다. 결국 자이언 캐년은 포기하고 브라이스 캐년Bryce canyon으로 행선지를 바꿔서 출발했다. 그곳에 도착하니 12시 20분이었다. 피곤이 밀려왔다. 안내소Visitor center에 들러 셔틀을 타기로 했다. 일몰 명소와 일출 명소, 또 명소 한 곳을 더 보았다. 아이들은 레인저 프로그램을 받았다. 5시까지 안내소로 가면 배지를 받을 수 있었는데 그곳에 도착하니 5시 15분이었다. 안내소가 문이 닫혀서 아깝게 배지를 받지 못했다. 아쉽지만 브라이스 캐년의 꼭대기에 있는 무지개 명소로 차를 돌렸다. 입구에서 10마일 정도의 거리였다. 몇 개의 명소들에서 사진을 찍었다. 카나브Kanab에 있는 숙소로 이동했다. 66달러에 호텔을 잡았다. 브라이스나 페이지 주변은 약 150달러로 더 비쌌다. 카나브에 도착하니 8시였다. 나는 완전히 탈진 상태가 되었다.

3일차(6/3, 월) 애리조나 페이지Page를 향해 떠났다. 목적지를 찾지 못해 헤매다가 겨우 투어 에이전시들이 모여 있는 곳을 찾았다. 1시 30분에 앤텔로프 캐년Antelope Canyon 투어를 예약했다. 도착한 시간이 오전 9시 40분이었고, 유타와 애리조나가 한 시간의 시차가 있기 때문에 카나브는 오전 10시 40분이었다. 앤텔로프 캐년 투어까지는 시간이 많이 남아 있었다. 그래서 우리는 홀슈 벤드horseshoe bend에 가기로 했다. 주차를 하고 홀슈 벤드까지 걸어가는 데 15분이 걸렸다. 날씨는 뜨겁고 모랫길이었지만 아름다웠다. 차로 다시 돌아올 때는 준

성이를 업고 걸었다. 숨이 차서 죽을 것 같았다. 점심은 중국 뷔페 레스토랑에서 먹었다. 가격은 어른이 7달러였다. 저렴하고 음식들도 맛있었다. 점심을 먹은 후 투어 에이전시에게로 갔다. 앤텔로프 캐년으로 떠나기 위해 트럭을 탔다. 준성이는 트럭 짐칸에 타고 싶어 했는데 베이비시트에 앉아야 해서 실망했다. 돌아오는 길에는 준성이 소원대로 트럭 뒤에 준성이를 태웠다. 가이드의 허락 덕분이었다. 모래 먼지가 심했는데도 준성이는 좋아했다. 다운타운과 앤텔로프 사이의 길은 사막이었다. 그때가 오후 3시 30분이었다. 우리는 라스베이거스로 향했다. 트레저 아일랜드 호텔Treasure island hotel에 도착하니 저녁 8시였다.

홀슈 벤드는 주차를 하고 걸어 올라가야 한다. 지우가 어디 가느냐고 물어서
여기 온 이유는 사실 지우를 버리러 온 거라고 장난을 쳤다. 지우는 날 버리지 말라며 울었다.
홀슈 벤드에 도착해서 안 버리겠다고 했더니 그제야 기분이 풀려서 사진을 찍었다.

4일차(6/4, 화) 아울렛으로 쇼핑하러 갔다. 내 샌들을 사고, 마키노Makino 스시 뷔페에서 점심을 먹었다. 정말 맛있었다. 음식 값은 74달러였다. 그 후에 M&M 초콜릿 공장에 갔다가 잠깐 쉬고 수영장으로 갔다. 저녁 7시에 문을 닫는다고 해서 30분 정도밖에 놀지 못했다. 샤워하고 호텔 주변을 걸었다. 먼저 베네치아 호텔로 갔다. 호텔 안은 말로 표현할 수 없이 웅장했다. 밤 10시에는 예린이, 지우와 함께 트레저 아일랜드 호텔 앞에서 해적선 공연을 보았다.

5일차(6/5, 수) 호텔 체크아웃을 하고 M 리조트 호텔로 점심 뷔페를 먹으러 갔다. 다른 주에서 여행 온 사람들에게는 20달러 할인을 해줘서 식사비용은 모두 38달러였다. 음식 종류가 매우 많았지만 내 입에는 맞지 않았다. 저녁에는 트로피카나 호텔에 체크인을 하고, 벨라지오 호텔에서 펼쳐진 분수쇼를 관람했다.

트로피카나 호텔에서 바라본 전경

6일차(6/6, 목) 아울렛에서 쇼핑을 하고 또 마키노에서 점심을 먹었다. 오후에는 럭소 호텔을 돌아다니고 만델레이 베이 호텔, 럭소 호텔, 엑스칼리버 호텔로 연결되는 모노레일을 탔다. 저녁에는 쇼핑 퀸인 집사람을 위해 10마일 떨어진 노드스트롬 랙Nordstrom Rack에 쇼핑을 갔다. 늦은 밤엔 예린이, 지우와 기프트숍에 가서 예린이 친구 아브리의 선물을 샀다.

7일차(6/7, 금) 라스베이거스를 떠났다. 9시간을 운전해 집에 도착하니 저녁 8시였다. 운전하는 길에 작은 돌이 시에나 앞 유리를 쳐서 작은 크랙이 생겼다.

2013년 7월 17일 화요일

쉬는 날이어서 젤리벨리 공장과 식스플래그에 갔다. 지난주 수요일(7월 10일)에는 누나와 조카가 샌프란시스코에 왔다. 도착하기 전 주 금요일에 아시아나가 샌프란시스코 공항에 착륙하는 과정에서 큰 사고가 있어서 걱정을 했는데 무사히 도착해서 다행이었다. 13일(목요일)에는 핑거프린트를 했다. 지금은 영주권 발급을 기다리고 있다. 레지던트 지원 전까지 영주권이 나와야 한다. 준성이 예방접종immunization과 신체검사physical 예약을 했다. 그리고 나는 영어 튜터를 구해 공부하기로 했다. 아흐마드에게 튜터를 부탁했는데 수락해 주었다. 한 주에 한 번 2시간 수업에 50달러를 주기로 했다.

2013년 7월 18일 목요일

어제와 오늘은 PCR과 랩 미팅 하느라 매우 바빴다. 추천서Letter of Recommendations에 관한 이메일을 받았다. 정진홍, 장병익 교수님의 추천서를 업로드했다. 지금은 MSPE를 준비하고 있다. 김민지 선생님의 MSPE를 받았다. 티아를 만났는데 다음 주부터 일을 시작한다고 한다. 내가 준비한 선물을 건넸다.

2013년 7월 26일 금요일

어제 우리 가족의 영주권이 승인되었다 USCIS 웹페이지에 접속하니 우리 가족 프로세스가 'card production'으로 되어 있어 놀랐다. 그저께는 'Acceptance'로 되어 있었다. 잠시 가족들과 기쁨을 나눴다. 오후 2시 데이비스 클리닉에 디스카운트 카드MediCal를 신청하러 가야 한다. 정 선생님은 랩에서 플로우 사이토메트리flow cytometry를 해야 해서 클리닉에 가는 길에 정 선생님 사모님을 픽업하기로 했다. 5시간쯤 걸리는 작업이어서 정 선생님이 내게 사모님 픽업을 부탁한 것이다. 저녁에는 캘리포니아 패키지 여행을 마치고 돌아오는 누나와 조카 유정이를 데리러 오클랜드에 가야 한다.

2013년 7월 28일 일요일

샌프란시스코에 바람 쐬러 갔다.

2013년 9월 7일 토요일

예린이와 지우 축구대회가 있었다. 학부모들이 심판을 봐주는데 아이들과 함께 시간을 많이 보내는 것이 부러웠다.

2013년 10월 31일 목요일

오늘은 할로윈데이다.

2013년 10월 29일 화요일

오전에 머리를 자르고 엔진오일을 갈았다. 1~3시까지 PCR 예약이 있어서 11시 30분에 시작했는데 실패했다. 아흐마드에게 영어과외를 받았다. 크라이슬러를 팔려고 KBB에 가격을 알아봐야 하고, 은행 잔고가 떨어져 가고 있어서 한국에 내시경 아르바이트 자리를 알아봐야 한다.

2013년 11월 7일 목요일

샘플 리스트를 정리한 파일을 닥터 듀안Duan에게 주었다. 샌프란시스코 영사관에 제출할 여권갱신 서류를 확인해서 출력했다.

2013년 11월 10일 일요일

샌프란시스코 하프문베이에 놀러 갔다. 오전 9시에 출발해서 11시 30분에 리츠칼튼 호텔에 도착했다. 해변가에서 놀다가 오후 4시경 클램차우더를 먹고 리버모어를 거쳐서 오려고 했는데 취소했다.

2013년 11월 11일 월요일

원래 연어를 보러 가려 했지만 피곤하기도 하고 아이들도 감기 기운이 있어서 취소하고 집에서 쉬었다.

2013년 11월 12일 화요일

닥터 전을 만나 이야기를 나눴다. 아이들을 픽업하고 코스트코에 가서 간단히 장을 보고 클라이슬러 실내를 세차했다. 세차 요금은 19,99달러였다. '도시락'에서 제육볶음과 BBQ 치킨을 사서 집으로 돌아왔다.

2013년 11년 13일 수요일

튜터 후 집에 들렀다가 새크라멘토 한인회 사무실(9225 Folsom Blvd, Sacramento, CA 95826, 916-363-4413) 순회영사에 예린이와 지우 여권을 발급 받으러 갔다. 비용은 45달러씩 2명과 이외의 비용까지 약 109달러가 들었다. 스마일마켓에 들러 장을 보았다.

2013년 11월 22일 금요일

제이드가든에서 정 선생님 가족과 함께 저녁을 먹었다.

2013년 11월 23일 토요일

식스플래그에 가서 놀고 리버모아에서 쇼핑하고 오는 길에 '도시락'에서 저녁을 먹었다.

2013년 11월 27일~12월 1일(수요일~일요일)

LA로 여행을 떠났다.

11/27(수) 몬트레이Monterey에서 점심을 먹고 크리크 브리지Creek Bridge에 갔다가 트래블로지 모로베이Moro Bay에 숙박했다. 40달러를 추가했는데도 숙박시설은 좋지 않았다.

11/28(목) 모로베이를 구경했다. 락Rock 파도가 인상적이었다. 솔뱅Solvang에서 카마릴로Camarillo로 이동했다. 홀리데이 인 숙박은 좋았다. 추수감사절이라 밤에 아울렛으로 쇼핑하러 갔다.

11/29(금) 카마릴로Camarillo 쇼핑을 하고, 오후 12시에 LA 홀리우드Hollywood로 이동했다. 오후 2시에 차이니즈 시어터Chinese Theater, 저녁엔 산타모니카 3번가 구경을 하다가 LA 윌셔 호텔Wilshire Hotel에 묵었다.

11/30(토) 오후 4시에 유니버셜 스튜디오Universal Studio 구경하다가 8시까지 그리피스 천문대Griffith Observatory에 있었다. 연경반점에서 짜장면과 짬뽕을 먹었다. 정말 맛있었다.

12/1(일) 한남체인에서 장을 보고 11시에 출발했는데 오후 7시 40분쯤 집에 도착했다. 차가 많이 막혔다.

2013년 12월 2일 월요일

월세Rental check 1,395달러를 냈다. 시에나 엔진오일도 체크했다.

2013년 12월 4일 수요일

아침 7시 반에 정 선생님을 공항에 데려다 주었다. 집에 오니 11시 40분이었다.

2013년 12월 5일 목요일

DMV 집사람 필기시험이 있었다. 합격해서 면허증을 받을 예정이다.

2013년 12월 6일 금요일

지우가 애나야Anaya 집에서 자고 오기로 했다.

2013년 12월 7일 토요일

지우가 집에 오지 않아 오후 1시에 데리러 갔는데, 집에 오지 않겠다고 소리를 질렀다. 집에 데리고 와서 혼내 주었다. 레지던트 인터뷰 호텔을 예약했다.

2013년 12월 8일 일요일

샘스클럽에서 쇼핑했다. 항공권과 렌트카도 예약했다.

2013년 12월 9일 월요일

오전 10시 50분에는 준성이 상담이 있었다. 오후에는 레지던트 인터뷰 연습을 했다.

2013년 12월 11일 수요일

오전에 영어 과외를 받고 쌍둥이네(여진, 윤서)와 점심을 먹고 오후에는 코스트코에 갔다.

2013년 12월 12일 목요일

랩 샘플을 정리했고, 유유가 논문을 투고했다. 이발을 한 뒤 시에나 엔진오일 교환하고, 고장 난 뒷좌석도 고쳤다.

2013년 12월 13일 금요일

3시 30분에 코스트코에 갔다가 월마트에 들러 준성이 전동카를 75달러에 구입했다.

2013년 12월 15일 일요일

너무 피곤해서 10시에 일어나 3시까지 누워 있다가 두 시간 정도 밖에 나가서 놀았다. 저녁에 크리스마스 데코레이션을 디스플레이했다.

2013년 12월 16일 월요일

인터뷰 연습을 했다.

2014년 1월 2일 목요일

아덴몰 시어스Sears에 갔다. 크리스마스 용품이 75퍼센트나 세일 중이었다.

2014년 1월 3일 금요일

11시에 집에서 출발해서 타겟으로 갔다. 준성이 수업료를 내러 출납원 사무실

Cashier's office에 들렀다가 식스플래그에 갔다. 오는 길에 시어스와 타겟에 들렀다. 타겟에서 90퍼센트 세일을 하고 있었다. 캐셔 말을 못 알아들어서 슬펐다. 캐셔가 "craft this or later?"라고 물어봤는데 'Craft'가 뭔지 몰라 머뭇거리다 예린이한테 물었다. 예린이가 바로 "아빠 바보 같애"라고 해서 순간 충격을 받았다. 만들기를 지금 할 건지 나중에 할 건지 물어보는 거라고 예린이가 알려주었다.

2014년 1월 6일 월요일

개학 첫날이다.

2014년 1월 7일 화요일

귀국 준비를 했다. 메디게이트에 알바를 알아보았다(2월 말~3월 말)

15일까지 운전면허갱신, 택스Tax 신고, 자동차보험 갱신, 옷가지, 2만 달러 송금받기 등 할 일이 많다.

2014년 1월 23일 목요일

크라이슬러를 팔았다.

2014년 2월 2일 일요일

인터뷰하러 뉴욕에 갔다. 코니 아일랜드Coney Island는 러시아 이민자들이 많이 사는 지역이라고 한다. 숙박 시설도 러시아인이 운영하는 곳이었다.

도착 후에 바로 병원에 사전 답사하러 갔다. 근처는 해안가로 놀이시설이 있었는데 너무 추웠다.

2014년 2월 5일 수요일

순천 모두편한내과에서 아르바이트를 하기로 했다.

* 환자가 많아 힘들었지만 원장님과 직원들이 친절하게 잘 대해주었고, 외래진료도 좋은 경험이었다. 나의 무엇을 믿었는지 급여도 근무 중에 선지급해 주었다. 생활비에 큰 보탬이 되었다.

2014년 2월 26일 수요일

첫 근무를 시작했다. 오랜만이라 오전 내시경이 힘들었다. 대장 4케이스, 위 6케이스를 했는데 시스템 익히는 것도 힘들었다. 외래를 어떻게 볼지 걱정이 된다. 순천 드라마촬영장이 있는데 순천역 앞에서 77번, 99-1번 버스를 타고 30분이면 갈 수 있는 거리에 있다.

이렇게 미국생활을 방황하며 2년을 보냈다.

2014/02/28

USMLE Step 3와 PTAL 승인 절차

2012년 12월에 영주권이 승인되었고, 2013년 2월에 ECFMG 자격증certificate을 받았다. 이제 레지던트 지원에 필요한 최소한의 자격요건을 갖춘 셈이다. 7월 접수까지 영어공부와 함께 Step 3와 PTAL를 받아두기로 했다. PTALPostgraduate Training Authorization Letter, 일명 California letter이 레지던트 지원에 큰 의미는 없겠지만 혹시 도움이 될까 해서 받아놓기로 했다. 우선 2013년 2월 3일, Step 3를 접수했다. 접수를 어떻게 했는지 기억나지 않지만 어렵지는 않았던 것 같다. FSMBFederation of State Medical Boards 사이트 안내에 따라 접수했다.

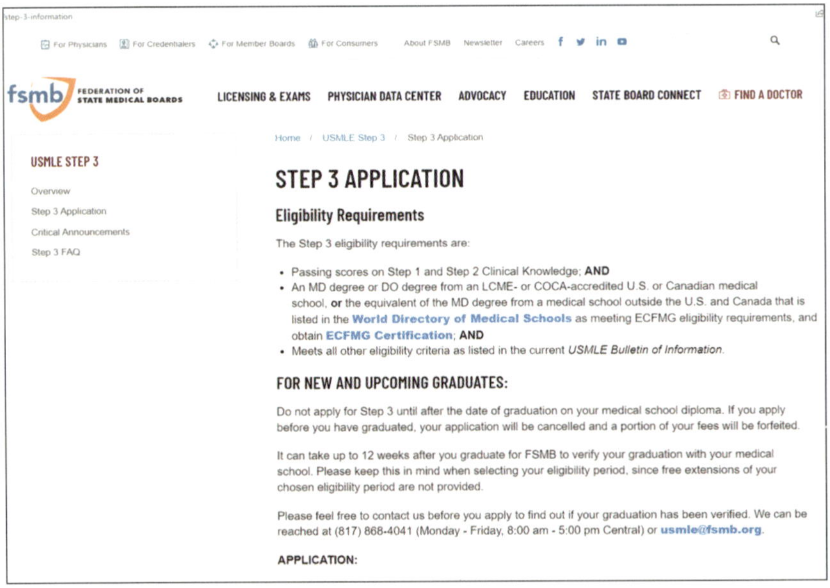
step-3-information

For Physicians | For Credentialers | For Member Boards | For Consumers | About FSMB | Newsletter | Careers

fsmb FEDERATION OF STATE MEDICAL BOARDS

LICENSING & EXAMS | PHYSICIAN DATA CENTER | ADVOCACY | EDUCATION | STATE BOARD CONNECT | FIND A DOCTOR

Home / USMLE Step 3 / Step 3 Application

USMLE STEP 3

Overview

Step 3 Application

Critical Announcements

Step 3 FAQ

STEP 3 APPLICATION

Eligibility Requirements

The Step 3 eligibility requirements are:

- Passing scores on Step 1 and Step 2 Clinical Knowledge; **AND**
- An MD degree or DO degree from an LCME- or COCA-accredited U.S. or Canadian medical school, **or** the equivalent of the MD degree from a medical school outside the U.S. and Canada that is listed in the **World Directory of Medical Schools** as meeting ECFMG eligibility requirements, and obtain **ECFMG Certification**; **AND**
- Meets all other eligibility criteria as listed in the current *USMLE Bulletin of Information*.

FOR NEW AND UPCOMING GRADUATES:

Do not apply for Step 3 until after the date of graduation on your medical school diploma. If you apply before you have graduated, your application will be cancelled and a portion of your fees will be forfeited.

It can take up to 12 weeks after you graduate for FSMB to verify your graduation with your medical school. Please keep this in mind when selecting your eligibility period, since free extensions of your chosen eligibility period are not provided.

Please feel free to contact us before you apply to find out if your graduation has been verified. We can be reached at (817) 868-4041 (Monday - Friday, 8:00 am - 5:00 pm Central) or **usmle@fsmb.org**.

APPLICATION:

당시 결제 금액이 총 845달러(780+65달러)였다.

Federation of STATE MEDICAL BOARDS

RECEIPT OF PAYMENT

Customer: Jong Ryeol Eun
USMLE ID:
Receipt for: United States Medical Licensing Examination Step 3 Application
Sponsored by: Medical Board of California

Amount Paid: $780.00
Balance Due: $0.00

Payment Date: 2/3/2013 10:12 PM
Payment Reference Number: VUYAA4DF6755

Federation of STATE MEDICAL BOARDS

RECEIPT OF PAYMENT

Customer: Eun, Jong Ryeol
USMLE ID:
Receipt for: Transcript Request

Total transcripts: 1
Total express fees: 0
Amount Paid: $65.00
Balance Due: $0.00

Payment Date: 2/6/2013 1:56 AM
Payment Reference Number: VSYAA3B9B795

결제하고 나면 다음과 같이 보내야 할 서류 안내가 온다. USMLE Step 1 & 2score와 ECFMG 자격증을 보내라고 한다. 우체국에서 공증하고 발송했다.

Additional Documents Are Required For Your Step 3 Application

Your application will not be completed until you print, sign, and mail these documents:

Dear Jong Ryeol Eun

Thank you for using the Federation of State Medical Boards (FSMB) online Step 3 application. Processing of your USMLE Step 3 application cannot be completed until all required documents are received.

- The **Certification of Identity form (CID) is required** for all applications. If you were unable to print the CID and one is no already on file with FSMB, you may use the following link to obtain a copy: Certificate of Identity
- **Additional forms may be required** for your application - please use the following link to access these forms: Additional Forms

Please mail your notarized USMLE Step 3 CID form and any additional required documents to

FSMB
Attn: Assessment Services
400 Fuller Wiser Road, Suite 300
Euless, TX 76039

For your convenience, a summary of your payment and application information are included below. We will send you another email within the next 3-4 business days once we have begun processing your application. If you have any further questions, please do no hesitate to contact us at usmle@fsmb.org or at (817) 868-4041 between the hours of 8:00 am and 5:00 pm (central), Monday throu Friday

We appreciate this opportunity to serve you

Assessment Services
Federation of State Medical Boards

Need Help? Have A Question? Contact Us

Payment Summary

Transaction Date: 2/3/2013 10:12 PM
Total: $780.00
Balance: $0.00
Payment Type: VISA
Account: ********2179
Payment Reference Number: VUYAA4DF6755

Personal Information

Name	Jong Ryeol Eun
Alternate Name	None
Gender	Male
Born	August 6, 1972 Daegu, Daegu Gwang'yeogsi [Taegu-Kwangyokshi] South Korea
Social Security Number	
USMLE ID	08251761
Address (Home)	320 Cambridge Terrace Apt A Davis, California 95618 United States
Phone Number (Mobile)	(530) 304-5754
Email Address	dreundavis@gmail.com
Ethnicity	Asian
English as native language?	No

Education

Medical School	Yeungnam University Taegu, Gyeongsangbugdo [Kyongsan Korea, Republic Of
Attended	Start: March 01, 1991 Finish: February 25, 1997
Graduated	February 25, 1997
Degree	Doctor of Medicine (MD)
Citizenship upon entering medical school	Korea, Republic Of
ECFMG Certificate	
ECFMG Issue Date	Jan 31 2013

Post Graduate Programs

Specialty

Planned Specialty	Internal Medicine

2013년 2월 14일에 Step 3 접수가 승인되었다는 이메일을 받았다.

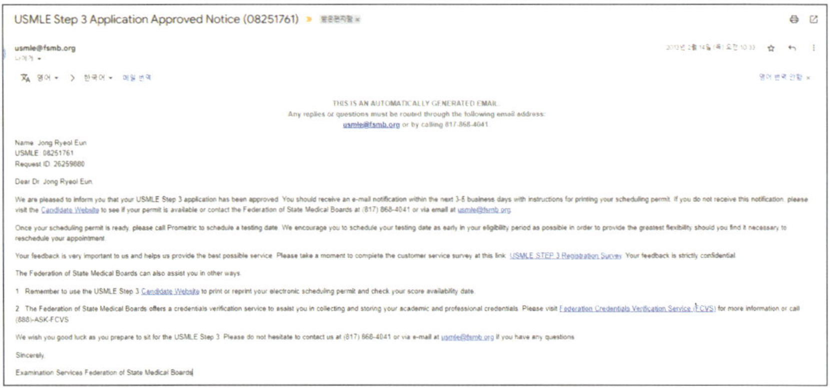

USMLE Step 3 Application Approved Notice (08251761)

usmle@fsmb.org

THIS IS AN AUTOMATICALLY GENERATED EMAIL.
Any replies or questions must be routed through the following email address:
usmle@fsmb.org or by calling 817-868-4041.

Name: Jong Ryeol Eun
USMLE: 08251761
Request ID: 26259880

Dear Dr. Jong Ryeol Eun:

We are pleased to inform you that your USMLE Step 3 application has been approved. You should receive an e-mail notification within the next 3-5 business days with instructions for printing your scheduling permit. If you do not receive this notification, please visit the Candidate Website to see if your permit is available or contact the Federation of State Medical Boards at (817) 868-4041 or via email at usmle@fsmb.org.

Once your scheduling permit is ready, please call Prometric to schedule a testing date. We encourage you to schedule your testing date as early in your eligibility period as possible in order to provide the greatest flexibility should you find it necessary to reschedule your appointment.

Your feedback is very important to us and helps us provide the best possible service. Please take a moment to complete the customer service survey at this link: USMLE STEP 3 Registration Survey. Your feedback is strictly confidential.

The Federation of State Medical Boards can also assist you in other ways:

1. Remember to use the USMLE Step 3 Candidate Website to print or reprint your electronic scheduling permit and check your score availability date.

2. The Federation of State Medical Boards offers a credentials verification service to assist you in collecting and storing your academic and professional credentials. Please visit Federation Credentials Verification Service (FCVS) for more information or call (888)-ASK-FCVS.

We wish you good luck as you prepare to sit for the USMLE Step 3. Please do not hesitate to contact us at (817) 868-4041 or via e-mail at usmle@fsmb.org if you have any questions.

Sincerely,

Examination Services Federation of State Medical Boards

2013년 2월 19일에는 시험 예약 안내Scheduling permit notice를 받았다.

USMLE Step 3 Scheduling Permit Notice (08251761)

usmle@fsmb.org

THIS IS AN AUTOMATICALLY GENERATED EMAIL.
Any replies or questions must be routed through the following email address:
usmle@fsmb.org or by calling 817-868-4041.

Name: Jong Ryeol Eun
USMLE: 08251761
Request ID: 26259880

Dear Dr. Jong Ryeol Eun:

Important Note: Changes will occur to the USMLE Step 3 resulting in a delay in score reporting for most Step 3 examinations administered from February 11, 2013 through early May 2013. The target date for reporting Step 3 scores for most examinees testing during that interval is **Wednesday, June 5, 2013. Please monitor www.fsmb.org for further updates.**

Your USMLE Step 3 **Scheduling Permit is now available** on the USMLE Step 3 Candidate Website. Please note that an additional 15 days have been added to your 90-day eligibility period to account for processing time. You will **not** receive a scheduling permit for this exam by mail.

Available test center exam slots fill up quickly, so please be sure to schedule a date as soon as possible. This also will provide you with the greatest flexibility in case you need to reschedule your appointment. Please remember that you are responsible for observing all scheduling, rescheduling and cancellation procedures listed on the scheduling permit. Failure to do so may result in a rescheduling fee charged by Prometric.

You must print your Scheduling Permit and bring it with you to the test center on your scheduled test dates. You will be **unable to test** if you do not bring your scheduling permit and a government issued form of ID (such as a driver's license or passport) that includes a recent photograph and signature. The name on your ID **must match exactly** the name on your scheduling permit.

Check-In Process at Prometric Test Centers
The Test Center Administrator (TCA) will ask you to write your Candidate ID Number(CIN) on the laminated writing surface provided for making notes. After you write your CIN on the laminated surface, the TCA will collect your permit, thereby eliminating the need for paper in the testing room. Do not erase your CIN until the end of your test day, as you may need to enter it several more times during the day. Because USMLE Step 3 is a multiple-day examination you will need to repeat this process on the following test day(s). Be sure to ask the TCA to return your permit to you at the end of your test day.

Your feedback is very important to us and helps us provide the best possible service. Please take a moment to complete the customer service survey at this link: USMLE STEP 3 Registration Survey. The information you provide helps us achieve our goal of service excellence. Your feedback is strictly confidential.

If you have any question about your scheduling permit, please do not hesitate to contact us at (817) 868-4041 or via e-mail at usmle@fsmb.org.

Sincerely,

Examination Services
Federation of State Medical Boards

이번에는 별도의 책으로는 공부하지 않고 UW를 결제했다. 반복해서 컴퓨터로 문제를 풀고 소프트웨어 프로그램을 연습했다. 시험 직전인 2013년 4월 19일에 시험 알림reminder과 안내가 왔다.

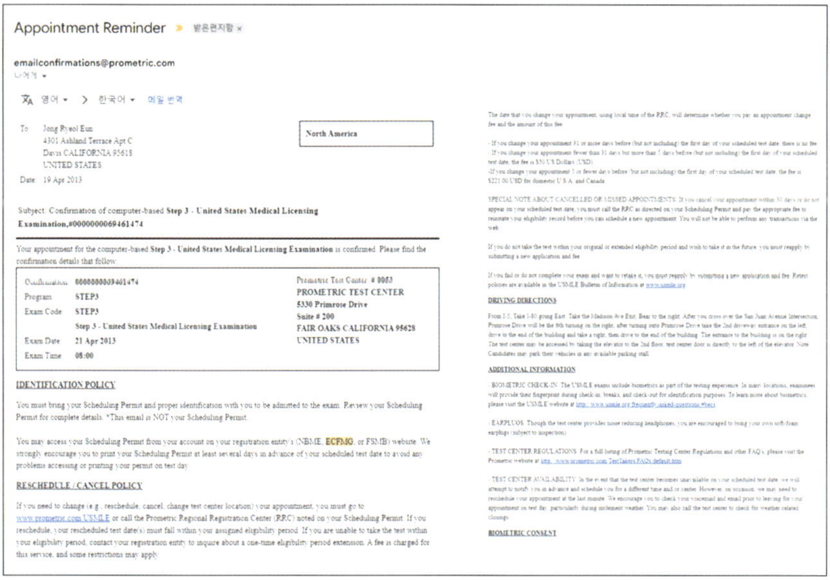

Appointment Reminder 받은편지함 ×

emailconfirmations@prometric.com
나에게

영어 > 한국어 메일 번역

To Jong Ryeol Eun
4301 Ashland Terrace Apt C
Davis CALIFORNIA 95618
UNITED STATES

Date 19 Apr 2013

North America

Subject: Confirmation of computer-based **Step 3 - United States Medical Licensing Examination,#0000000069461474**

Your appointment for the computer-based **Step 3 - United States Medical Licensing Examination** is confirmed. Please find the confirmation details that follow:

Confirmation	**0000000069461474**	Prometric Test Center # 0063
Program	**STEP3**	**PROMETRIC TEST CENTER**
Exam Code	**STEP3**	**5330 Primrose Drive**
	Step 3 - United States Medical Licensing Examination	**Suite # 200**
Exam Date	**21 Apr 2013**	**FAIR OAKS CALIFORNIA 95628**
Exam Time	**08:00**	**UNITED STATES**

IDENTIFICATION POLICY

You must bring your Scheduling Permit and proper identification with you to be admitted to the exam. Review your Scheduling Permit for complete details. *This email is NOT your Scheduling Permit.

You may access your Scheduling Permit from your account on your registration entity's (NBME, ECFMG, or FSMB) website. We strongly encourage you to print your Scheduling Permit at least several days in advance of your scheduled test date to avoid any problems accessing or printing your permit on test day.

RESCHEDULE / CANCEL POLICY

If you need to change (e.g., reschedule, cancel, change test center location) your appointment, you must go to www.prometric.com/USMLE or call the Prometric Regional Registration Center (RRC) noted on your Scheduling Permit. If you reschedule, your rescheduled test date(s) must fall within your assigned eligibility period. If you are unable to take the test within your eligibility period, contact your registration entity to inquire about a one-time eligibility period extension. A fee is charged for this service, and some restrictions may apply.

The date that you change your appointment, using local time of the RRC, will determine whether you pay an appointment change fee and the amount of this fee.

- If you change your appointment 31 or more days before (but not including) the first day of your scheduled test date, there is no fee.
- If you change your appointment fewer than 31 days but more than 5 days before (but not including) the first day of your scheduled test date, the fee is $50 US Dollars (USD).
-If you change your appointment 5 or fewer days before (but not including) the first day of your scheduled test date, the fee is $221.00 USD for domestic U.S.A. and Canada.

SPECIAL NOTE ABOUT CANCELLED OR MISSED APPOINTMENTS: If you cancel your appointment within 30 days or do not appear on your scheduled test date, you must call the RRC as directed on your Scheduling Permit and pay the appropriate fee to reinstate your eligibility record before you can schedule a new appointment. You will not be able to perform any transactions via the web.

If you do not take the test within your original or extended eligibility period and wish to take it in the future, you must reapply by submitting a new application and fee.

If you fail or do not complete your exam and want to retake it, you must reapply by submitting a new application and fee. Retest policies are available in the USMLE Bulletin of Information at www.usmle.org.

DRIVING DIRECTIONS

From I-5, Take I-80 going East. Take the Madison Ave Exit. Bear to the right. After you cross over the San Juan Avenue Intersection, Primrose Drive will be the 6th turning on the right, after turning onto Primrose Drive take the 2nd driveway entrance on the left, drive to the end of the building and take a right, then drive to the end of the building. The entrance to the building is on the right. The test center may be accessed by taking the elevator to the 2nd floor, test center door is directly to the left of the elevator. Note: Candidates may park their vehicles in any available parking stall.

ADDITIONAL INFORMATION

- BIOMETRIC CHECK-IN: The USMLE exams include biometrics as part of the testing experience. In many locations, examinees will provide their fingerprint during check-in, breaks, and check-out for identification purposes. To learn more about biometrics, please visit the USMLE website at http://www.usmle.org/frequently-asked-questions/#bcs

- EARPLUGS: Though the test center provides noise reducing headphones, you are encouraged to bring your own soft-foam earplugs (subject to inspection).

- TEST CENTER REGULATIONS: For a full listing of Prometric Testing Center Regulations and other FAQ's, please visit the Prometric website at http://www.prometric.com/TestTakers/FAQs/default.htm

- TEST CENTER AVAILABILITY: In the event that the test center becomes unavailable on your scheduled test date, we will attempt to notify you in advance and schedule you for a different time and/or center. However, on occasion, we may need to reschedule your appointment at the last minute. We encourage you to check your voicemail and email prior to leaving for your appointment on test day, particularly during inclement weather. You may also call the test center to check for weather-related closings.

BIOMETRIC CONSENT

2013년 4월 21일(일요일)과 24일(수요일), 이틀에 걸쳐 시험을 보았다. 다행히 시험장이 데이비스 집 가까운 곳에 있어 시험 보기는 편했다.

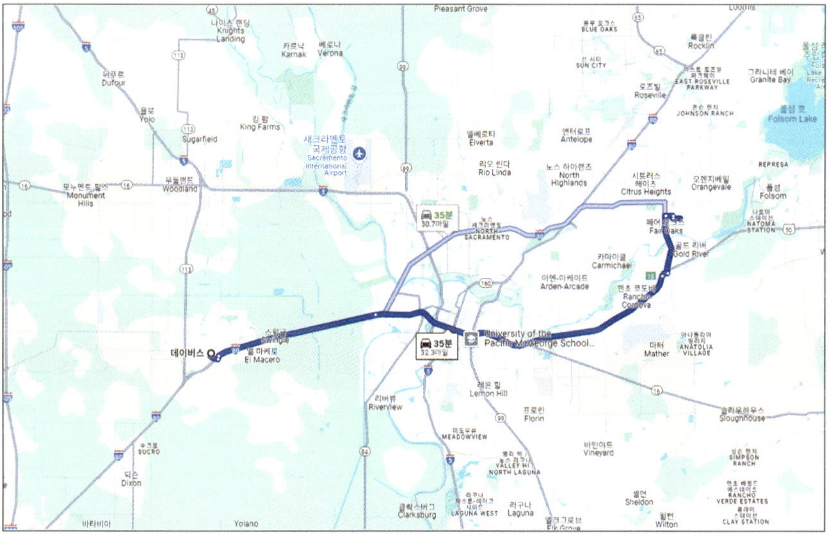

일기장을 보니 다음과 같이 기록되어 있다.

2013년 4월 25일, 목요일

지난 일요일과 어제 이틀에 걸쳐 USMLE Step 3를 보았다. Step 3는 이틀에 걸쳐서 치러진다. 첫날은 다소 어려웠다. 시간이 부족해 몇 문제는 읽을 시간이 없었다. 그나마 어제는 좀 편했다. 시간이 부족했지만 아주 쫓길 정도는 아니었다. CCS는 힘들지 않았다. 소프트웨어 프로그램을 여러 번 연습해서 익숙했던 것 같다. 점수를 확신할 수는 없지만 큰 어려움 없이 마쳤다.

점수는 219점으로 그리 좋은 편은 아니었다.

Step 3 시험 준비와 함께 캘리포니아 주 면허를 받기 위해 PTAL California letter를 신청했다. 2013년 2월 5일에 신청하고 4월 26일 승인되었다. 본인이 준비해야 하는 서류들도 있지만 의과대학에서 준비해 줘야 하는 서류들이 있어 조금 친분이 있는 행정실 담당 선생님에게 부탁했다. 2013년 2월 5일, 인터넷으로 신청하고 결제 영수증을 받았다. 491달러가 결제되었다. 매번 돈이 많이 들었던 것 같다.

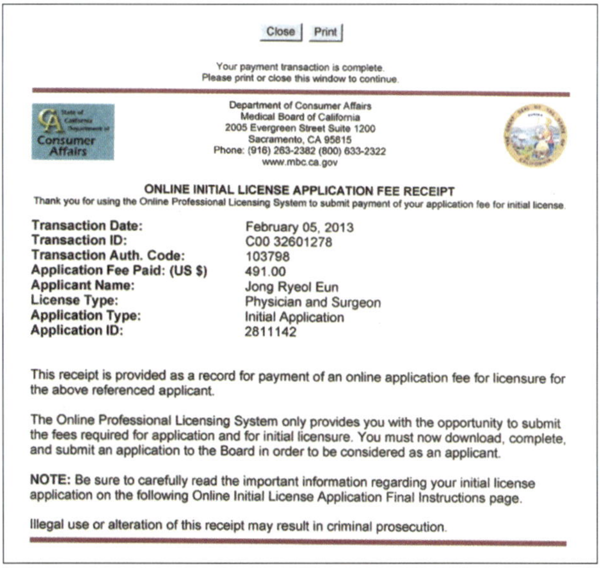

Close | Print

Your payment transaction is complete.
Please print or close this window to continue.

Department of Consumer Affairs
Medical Board of California
2005 Evergreen Street Suite 1200
Sacramento, CA 95815
Phone: (916) 263-2382 (800) 633-2322
www.mbc.ca.gov

ONLINE INITIAL LICENSE APPLICATION FEE RECEIPT

Thank you for using the Online Professional Licensing System to submit payment of your application fee for initial license.

Transaction Date:	February 05, 2013
Transaction ID:	C00 32601278
Transaction Auth. Code:	103798
Application Fee Paid: (US $)	491.00
Applicant Name:	Jong Ryeol Eun
License Type:	Physician and Surgeon
Application Type:	Initial Application
Application ID:	2811142

This receipt is provided as a record for payment of an online application fee for licensure for the above referenced applicant.

The Online Professional Licensing System only provides you with the opportunity to submit the fees required for application and for initial licensure. You must now download, complete, and submit an application to the Board in order to be considered as an applicant.

NOTE: Be sure to carefully read the important information regarding your initial license application on the following Online Initial License Application Final Instructions page.

Illegal use or alteration of this receipt may result in criminal prosecution.

2013년 2월 7일, 행정실 담당선생님에게 이메일로 부탁했다.

보낸사람 은종렬<dreun@ynu.ac.kr>

보낸날짜 2013. 2. 7 오후 2:16:20

받는사람 주소록추가 이장숙<leejs@medical.yu.ac.kr>

이장숙 선생님께,

안녕하세요? 내과학교실 은종렬입니다.
저는 2012년 3월 미국 캘리포니아 새크라멘토로 연수를 와 있습니다.
USMLE 접수로 여러번 부탁했었었는데 덕분에 출국 전에 step 1, 2CK합격하고,
얼마전 Step2CS 합격하여 드디어 ECFMG certificate를 받았습니다.
많이 도와주신 점 다시한번 감사드립니다.

결국 아시게 되겠지만 저는 2월 28일자로 사직합니다.
병원 사직 전에 긴히 부탁을 드리고자 메일을 드립니다.

저는 지금 캘리포니아 주 면허를 신청하기 위해 서류를 접수하였습니다.
캘리포니아 주면허 신청은 매우 까다롭고, 심사가 엄격합니다.
혹시 캘리포니아 레터(PTAL) 서류 작성해 보신 경험이 있으신지요?
많은 학생들이 USMLE를 준비하는 일부 의과대학에서는 PTAL 경험이 많은 담당자가 있어
수월하게 서류를 처리하기도 한다고 들었는데, 영남의대 출신중에서 USMLE를 준비하거나
certificate을 받은 사람은 꽤 있는 것으로 알지만 PTAL를 준비 한다는 이야기는 잘 못들어봤네요.

제가 준비해야 하는 서류는 모두 California Medical Board로 보냈습니다.
출신의과대학에서 보내야 하는 서류를 부탁드립니다.
혹시 해서 <준비해야 하는 서류와 요령>을 정리해 보았습니다.
의문사항 있으시면 메일 주시면 감사하겠습니다.
** USMLE접수와 마찬가지로 기관에 등록된 학장님과 현재 학장님 사인이 일치하여야 합니다.

9월 1일이 레지던트 지원일이고, 7월까지는 모든 서류가 완료되어야
8월에 ERAS에 서류를 업로드 시킬 수 있습니다.
PTAL심사가 평균 5-9개월 걸리므로 시간이 다소 촉박하여 다시한번 부탁드립니다.

이영환 학장님께 사인에 관해서 따로 부탁드리겠습니다.

감사합니다.

은종렬 드림

행정실 담당 선생님에게 첨부파일로 부탁한 내용이다.

캘리포니아 주 면허 신청 서류 및 절차

: PTAL (Postgraduate Training Authorization Letter, 일명 캘리포니아 레터)

I. 캘리포니아 주 면허 신청시 필요한 서류

1. 본인이 준비하여 California Medical Board로 보내야 하는 서류
   1) L1A-L1F
   2) Live Scan Request Form (캘리포니아 주민일 경우)
   3) Receipt of Fee($491)
   4) Timeline of activity

2. FSMB (Federation of State Medical Board)에 요청하여
   California Medical Board로 보내야 하는 서류: USMLE 시험 성적표

3. 출신학교에서 California Medical Board로 직접 보내야 하는 서류
   1) Form L2
   2) Official Medical School Transcript
      - Dean's signature(학장사인), 학교직인, Curriculum, a transcript 포함
   3) Certified Copy of Medical School Degree
      - Dean's signature, authenticity, 학교직인
   4) Form L5

II. Form L2 작성 요령 : 첨부된 Form L2 참조

1) 첨부된 PTAL pdf파일을 열어 L2 페이지를 찾는다.

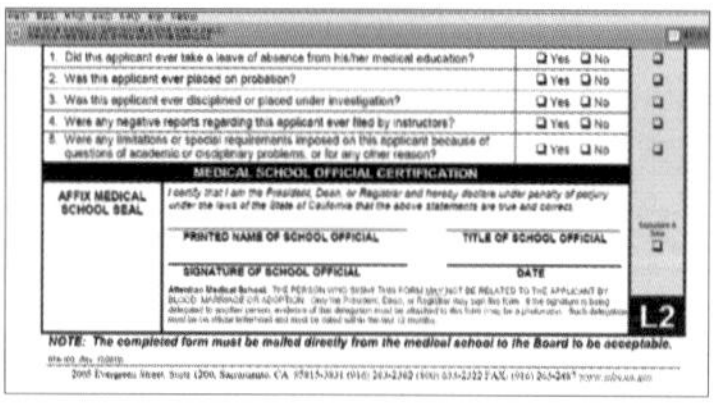

1. Did this applicant ever take a leave of absence from his/her medical education?	❑ Yes ❑ No	❑
2. Was this applicant ever placed on probation?	❑ Yes ❑ No	❑
3. Was this applicant ever disciplined or placed under investigation?	❑ Yes ❑ No	❑
4. Were any negative reports regarding this applicant ever filed by instructors?	❑ Yes ❑ No	❑
5. Were any limitations or special requirements imposed on this applicant because of questions of academic or disciplinary problems, or for any other reason?	❑ Yes ❑ No	❑

MEDICAL SCHOOL OFFICIAL CERTIFICATION

AFFIX MEDICAL SCHOOL SEAL

I certify that I am the President, Dean, or Registrar and hereby declare under penalty of perjury under the laws of the State of California that the above statements are true and correct.

PRINTED NAME OF SCHOOL OFFICIAL — TITLE OF SCHOOL OFFICIAL

SIGNATURE OF SCHOOL OFFICIAL — DATE

L2

NOTE: The completed form must be mailed directly from the medical school to the Board to be acceptable.

2) 상단에 이름, 생일, 사회보장번호, 출신학교란에 첨부된 Form L2를 참조하여
   Eun Jong Ryeol 08/06/1972 870-**-9**6
   Yeungnam Univeristy College of Medicine이라고 입력한 후 L2 쪽만 출력한다.
3) 첨부된 L2 폼을 참조하여 빈칸을 기입한다.
4) 아래에 학교담당자 사인에 담당자 또는 학장님 사인을 한다.

5) 학교직인(종이가 눌리는)을 찍는다.

III. Official Medical School Transcript
1) 첨부된 블로그(PTAL 작성요령 p51, 52, 53 참조하시면 되고,
http://www.slideshare.net/maxedmond/PTAL-step-by-step-application-guide-line-presentation)
영문성적표에 학장님 사인(Dean's signature), 학교직인이 반드시 있어야 합니다.
2) 제가 학교다닐 당시(1993-1996)의 Curriculum이 첨부되어야 합니다.

IV. Certified Copy of Medical School Degree
학장님 사인, 학교직인
이 사본이 원본과 동일하다는 문구가 포함되어야 한다고 하는데...

V. Form L5 (임상실습기록)
1) PTAL pdf 파일에서 L5부분 찾는다.
2) L2처럼 기본 신상 입력 후 현재 페이지로 출력한다.
3) 최소 72주 이상 만족해야 하고, 핵심과목은 최소 40주 이상을 이수하여야 한다.
(내과 8주, 외과 8주, 소아과 6주, 산부인과 6주, 정신과 4주, 가정의학 4주)
단, 가정의학은 1999년 이후 졸업자에 해당하므로 저에게는 해당이 없습니다.
** 옛날 제가 실습했던 시간표(1995년, 1996년)가 없어서 이 부분 좀 부탁드립니다.
: 실습 시작일과 종료일은 대략 채우면 될 것 같습니다.
** 제 기억으로는 최소 요건을 충분히 채웠던 것으로 기억합니다.
4) 마찬가지로 학장님 또는 담당자 사인과 학교직인이 있어야 합니다.

서류가 완료되면 다음의 주소로 보내주시면 됩니다.

Department of Consumer Affairs
Medical Board of California
2005 Evergreen Street Suite 1200
Sacramento, CA 95815, USA
(916) 263-2382 (800) 633-2322

감사합니다.

첨부파일
1. PTAL 작성요령 블로그:
http://www.slideshare.net/maxedmond/PTAL-step-by-step-application-guide-line-presentation
2. PTAL pdf 파일
3. Form L2 예시
4. Form L5 예시

실시간 스캔 요청 양식Live scan request form은 직접 작성하는 항목이다.

STATE AND CONSUMER SERVICES AGENCY - *Department of Consumer Affairs* EDMUND G. BROWN JR., *Governor*

MEDICAL BOARD OF CALIFORNIA
Licensing Program

PHYSICIAN'S & SURGEON'S
LIVE SCAN INFORMATION

California's Department of Justice (DOJ) provides statewide Live Scan, which is an electronic fingerprinting system with a subsequent automated background check and response. This system significantly expedites the fingerprint clearance process. **APPLICANTS WHO RESIDE IN CALIFORNIA MUST COMPLETE THE ELECTRONIC LIVE SCAN FINGERPRINT PROCESS.** Applicants residing outside of California may choose this option if visiting the state.

· CALIFORNIA DOES NOT HAVE LIVE SCAN LINKS TO ANY OTHER STATES·

The "Request For Live Scan Service" form (below) is required to have your fingerprints processed by Live Scan. This form must be completed in triplicate; therefore, THREE copies will be printed automatically when printing the form. Please ensure that all personal data (name, AKA's, date of birth, sex, height, weight, eye color, hair color, place of birth, social security number, California driver's license number and home address) is provided on *each of the three forms*. The last section of the form requires information from the fingerprint agency; please ensure this information is completed or the forms will be void. **It is the responsibility of the applicant to ensure that the person scanning the fingerprints submits TWO digital prints, one for the DOJ and one for the FBI.**

Applicants can access the Web site, http://ag.ca.gov/fingerprints/publications/contact.htm to obtain the names and location of approved fingerprint sites. Information pertaining to the need for appointments, hours of availability, and rolling fees are also available through that Web site. **After completing the Live Scan process, applicants must submit ONE of the THREE pages with the initial application (Forms L1A-L1E) to document the scanning of their fingerprints.** The results of Live Scan fingerprints are generally received within five (5) days.

If you do not reside in California, you have the option of completing the paper fingerprint cards. You may contact the Board's Consumer Information Unit at (916) 263-2382 to request the paper fingerprint cards. The results of paper fingerprint cards are generally received within twelve 12 weeks.

Whether you use Live Scan or paper fingerprint cards, you will be charged an administrative fee by the local agency that scans the prints or provides the inked impressions. This is in addition to the fingerprint processing fee that must be paid to the Medical Board of California with your application. For information about the fingerprint clearance process and time frames, please see:

http://ag.ca.gov/consumers/morefaqs.php

Because applicants from the medical professions must be concerned with sanitary issues, they wash and scrub their hands so much that images of their fingerprints are often difficult to read. When the impressions are of such poor quality that they cannot be searched in DOJ's fingerprint data base, the fingerprints (whether Live Scan or paper card) are rejected and reprints will be necessary. Therefore, please advise the person processing your fingerprints that extra care needs to be given to ensure that clear impressions have been made.

FINGERPRINT CLEARANCES FROM BOTH THE DOJ AND THE FBI MUST BE RECEIVED PRIOR TO THE ISSUANCE OF A PHYSICIAN'S AND SURGEON'S MEDICAL LICENSE IN CALIFORNIA

If you have ever been convicted of a misdemeanor or felony, the record of conviction will be reported to the Board as a result of your fingerprint inquiry.

Revised 06/2011

2005 Evergreen Street, Suite 1200, Sacramento, CA 95815-3831 (916) 263-2382 (800) 633-2322 FAX: (916) 263-2944 www.mbc.ca.gov

REQUEST FOR LIVE SCAN SERVICE
Applicant Submission

ORI: A0383 Type of Application: LICENSE, CERTIFICATION, PERMIT

Job Title or Type of License, Certification or Permit: PHYSICIAN & SURGEON

Agency Address Set Contributing Agency:

MEDICAL BOARD OF CALIFORNIA — 05612
2005 EVERGREEN STREET, SUITE 1200 — CINDY ROGALSKI
SACRAMENTO CA 95815

Name of Applicant: ______ (Last / First / MI)

Alias: ______ (Last / First) Driver's License No.: ______

Date of Birth: ______ Sex: ☐ Male ☐ Female Misc. No. BIL - 130065

Height: ______ Weight: ______ Misc. No: ______

Eye Color: ______ Hair Color: ______ Home Address: ______

Place of Birth: ______ (City, State and Zip Code)

SOC: ______

Your Number: ______

If resubmission, list Original ATI No. ______ Level of Service ☒ DOJ ☒ FBI

Employer: (Additional response for agencies specified by statute)

Live Scan Transaction Completed By: ______ Date: ______

Form L5는 행정실에서 작성해 주어야 한다. 양식은 내가 작성하고, 행정실에서는 직인을 찍어 캘리포니아 의료 위원회Medical Board of California로 우편으로 보내주도록 부탁했다.

STATE AND CONSUMER SERVICES AGENCY- *Department of Consumer Affairs* EDMUND G. BROWN JR., *Governor*

MEDICAL BOARD OF CALIFORNIA
Licensing Program

CERTIFICATE OF CLINICAL TRAINING
(This form is only required of international medical school graduates)

Type or Print Legibly — APPLICANT INFORMATION			MBC Use Only
Name: Last Eun	First Jong Ryeol	Middle	Personal Data ☐
Date of Birth (m/dd/yyyy)	U.S. Social Security Number	Medical School of Graduation	
08/06/1972	870-51-9006	Yeungnam University College of Medicine	

MEDICAL SCHOOL: PLEASE COMPLETE THIS FORM IN THE ENGLISH LANGUAGE

Report undergraduate clinical clerkships in which the applicant participated in DIRECT, HANDS-ON DIAGNOSIS OR TREATMENT OF PATIENTS IN A CLINICAL SETTING. *Please use as many forms as necessary to document ALL undergraduate clinical clerkships completed during enrollment in medical school.*

Note: Section 2089.5(c) of the Business and Professions Code requires that instruction in the clinical courses shall total a minimum of 72 weeks. Instruction in the core clinical courses shall total a minimum of 40 weeks in length with a minimum of (8) weeks of medicine, (8) weeks of surgery, (6) weeks of pediatrics, (6) weeks of ob/gyn, (4) weeks of psychiatry, and (4) weeks of family medicine. (Family Medicine is required for applicants who graduated after June 30, 1999)

Clinical Subject (List one subject per line)	Facility Name City/State/Province/Country	Dates of Attendance in Chronological Order (mm/dd/yyyy)	Weeks or Weekly Clinical Hours	
ENT		Start: __/__/____ End: __/__/____		☐
Emergency Medicine		Start: __/__/____ End: __/__/____		☐
Orthopedics		Start: __/__/____ End: __/__/____		☐
Neurology		Start: __/__/____ End: __/__/____		☐
Neurosurgery		Start: __/__/____ End: __/__/____		☐
Ophthalmology		Start: __/__/____ End: __/__/____		☐

MEDICAL SCHOOL OFFICIAL CERTIFICATION

AFFIX MEDICAL SCHOOL SEAL

I certify that I am the President, Dean, or Registrar and hereby declare under penalty of perjury under the laws of the State of California that the above statements are true and correct.

PRINTED NAME OF SCHOOL OFFICIAL　　TITLE OF SCHOOL OFFICIAL

SIGNATURE OF SCHOOL OFFICIAL　　DATE

Attention Medical School THE PERSON WHO SIGNS THIS FORM MAY NOT BE RELATED TO THE APPLICANT BY BLOOD, MARRIAGE OR ADOPTION. Only the President, Dean, or Registrar may sign this form. If the signature is being delegated to another person, evidence of that delegation must be attached to this form (may be a photocopy). Such delegation must be on official letterhead and must be dated within the last 12 months.

Signature and Date ☐
Seal ☐

L5

NOTE: The completed form must be mailed directly from the medical school to the Board to be acceptable.

07A-100 (Rev. 10/2012)

2005 Evergreen Street, Suite 1200, Sacramento, CA 95815-3831 (916) 263-2382 (800) 633-2322 FAX (916) 263-2487 www.mbc.ca.gov

Form L2도 마찬가지다.

STATE AND CONSUMER SERVICES AGENCY - *Department of Consumer Affairs* EDMUND G. BROWN JR., *Governor*

MEDICAL BOARD OF CALIFORNIA
Licensing Program

CERTIFICATE OF MEDICAL EDUCATION

Check one: ☐ U.S. or Canadian Medical School Graduate ☑ International Medical School Graduate

APPLICANT INFORMATION (Type or Print Legibly) — MBC Use Only

NAME: Last *Eun* First *Jong Ryeol* Middle

Date of Birth (mm/dd/yyyy)	U.S. Social Security Number	Medical School of Graduation
08/06/1972	*870-51-9006*	*Yeungnam University College of Medicine*

MEDICAL SCHOOL: PLEASE COMPLETE THIS FORM IN THE ENGLISH LANGUAGE

Name of Medical School	Yeungnam University College of Medicine
State/Province/Country	Daegu, South Korea
Did the applicant complete an English Language program?	☐ Yes ☒ No

The undersigned further certifies that the records of this institution show that the applicant attended in this institution __4__ years of resident instruction, completing at least 4,000 hours, of which at least 80 percent actual attendance is required in the subjects set forth hereunder (Business and Professions Code Sections 2089, 2089.5, 2089.7, 2090, 2091.1, 2091.2). **The standard duration of the curriculum at this institution is __4__ years.**

Anatomy, Otolaryngology, Obstetrics and Gynecology, Radiology, including Radiation Safety, Tropical Medicine, Physiology, Biochemistry, Pathology, Bacteriology, and Immunology, Ophthalmology, Dermatology, Embryology, Histology, Human Sexuality, Medicine, Surgery, including Orthopedic Surgery, Urology, Psychiatry, Neurology, Alcoholism and Chemical Dependency, Preventative Medicine, including Nutrition, Physical Medicine, Therapeutics, Neuroanatomy, Child Abuse Detection and Treatment, Geriatric Medicine, Pediatrics, Pharmacology, Anesthesia, Spousal Partner Abuse Detection & Treatment*, Family Medicine**, Pain Management and End-of-Life-Care***

* ONLY applicable to medical students who enrolled in medical school on or after September 1, 1994
** ONLY applicable to medical students who graduated from medical school on or after June 30, 1999
*** ONLY applicable to medical students who enrolled in medical school on or after June 1, 2000

Date the applicant enrolled in medical school:	03/01/1991
Date the applicant was issued the diploma of Bachelor/Doctor of Medicine:	02/22/1997
Date the applicant withdrew from medical school (if applicable):	__/__/____

UNUSUAL CIRCUMSTANCES DURING MEDICAL SCHOOL

Any "Yes" response below requires a signed and dated letter of explanation by school official.

1. Did this applicant ever take a leave of absence from his/her medical education?	☐ Yes ☒ No
2. Was this applicant ever placed on probation?	☐ Yes ☒ No
3. Was this applicant ever disciplined or placed under investigation?	☐ Yes ☒ No
4. Were any negative reports regarding this applicant ever filed by instructors?	☐ Yes ☒ No
5. Were any limitations or special requirements imposed on this applicant because of questions of academic or disciplinary problems, or for any other reason?	☐ Yes ☒ No

MEDICAL SCHOOL OFFICIAL CERTIFICATION

AFFIX MEDICAL SCHOOL SEAL

I certify that I am the President, Dean, or Registrar and hereby declare under penalty of perjury under the laws of the State of California that the above statements are true and correct.

PRINTED NAME OF SCHOOL OFFICIAL TITLE OF SCHOOL OFFICIAL

SIGNATURE OF SCHOOL OFFICIAL DATE

Attention Medical School: THE PERSON WHO SIGNS THIS FORM MAY NOT BE RELATED TO THE APPLICANT BY BLOOD, MARRIAGE OR ADOPTION. Only the President, Dean, or Registrar may sign this form. If the signature is being delegated to another person, evidence of that delegation must be attached to this form (may be a photocopy). Such delegation must be on official letterhead and must be dated within the last 12 months.

L2

NOTE: The completed form must be mailed directly from the medical school to the Board to be acceptable.

2013년 3월 14일, 우편으로 필요한 서류를 보내니 PTAL 접수가 되었다는 편지가 우편으로 왔다.

STATE AND CONSUMER SERVICES AGENCY- *Department of Consumer Affairs* EDMUND G. BROWN JR., *Governor*

MEDICAL BOARD OF CALIFORNIA
Licensing Program

March 14, 2013 File#: 289930

JONG RYEOL EUN
320 CAMBRIDGE TERRACE # A
DAVIS, CA 95618

Dear Applicant:

This is to inform you of the current status of your application for a Postgraduate Training Authorization Letter.

Based on a review of your application and supporting documents, it will be necessary for you to submit the following item(s) so we may further process your application:

1. Certification Status Report sent directly to the Board from the Educational Commission for Foreign Medical Graduates (ECFMG) to verify the current status of ECFMG certification. The ECFMG may be reached by telephone at 215-386-5900 or on their Web site at www.ecfmg.org.

2. Please submit a signed and dated Curriculum Vitae (CV).

3. Certificate of Medical Education, Form L2, signed, dated and affixed with the official medical school seal. The questions under "Unusual Circumstances" must be answered by the school official. Please request that this item be mailed directly to the Board from the medical school.

4. Original, official medical school transcript documenting all of the basic science and clinical courses completed during the medical curriculum and the grades/hours/credits you received in each subject. The transcript shall be mailed directly from the medical school to the Board.

5. A certified copy of your medical school degree. The certified copy must have the original signature of the dean or registrar of the medical school; be affixed with the official school seal; and include a statement attesting that the copy is a true and correct copy of the original. The certified copy of your diploma shall be mailed directly from the medical school to the Board.

6. Certificate of Clinical Clerkship, Form L5, signed, dated and affixed with the official medical school seal to document all of your undergraduate clinical rotations completed during your enrollment in medical school. Section 2089.5 of the Business and Professions Code requires that you complete the following clinical clerkship training: eight weeks medicine, eight weeks surgery, six weeks pediatrics, six weeks ob/gyn, four weeks psychiatry, and 40 weeks of clinical elective training. Applicants who graduated June 1999 or later also are required to complete four weeks of family medicine. The Form(s) L5 must be mailed directly from the medical school to the Board to be acceptable.

Pursuant to Section 1306 of Title 16 of the California Code of Regulations, if you fail to complete your application within the specified time frame, your file will be deemed abandoned and confidentially destroyed. If you later decide to reapply for a Postgraduate Training Authorization Letter (PTAL), you will be required to submit a new application, submit new fingerprints, submit new applicable fees and you will be required to comply with any new requirements in effect at the time of reapplication.

Upon receipt and approval of the above items, you will be advised of your eligibility to commence postgraduate training in California. If you have any questions please contact me by telephone at (916) 263-2596 or in writing at the address noted in this letter. The Medical Board of California encourages applicants to check your application status online at https://www2.mbc.ca.gov/WAAS/ .

Sincerely,

Dyian Thompson for

Dyian Thompson for
Dalia Demian, Licensing Analyst
Licensing Program

2013년 4월 26일, PTAL 승인 편지를 받았다.

STATE AND CONSUMER SERVICES AGENCY - *Department of Consumer Affairs* EDMUND G. BROWN JR., *Governor*

MEDICAL BOARD OF CALIFORNIA
Licensing Program

POSTGRADUATE TRAINING AUTHORIZATION LETTER

April 26, 2013

ATS#: 289930

Jong Ryeol Eun
4301 Ashland Terrace, Apt. C
Davis, CA 95618

Dear Applicant:

Your application for a Postgraduate Training Authorization Letter (PTAL) has been reviewed. Our evaluation has determined that your undergraduate medical education and clinical training satisfies the requirements of Sections 2089 and 2089.5 of the Business and Professions Code (B&P Code). Therefore, you are eligible to commence ACGME-accredited postgraduate training in California should a position be offered to you.

Acceptance into an ACGME-accredited postgraduate training program is not assured by issuance of a PTAL. All requirements imposed by the program must be met and independently satisfied. You should directly contact the appropriate officials in the training program at those institutions to which you wish to apply.

Once you are formally admitted to an ACGME-accredited postgraduate training program, you must complete and return the enclosed Postgraduate Training Registration Form to fulfill the registration requirement specified by law.

To satisfy the postgraduate training requirements for California medical licensure, you must satisfactorily complete two years of ACGME-accredited postgraduate training. In accordance with Title 16, Section 1321 (d) of the California Code of Regulations, each year of postgraduate training must consist of 12 months of satisfactory continuous training within the same program.

In addition, applicants must complete at least four months of postgraduate training in GENERAL MEDICINE as part of the two-year requirement. The GENERAL MEDICINE requirement may be satisfied by actual clinical practice where the applicant has direct patient care responsibilities in any particular specialty or sub-specialty area for at least four months.

Section 2066 of the B&P Code allows graduates of international medical schools to engage in three years of ACGME-approved postgraduate training without a license. At the end of the three-year period, you must be licensed or all clinical service in California facilities must cease. In calculating the maximum three years of training, the Medical Board includes all approved training undertaken in the United States or Canada.

Pursuant to Section 1306 of Title 16 of the California Code of Regulations, if you fail to complete your application within the specified time frame, your file will be deemed abandoned and confidentially destroyed. If you later decide to reapply for licensure or a Postgraduate Training Authorization Letter (PTAL), you will be required to submit a new application, submit new fingerprints, submit new applicable fees and you will be required to comply with any new requirements in effect at the time of reapplication.

Please be advised that you will be required to comply with any new policy, statutory, or regulatory requirements that come into effect prior to your licensure.

Should you have any questions regarding the above information, please contact me at the address noted below or by telephone at (916) 263-2596. You may also contact me at my e-mail address, Dalia.Demian@mbc.ca.gov.

The Medical Board of California encourages applicants to check your application status online at https://www2.mbc.ca.gov/WAAS/.

Sincerely,

Dalia Demian, Analyst
Licensing Program
Enclosures

이제부터 USMLE 전 과정을 마치고 본격적으로 레지던트 지원 준비를 시작한다.

레지던트 지원과 인터뷰: CV, PS, LoR, MSPE 준비

레지던트 지원자 1만 명 가운데 3천 명은 노 인터뷰다. 인터뷰를 받은 7천 명 가운데 4천 명은 실패하고, 3천 명은 매치에 성공한다고 한다. 9월 15일에 시작해 11월에서 1월은 인터뷰 기간이다. 2월 NRMP 지원 목록rank order을 넣는다. 인터뷰 한 개를 받을 때마다 25퍼센트 매치 확률이라고 생각하면, 5개 받으면 75퍼센트, 10개 받으면 대부분 매치된다고 한다. 나는 2013년에 1개, 2014년에는 2개를 받았다. 오랜만에 레지던트 지원사이트에 들어가 보았다. 나의 AAMC ID가 살아 있는 게 신기했다.

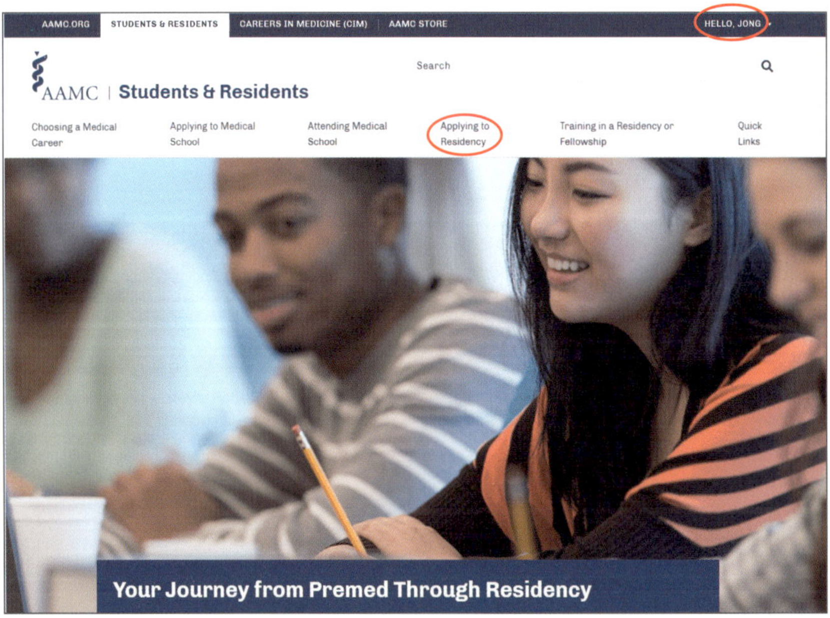

2013년 7월 2일 ERASElectronic Residency Application Service에 필요한 서류를 업로드하라는 안내를 받았다. 그전에 필요한 서류들(CV, PS, LoR, MSPE)을 미리 준비해 두었다.

myERAS에 등록하면 ID 번호를 받고 지원 절차에 대한 안내가 온다.

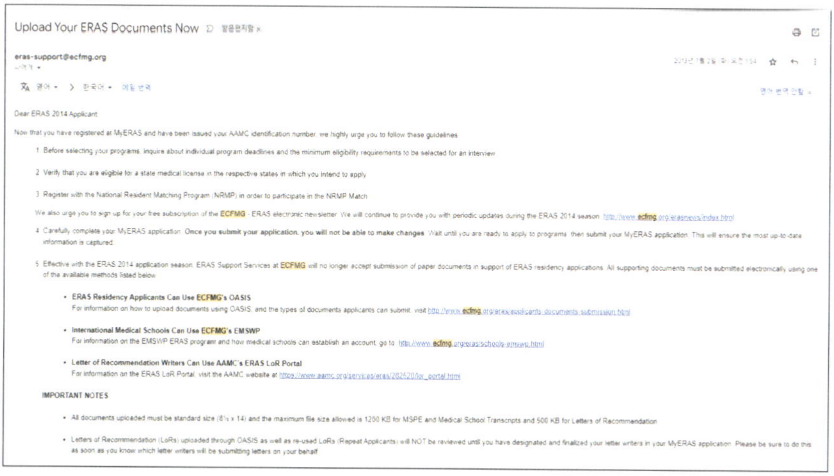
Upload Your ERAS Documents Now

eras-support@ecfmg.org

Dear ERAS 2014 Applicant

Now that you have registered at MyERAS and have been issued your AAMC identification number, we highly urge you to follow these guidelines

1 Before selecting your programs, inquire about individual program deadlines and the minimum eligibility requirements to be selected for an interview

2 Verify that you are eligible for a state medical license in the respective states in which you intend to apply

3 Register with the National Resident Matching Program (NRMP) in order to participate in the NRMP Match

We also urge you to sign up for your free subscription of the ECFMG - ERAS electronic newsletter. We will continue to provide you with periodic updates during the ERAS 2014 season. http://www.ecfmg.org/erasnews/index.html

4 Carefully complete your MyERAS application. **Once you submit your application, you will not be able to make changes.** Wait until you are ready to apply to programs, then submit your MyERAS application. This will ensure the most up-to-date information is captured

5 Effective with the ERAS 2014 application season, ERAS Support Services at ECFMG will no longer accept submission of paper documents in support of ERAS residency applications. All supporting documents must be submitted electronically using one of the available methods listed below

- **ERAS Residency Applicants Can Use ECFMG's OASIS**
  For information on how to upload documents using OASIS, and the types of documents applicants can submit, visit http://www.ecfmg.org/eras/applicants-documents-submission.html
- **International Medical Schools Can Use ECFMG's EMSWP**
  For information on the EMSWP ERAS program and how medical schools can establish an account, go to http://www.ecfmg.org/eras/schools-emswp.html
- **Letter of Recommendation Writers Can Use AAMC's ERAS LoR Portal**
  For information on the ERAS LoR Portal, visit the AAMC website at https://www.aamc.org/services/eras/282520/lor_portal.html

IMPORTANT NOTES

- All documents uploaded must be standard size (8½ x 14) and the maximum file size allowed is 1200 KB for MSPE and Medical School Transcripts and 500 KB for Letters of Recommendation
- Letters of Recommendation (LoRs) uploaded through OASIS as well as re-used LoRs (Repeat Applicants) will NOT be reviewed until you have designated and finalized your letter writers in your MyERAS application. Please be sure to do this as soon as you know which letter writers will be submitting letters on your behalf

1. 이력서Curriculum Vitae

다음과 같은 형식으로 만들었다.

Curriculum Vitae

NAME: Jong Ryeol Eun

HOME ADDRESS: 4301 Ashland Terrace Apt C, Davis, CA95618, USA

CELLPHONE: 530-304-5754

E-MAIL: dreundavis@gmail.com

DATE OF BIRTH: 08/06/1972

GENDER: Male

PLACE OF BIRTH: Daegu, South Korea

HEALTH: Good

MARRITAL STATUS: Married

FAMILY: Wife, two daughters and one son

PRESENT STATUS: Research Fellow & Visiting Scholar, GI/Hepatology, UC DavisMedicalCenter

EDUCATION
03/2010-02/2012 GRADUATE (PhD course) Kyungpook National University, Daegu, S. Korea
03/1999-02/2002 GRADUATE (Master degree) Yeungnam University, Daegu, S. Korea
03/1991-02/1997 UNDERGRADUATE (MD) Yeungnam University College of Medicine, Daegu, S. Korea

LICENSURE AND CERTIFICATION
2013 ECFMG Certificate, USA
2007 Gastroenterology and Hepatology Specialist, South Korea (No.1-071**1)
2006 Board of Gastrointestinal Endoscopy,South Korea (No.2006-3**2)
2002 Internal Medicine Specialist, South Korea (No.7**8)
1997 M.D., South Korea (No.61**9)

MEMBERSHIP OF MEDICAL SOCIETY
The Korean Medical Association
The Korean Association of Internal Medicine
The Korean Society of Gastroenterology, Gastrointestinal Endoscopy
The Korean Association for the Study of Liver Disease
The Asian-Pacific Association for the Study for the Liver (APASL)

TRAINING
05/2005-08/2006 FELLOWSHIP Gastroenterology and Hepatology, Internal Medicine, Yeungnam University Hospital, Daegu, South Korea
03/1998-02/2002 RESIDENCY Internal Medicine, Yeungnam University Hospital, Daegu, S. Korea
03/1997-02/1998 INTERNSHIP Yeungnam Univeristy Hospital, Daegu, South Korea

Army Service: Public Doctor
04/2003-04/2005 Andong Sunso General Hospital, Kyungsangpook-do, South Korea
04/2002-03/2003 Gunwi Public Heath Service, Gunwi, Kyungsangpook-do,South Korea

CAREER
03/2012–Present Research Fellow, GI/Hepatology, Internal Medicine, University of California, Davis Medical Center, CA, USA
09/2012–02/2013 Associate Professor, Division of Gastroenterology and Hepatology, Internal Medicine, Yeungnam University College of Medicine, Daegu, South Korea
09/2009–08/2012 Assistant Professor, Division of Gastroenterology and Hepatology, Internal Medicine, Yeungnam University College of Medicine, Daegu, South Korea
09/2006–08/2008 Full-time Lecturer. Division of Gastroenterology and Hepatology, Internal Medicine, Yeungnam University College of Medicine, Daegu, South Korea

SCHOLARSHIPS AND AWARDS
2011 KASL-GSK scholarship for abroad research scholar ($15,000)
2011 Best reviewer award for the Korean Journal of Hepatology

RESEARCH GRANT

2009-2011 Korea Research Foundation ($130,000)

2009 Yeungnam University School of Medicine Chunma Grant ($5,000)

2009 Yeungnam UniversityS chool of Medicine Research Fund ($10,000)

2008 Yeungnam University Medical Center Research Fund ($15,000)

2006 Yeungnam University Research Fund for New Scholar ($7,000)

INTELLECTUAL PROPERTY (PATENT)

Cilostazol for alcoholic-induced liver injury (registered) Korean Intellectual Property Office (No. 10-1094934)

Cilostazol for alcohol-induced liver injury (in process) Patent Cooperation Treaty (No. PCT/KR2011/007441)

BOOK PUBLICATION

14-day course of abdominal ultrasound (2008, E-Public,Korea)

PUBLICATIONS (selected from >50 publications)

Lee YJ, **Eun JR**. Cilostazol Decreases Ethanol-Mediated TNFalpha Expression in RAW264.7 Murine Macrophage and in Liver from Binge Drinking Mice. Korean J Physiol Pharmacol 2012;16:131-138.PMID: 22563259

Kang MK, Kim MS, Kim SK, Ye GW, Lee HJ, Kim TN, **Eun JR**. High-dose radiotherapy with intensity-modulated radiation therapy for advanced hepatocellular Carcinoma. Tumori 2011;97:724-731. PMID: 22322838

Jun DW, Cho YK, Sohn JH, Lee CH, Kim SH, **Eun JR**. A study of the awareness of chronic liver disease among Korean adults. Korean J Hepatol 2011;17:99-105. PMID: 21757980

Choi EJ, Lee HJ, Kim KO, Lee SH, **Eun JR**, Jang BI, Kim TN. Association between acid suppressive therapy and spontaneous bacterial peritonitis in cirrhotic patients with ascites. Scand J Gastroenterol 2011;46:516-620. PMID: 21275825

Eun JR, Kim YG, Kim TN, Lee HJ, Kim JW, Chang JC, Yun SS, Choi JH. Pathological complete remission of advanced hepatocellular carcinoma with main portal vein tumor thrombosis by hepatic arterial infusion chemotherapy. Gut Liver. 2010;4:266-269. PMID: 20559534

Eun JR, Lee HJ, Kim TN, Lee KS. Risk assessment for the development of hepatocellular carcinoma: according to on-treatment viral response during long-term lamivudine therapy in hepatitis B virus-related liver disease. J Hepatol. 2010;53:118-125. PMID: 20471129

Eun JR, Lee HJ, Moon HJ, Kim TN, Kim JW, Chang JC. Hepatic arterial infusion chemotherapy using high-dose 5-fluorouracil and cisplatin with or without interferon-alpha for the treatment of advanced hepatocellular carcinoma with portal vein tumor thrombosis. Scand J Gastroenterol 2009;44:1477-1486. PMID: 19958061

Eun JR, Jang BI, Lee JY, Kim KO, Lee SH, Kim TN, Lee HJ. Clinical characteristics of intrahepatic cholangiocarcinoma and prognostic factors in patients who received non-surgical treatment. Korean J Gastroenterol 2009;54:227-234. PMID: 19844142

Eun JR, Kim DH, Moon HJ, Oh HJ, Kim YK, Jang BI, Kim TN, Lee HJ. A case of peritoneal seeding from a ruptured hepatocellular carcinoma with direct invasion into the stomach causing gastrointestinal hemorrhage, Korean J Gastroenterol 2009; 53; 194-197. PMID: 19835221

Choi EJ, Lee HJ, Kim KO, Lee SH, **Eun JR**, Jang BI, Kim TN. Long-term clevudine therapy in nucleos(t)ide-naïve and lamivudine-experienced patients with hepatitis B virus-related chronic liver diseases Korean J Hepatol. 2009;15:179-192. PMID: 19581770

Kim MK, Lee KH, Jang BI, Kim TN, **Eun JR**, Bae SH, Ryoo HM, Lee SA, Hyun MS. S-1 and gemcitabine as an outpatient-based regimen in patients with advanced or metastatic pancreatic cancer. Jpn J of Clin Oncol 2009;39:49-53. PMID: 19060295

Lee KH, Choi EY, Hyun MS, **Eun JR**, Jang BI, Kim TN, Lee HJ, Lee DS, Yun SS, Kim HJ, Kim JH, Kim JR. Cellular mechanisms of hepatocyte growth factor-mediated urokinase plasminogen activator secretion by MAPK signaling in hepatocellular carcinoma. Tumori 2008;94:523-530. PMID: 18822689

Lee KH, Choi EY, Hyun MS, Jang BI, Kim TN, Lee HJ, **Eun JR**, Kim HG, Yoon SS, Lee DS, Kim JH, Kim JR. Role of hepatocyte growth factor/c-Met signaling in regulating urokinase plasminogen activator. Clin Exp Metastasis 2008;25:89-96. PMID: 17992475

Lee KH, Choi EY, Kim MK, Hyun MS, **Eun JR**, Jang BI, Kim TN, Kim SW, Song SK, Kim JH, Kim JR. Hepatocyte growth factor promotes cell survival by phosphorylation of BAD in gastric cancer cells. Oncol Res, 2008: 25:89–96. PMID: 18488712

Lee SH, **Eun JR,** Lee HJ, Kim TN, Jang BI, Choi JW, Park YS, Kim KO, Lee GH, Moon HJ, Lee SH. The usefulness of transient elastography (Fibroscan) for predicting esophageal varices and esophageal variceal hemorrhage in patients with chronic liver diseases. Korean J Int Med 2008;74:491-499.

Lee HJ, **Eun JR**, Choi JW, Kim KO, Moon HJ. Comparison of therapeutic results between combination therapy of peginterferon alpha-2a plus ribavirin and interferon alpha-2b plus ribavirin according to treatment duration in patients with chronic hepatitis C. Korean J Hepatol 2008;14:46-57. PMID: 18367857

Eun JR, Lee HJ, Kim TH, Jang BI, Moon HJ. Clinical characteristics of adult patients with acute hepatitis A. Yeungnam Univ. J. of Med 2007; 24:170-178.

Eun JR. Comparison of clinical outcome between patients continuing and discontinuing lamivudine therapy in acute exacerbation after viral breakthrough during lamivudine therapy in chronic hepatitis B, Korean J Hepatol 2006;12:184-190. PMID: 16804343

Eun JR, Kim TN, Choi ST, Jang BI. The causes and endoscopic management of bile leak. Korean J Gastrointest Endosc 2006;33:346-352.

Eun JR, Jang BI. The usefulness of capsule endoscopy in diagnosis of small bowel diseases. Yeungnam Univ. J. of Med. 2006;23:45-51.

I certify that the information is complete and accurate to the best of my knowledge.

Signature ______________________ Date ______________________

2. 자기소개서 Personal Statement

부족한 영어로 직접 작성했다. 지금 읽어보니 영어도 조악하고 내용도 부끄러워서 얼굴이 화끈거린다.

PERSONAL STATEMENT

AAMC ID: 133**246
NAME: Jong Ryeol Eun

Looking back at my life in Korea, over the past 41 years, every step I came across was challenging, even though it may look easy to others. I have always tried my best and finally overcame every hurdle. Now I am going to try a new, amazing challenge to become a physician in the U.S.

I used to be a little shy and introverted in medical school. I enjoyed studying. I liked most subjects, except anatomy. In particular, I liked internal medicine. It was exciting to learn pathophysiology, diagnosis and treatment. Internal medicine was logical. That's why I did not hesitate to become an internal medicine resident. Five years of internship and residency training gave me invaluable experiences. I had a lot of hands-on experiences. I also participated in many procedures, including cardiac catheterization as an assistant. Meanwhile, I was interested in abdominal ultrasonography and echocardiography. I attended many lectures and programs to learn them. I was a member of the Ultrasonography Study Club for Internists. Also I was in echocardiography room every day in my cardiology rotation in the 3rd year residency. I became familiar with the equipment and could read the findings of liver, pancreas, biliary system, and kidneys. I also could measure cardiac wall motion and valve area. In my 4th year residency, I spent much time preparing for the board exam. I summarized all the 15th edition of Harrison's Textbook of Internal Medicine and uploaded the notes on my personal blog for Korean medical students and resident doctors. Online visitors recorded more than 100,000 hits on my blog. Although the website is not available now, the contents are still available on other websites. Many Korean medical students have used the contents for studying. That's why I am kind of a celebrity among Korean medical students. My most valuable experience, however, was how to communicate well with patients, their families, and hospital staff. That is the most invaluable asset in my career. Through the training, I learned all the skills I need to do my job efficiently.

I have always been interested in Gastroenterology and Hepatology and became a staff physician in Yeungnam University Hospital in 2006. I did my best in teaching students and residents, writing papers, and presenting my data at academic meetings as well as taking care of outpatients and inpatients. Taking care of patients was fruitful. Sometimes, however, I was frustrated when I could not help grave patients, like those with advanced liver cancers or severe alcoholic hepatitis. That's why I focused my research on liver cancers and alcoholic hepatitis. For advanced hepatocellular carcinomas (HCCs) and portal vein thrombosis, our protocol is based on hepatic arterial infusion chemotherapy. The therapy is popular in Korea and Japan. It improved tumor response rate by 40-60 percent, and increased survival by around 1.5 years in treatment responders. Four of my patients were cured by the chemotherapy alone or curative surgical resection after downstaging. I always felt happy whenever I met any of them in my office. On the other hand, I gathered the data about the HCC incidence in chronic hepatitis B patients treated with antiviral agents. I published the data in a high quality journal, Journal of Hepatology in 2010. I felt like walking on air when I saw my name on the paper. In addition, I paid attention to a drug called Cilostazol, a widely used antiplatelet drug. There are two options available for the treatment of severe alcoholic hepatitis at the moment, steroid and pentoxifylline. The main pathophysiology of alcoholic hepatitis is related to an increased TNF-alpha in Kupffer cells. I found that Cilostazol significantly inhibited TNF-alpha in Kupffer cell-like macrophages. I believe that Cilostazol might be a potential therapeutic drug for severe alcoholic hepatitis. I got a patent based on the data. It was an interesting experience. During the project, I learned how to propose a grant, how to perform basic research, and how to get a patent. I would like to continue my research to establish a possible clinical use.

I have been doing research about liver cancer/cancer stem cells at UC Davis Medical Center, Sacramento, California since I came to the U.S. in 2012. My research focus is to elucidate the origin of liver cancer/cancer stem cells. Our team got awesome results. I am thrilled that my research papers are going to be submitted soon. I am also happy to make friends with many people in the lab. It doesn't matter where they are from and what their ages are. We are just friends and colleagues. Meanwhile, I have been enjoying life with my family. My family loves their friends, school and life in America.

I am strongly motivated to be a doctor in a bigger world. I would like to build a new career in the U.S. with my family. I know it will be really tough and there are many obstacles to overcome, but I will do my best and overcome all of them as before. I believe my clinical, research and teaching experiences, and academic accomplishments will contribute to your internal medicine residency program.

2014년에는 매치에 실패하고, 2015년 지원 때는 다음과 같이 수정했다.

Personal Statement

I was full of confidence when I first stepped on the U.S. land two and a half years ago. I built a good career as an attending physician at a university hospital in Korea. For years I was a successful doctor in my province. However, I soon realized I was a 'frog in a small pond'.

In 2012, I came to the U.S. for basic research. I had been treating many patients with advanced liver diseases and liver cancers. I wanted to learn about stem cells and liver cancer stem cells. I applied for a position in Dr. Zern's lab at UC Davis Medical Center, and was accepted. As a foreign doctor, this was new environment for me. It was quite natural to feel cultural shock. To be honest, the biggest challenge was communicating well in English. I felt frustrated. It seemed I would never overcome my English hurdle. I have studied and practiced English ever since my arrival. I would have to admit it is still not perfect, but I believe I will be at an advanced level soon. While working in the lab, I became accustomed to the American culture and working environment.

Although I was satisfied with my professional career in Korea, I decided to build a new career as a doctor in the U.S. I have always dreamed of practicing medicine in this big world. Providing my children a better education was another reason.

Despite not being matched last year, I am determined to try again. Tenacity is my strongest strength. I have a history of overcoming all obstacles in my past.

I started an observership 09/02/2014 at UC Davis Medical Center, where I worked for. Besides my research mentor, Dr. Zern, Dr. Urayama, who is a GI specialist, accepted me. This is a great opportunity for me. Although it is not direct hands-on clinical experience, it is very helpful to learn the U.S. medical system and how hospitals function. I am attending at GI clinic and endoscopy unit. I was nervous at first, but was soon relieved because everyone was nice.

Lastly, I would like to finish this short description of me with my favorite proverb. "Slow and steady wins the race". I like the saying best. I believe it. Although the probability for me to get a resident job is extremely low, I will advance step by step like a turtle.

3. 추천서Letter of Recommendation

추천서 작성해 줄 사람을 입력하면 AAMC로부터 추천서를 부탁받은 교수님에게 추천서를 업로드하라는 이메일을 보낸다. 레지던트 지원에 필요한 추천서도 미리 준비했다. 영남대학교병원 교수님들께는 내가 미리 작성한 것으로 부탁해 사인을 받고 업로드하는 방식으로 진행했다. 영남대병원 로고를 배경으로 한 편지지를 만들어 작성했다. 2014년도에 지원할 때는 UC 데이비스 메디컬 센터의 닥터 우라야마가 직접 작성해서 업로드해 주었다.

AAMC

Dear Chung Jin Hong,

On Jul 18,2013 at 05:43:07 P.M. ET, you registered for an AAMC Account.

Your user name: IMMESUN

To complete your AAMC Account registration, please click on the link below or copy and paste it into your Web browser:

https://services.aamc.org/30/ssoLogin/home/verification/verifyEmail?verificationCode=SOPXXK92HD5DWA98&wamId=5002120438&gotoUrl=aHR0cHM6Ly9zZXJ2aWNlcy5hYW1jLm9yZy9lcmFzL2xvcnBvcnRhbC8%3D

If you have any questions about this process, please contact us through http://www.aamc.org/accounthelp.htm.

Thank you,
Association of American Medical Colleges (AAMC)
2450 N Street NW
Washington, DC 20037
www.aamc.org

June 28, 2013
AAMC ID: 13318246
Name: Jong Ryeol Eun
Re: Letter of Recommendation

Dear Program Director,

I am very pleased to provide a letter of recommendation for Dr. Jong Ryeol Eun's application for your internal medicine residency program. I am writing this recommendation letter as I truly believe Dr. Eun will be a great asset to the program.

Now I am the chairman at the department of internal medicine, Yeungnam University College of Medicine, Daegu, South Korea. I've been working for the hospital for over 20 years. I am afraid I don't remember him when he was a medical student because it was a long time ago. But I remember he was an excellent internal medicine resident. When he applied for residency, he was highly competitive in terms of his excellent medical school transcripts and good reputation from interns and other residents.

He completed rotations in pulmonology for two months in his 1st year of residency, and for one month each in his 2nd and 3rd year of residency. He was really hard working and diligent. In our division, the 1st and 2nd year residents are supposed to be responsible for patients care and report their new patients in the morning conference. He presented his cases articulately. His chest X-ray and CT reading skills were excellent. As far as inpatient care is concerned, his technical skills like pleural biopsy, central line placement, and intubation were excellent. Above all, he communicated well with patients and their families. When he was a 3rd grade resident, he tried his best to teach junior residents his clinical tips and skills. I was pleased to work with him.

Regretfully, however, Dr. Eun was more interested in GI/Hepatology field. He became a GI/Hepatology faculty staff in our hospital after completion of his fellowship. We worked in the department of internal medicine as colleagues for 6 years. During the junior faculty, he actively participated in teaching residents and clerkship students. Although he was really busy in his own job, he participated in many committees like the medical student education committee, the medical license examination study task force, the medical record committee and the hospice committee, etc.

Moreover, he made all efforts to organize and keep good cooperation between other professors. For instance, Yeungnam University Medical Center is a 975-bed of tertiary university hospital. To study and provide better treatment in the field of liver cancers, Yeungnam University Liver Cancer Study Group has been comprised by the faculties of internal medicine, surgery, radiology, pathology, and radiation oncololgy. The international symposium has been held annually. Dr. Eun arranged periodic conferences and annual meetings successfully for several years as a secretary.

Most of all, he was nice and really cared about the patients. He always responded promptly to consultation from other departments and gave them advices. He was also kind to hospital staff. That's why faculties and hospital staffs liked him.

우라야마에게 받은 추천서는 내가 보지 못해서 내용은 알 수 없다.

Letter Request Form

Electronic Residency Application Service ERAS | AAMC

ERAS Application Season: 2015

Applicants: If you have NOT waived your right to view this Letter of Recommendation (LoR) and you are uploading this letter yourself, proceed to page 2 for instructions on using the Letter of Recommendation Portal (LoRP).

Letter Authors: If you are uploading this letter on behalf of the applicant, you should review the information below before proceeding to the instructions on page 2.

Request From:
Jong Ryeol Eun
dreundavis@gmail.com
5309029370

To:
Shiro Urayama
Professor/Internal Medicine

With this form, I am requesting that you submit my Letter of Recommendation (LoR) to the Electronic Residency Application Service (ERAS), which transmits my LoR(s) to the residency programs to which I am applying.

If **"I waive"** is selected, I waive my right to view this letter now and in the future under the *Family Educational Rights and Privacy Act (FERPA)*. I acknowledge that this letter is for the specific purpose of supporting my application for residency.

__X__(I waive) my right to see this letter.
____(I do not waive) my right to see this letter.

Note:

- It is recommended that all letters be written and submitted on professional letterhead
- Letter should include a date
- Letter should be signed by the LoR Author
- Carefully review your letter for accuracy and grammatical errors before submitting
- **Do not submit LoR(s) by mail. Documents submitted to the ECFMG by mail will not be processed to the ERAS application.**
- LoR(s) submitted through the ERAS LoR Portal are expected to take two weeks to process.

Please see **Page 2 for instructions** on how to submit letters to ERAS.

Instructions for submitting LoR(s) to ERAS

- **ERAS LoR Portal**: This application enables LoR Authors to upload letters securely to ERAS. Please go to https://www.aamc.org/eras/lorp and click *Sign in to LoRP* on the upper right-hand side of the page.

Register for an AAMC Account and follow the directions on the site. If you already have an AAMC account, but forgot your user name or password, please use the 'Forgot your user name' and/or 'Forgot your password' links on the LoR Portal sign in page.

To submit your LoR using the LoR Portal, your letter must meet the following system requirements:
- File must be in a PDF format
- File size cannot exceed 500 KB.
- File cannot be password protected, encrypted and/or contain an electronic signature.
- Page size must be 8.5 x 11 inches.
- File name cannot contain spaces or special characters (i.e. hyphens, slashes, periods, etc.).

Standard Letter of Evaluation (SLOE):
If you were asked to submit a Standard Letter of Evaluation (SLOE) as well and would like to submit the form through the LoR Portal, the LoR and SLOE must be uploaded together in one single PDF file.

When uploading a letter to the LoR Portal, please have the information directly below available.

Applicant AAMC ID: 13676322
Applicant Name: Jong Ryeol Eun
ERAS Letter ID: 30nbba6d1
Specialty to which this letter will be assigned: Internal Medicine

*LoR(s) submitted through the ERAS LoR Portal are expected to take two weeks to process.

Once submitted through the LoR Portal, the LoR will display a watermark containing a date/time stamp of when it was received by ERAS, source of upload and name of the LoR Portal account holder.

Example: Received by ERAS: 12 JUN 2014 02:02 PM Source: LoR Portal Uploaded by: John Doe

Contact ERAS for LoR Portal Help

Letter Authors: 202-862-6249 or eraslorportal@aamc.org

Applicants: 202-862-6264 or eraslorportal@aamc.org

4. 의대 성과 평가 Medical Student Performance Evaluation

AAMC 가이드에 따라 MSPE를 만들었다. 다른 선생님이 만든 샘플을 참고했다.

AAMC ASSOCIATION OF AMERICAN MEDICAL COLLEGES

A Guide to the Preparation of the Medical Student Performance Evaluation

Yeungnam University College of Medicine

MEDICAL STUDENT PERFORMANCE EVALUATION

JONG RYEOL EUN

September 1, 2013

Identifying Information
Jong Ryeol Eun graduated in 1997 from Yeungnam University College of Medicine in Daegu, Republic of Korea.

Unique Characteristics
Throughout his medical training, Jong Ryeol Eun has demonstrated intellectual curiosity and leadership in his clinical, research, and service endeavors. He won two scholarships during the medical school from Korea Student Aid Foundation and MSD pharmaceutical company. Both of them are awarded for academically outstanding students. Mr. Eun demonstrated an excellent academic record. His rank increased with his advancement in the medical school, 17th in 1st grade, 7th in 2nd grade, 7th in 3rd grade, and 3rd in 4th grade. Overall, he graduated with being ranked 8th out of 68 classmates. Mr. Eun was a member of the pathology lab and performed as a teaching assistant during pathology laboratory classes. He also volunteered the research project during summer vacation in 1994. During the winter vacation in 1995, he took part in a project establishing order communication system (OCS) in Yeungnam University Hospital for one month. He entered ICD-10 codes and their descriptions into the computer. We are proud of him that the codes and the diseases names he had entered are still available in the system.

Academic History
Transfer student: Not applicable
Matriculation in Medical School: March 2, 1993
Graduation from Medical School: February 22, 1997
Extensions, Leave(s) of Absence, Gaps or Breaks: Not applicable
Dual/Joint/Combined Degree: Not applicable
Was this student required to repeat or otherwise remediate any coursework during his/her medical education? No
Was this student the recipient of any adverse action(s) by the medical school or its parent institution? No

Academic Progress
Yeungnam University College of Medicine uses both a scoring system and a ranking system. Jong Ryeol Eun completed all the courses successfully and ranked at the 8th place out of 68 classmates. His rank increased with his advancement in the medical school, and was 3rd place in 4th grade. Mr. Eun performed solidly throughout the basic science curriculum. He has continued the solid performance with ever increasing academic strength in the clinical portal of the curriculum.

Preclincal: Basic Science:
Jong Ryeol Eun passed all the pre-clinical courses without difficulty. He successfully completed the following courses: Anatomy, Physiology, Biochemistry, Microbiology, Neuroanatomy, Parasitology, Histology, Embryology, and Behavioral Science.

Clinical/Pre-Clerkship:
Jong Ryeol Eun satisfactorily completed introductory clinical courses in Internal Medicine, Pediatrics, Surgery, OB & GYN, E.N.T, Neurosurgery, Neuroscience, Psychiatry, Orthopedic surgery, Ophthalmology, Diagnostic Radiology, Therapeutic Radiology, Anesthesiology, Dermatology, Preventive medicine, Pathology, Diagnostic pathology, Forensic Medicine, Pharmacology, Thoracic Surgery, Public health law, Plastic Surgery, Neurology, Emergency Medicine, and Urology.

Clinical: Clinical Clerkships
Following are narrative evaluations of Jong Ryeol Eun's performance on the clerkships and electives.

Internal Medicine: Mr. Eun's overall performance in the Internal Medicine Clerkship was excellent. He showed an excellent understanding of the application of basic science in the clinical practice. He was hard working, motivated, and thorough. He was professional, empathetic, and diligent. He always had an extensive differential diagnosis and an appropriate diagnostic decision making plan. He had good clinical skills and demonstrated these skills in rounds several times. Moreover, he had excellent bedside manners and communicated well with the patients. At every subspecialty rotations, his presentations were excellent. He had excellent professionalism and performed well as a team member.

Surgery: Mr. Eun's overall performance in the Surgery Clerkship was excellent. He had a strong understanding of the scientific basis of medicine and easily applied it to the daily practice of medicine. He had excellent clinical skills that he applied on a daily basis. His case presentation was outstanding. He is diligent, pleasant and it was a true pleasure to work with him. He communicated well with patients. He had strong clinical reasoning and problem solving skills. He worked well with the residents while he was in service. He also worked well with the members of the team. He studied a lot on the rotation and was self-motivated.

Pediatrics: Mr. Eun's overall performance in the Pediatrics Clerkship was excellent. His strong sense of compassion and his enjoyment in working with children came through in his excellent clinical evaluations in pediatrics. He performed outstanding history taking and physical examination. He was very well liked by both patients and clinic staff, and was always eager to pitch in and help anywhere help was needed. He did an outstanding job in this rotation.

Obstetrics and Gynecology: Mr. Eun's overall performance in the Obstetrics and Gynecology Clerkship was excellent. He was clearly reading and was interested in expanding his knowledge base. He had a good understanding of the fundamentals of OB/GYN. He performed good physical exams in labor and delivery. His presentations were excellent. He was enthusiastic and an exceptionally hard worker who always maintained an outstanding standard of professional behavior.

Psychiatry: Mr. Eun's overall performance in the Psychiatry Clerkship was excellent. He was found to consistently demonstrate a professional level of conduct including confidence and responsibility. He was very well organized and thorough.

Neurology: Mr. Eun's overall performance in Neurology was excellent. He was a strong performer in his Neurology clerkship, exhibiting mastery of basic clinical skills in the neurological history taking and examination and demonstrating the ability to adequately analyze neurological cases. He always presented a history and physical write-up that included a well-reasoned analysis of the differential diagnosis.

Diagnostic Radiology: Mr. Eun's overall performance in Radiology Clerkship was excellent. He was an excellent medical student and a hard worker. He did not hesitate to ask questions. He had very good knowledge base. His X-ray reading skills were excellent.

E.N.T: Mr. Eun's overall performance in the ENT Clerkship was excellent. He was a very knowledgeable, personable and ambitious student. He consistently completed extra assignments promptly and was always available.

Ophthalmology: Mr. Eun's overall performance in the Oththalmology Clerkship was excellent. He was an excellent medical student and hard worker. His ability to elicit pertinent physical findings was appropriate and his patient presentations were satisfactory.

Neurosurgery: Mr. Eun's overall performance in Neurosurgery Clerkship was outstanding. He was a very knowledgeable student and a good team player. His case presentation was excellent.

Orthopedic Surgery: Mr. Eun's overall performance in Orthopedics Clerkship was excellent. He was professional, empathetic, and diligent. His case presentation was excellent.

Preventive Medicine: Mr. Eun's overall performance in Preventive Medicine was excellent. His presentation was excellent.

Therapeutic Radiology: Mr. Eun.s overall performance in Therapeutic Radiology Clerkship was excellent. He was a very bright and hard working student. He had an excellent fund of knowledge and was able to adjust it to clinical situations well.

Clinico-Pathologic Conference: Mr. Eun's overall performance in C.P.C Clerkship was excellent. He had very good knowledge base. His presentation was excellent. He was a very bright and hard working student.

Urology: Mr. Eun's overall performance in Urology Clerkship was excellent. He had a very good knowledge base. He was a hard working student.

Thoracic Surgery: Mr. Eun's overall performance in Thoracic Surgery Clerkship was excellent. He had a very good knowledge base. He was a hard working student.

Plastic Surgery: Mr. Eun's overall performance in Plastic Surgery Clerkship was excellent. His suturing skills were excellent. His case presentation was fantastic.

Anesthesiology: Mr. Eun's overall performance in Anesthesiology Clerkship was excellent. He was a very bright and hard working student. He had an excellent fund of knowledge. His intubation skills were excellent.

Dermatology: Mr. Eun's overall performance in Dermatology Clerkship was excellent. Mr. Eun was a very excellent student to work with. He completed interpreting all required skin lesions. He performed very well in oral test.

Summary

Throughout the basic courses and clinical rotations, Jong Ryeol Eun showed great performances consistently. He was very motivated and passionate towards medicine. Based on the entire review of Mr. Eun's academic record, his overall medical school performance was excellent in comparison to that of his peers at this institution.
After graduation in 1997, he completed internship, internal medicine residency, and GI/ Hepatology fellowship in Yeungnam University Hospital and became a faculty member of Yeungnam University College of Medicine in 2006. During 6 years of the faculty, he dedicated himself to teach medical students. Our overall evaluation of Jong Ryeol Eun's performance in mastering the competencies of our curriculum demonstrates that he is an excellent candidate for your internal medicine residency program.

Sincerely,

Young-Hwan Lee, MD, PhD
Professor of Pediatrics
Dean, College of Medicine, Yeungnam University
170 Hyunchungro Namgu, Daegu, South Korea 705-717
+82-53-620-4381
yhlee@med.yu.ac.kr

Attachments: MSPE Appendices

APPENDIX A

Graphic Representations of Comparative Performance in Preclinical/Basic Science Coursework

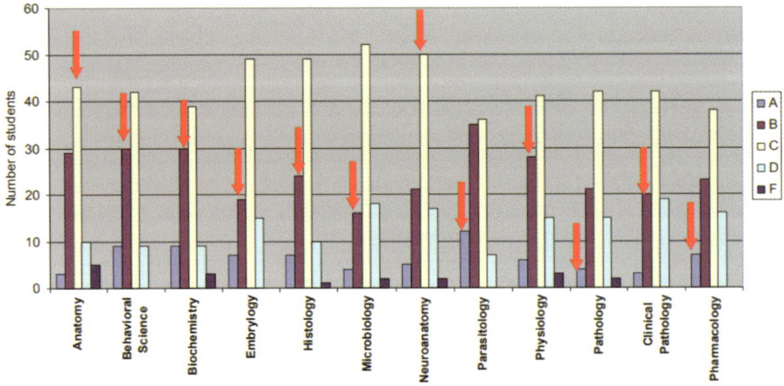

APPENDIX B

Graphic Representations of Comparative Performance in Clinical/Pre-Clerkship Coursework

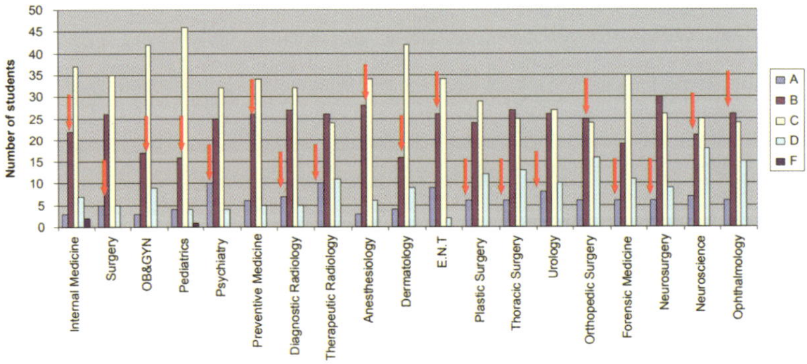

APPENDIX C

Graphic Representations of Comparative Performance in Clinical Clerkships Coursework

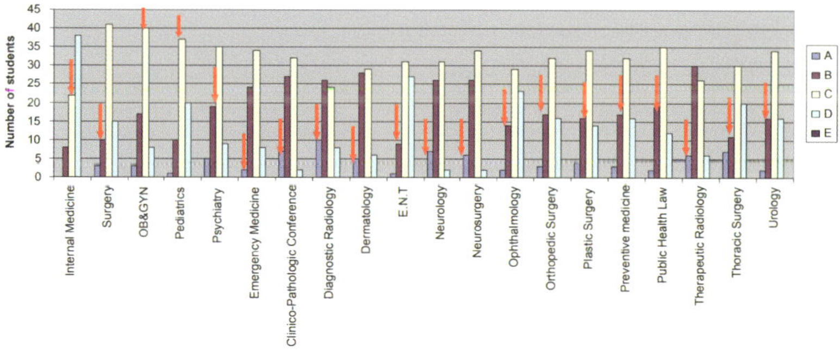

APPENDIX D

Graphic Representations of Comparative Performance in Professional Attributes

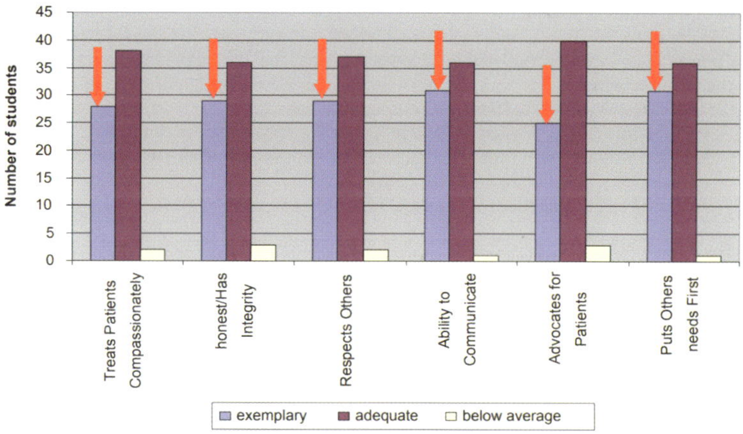

APPENDIX E

Graphic Representations of Comparative Performance in Medical School

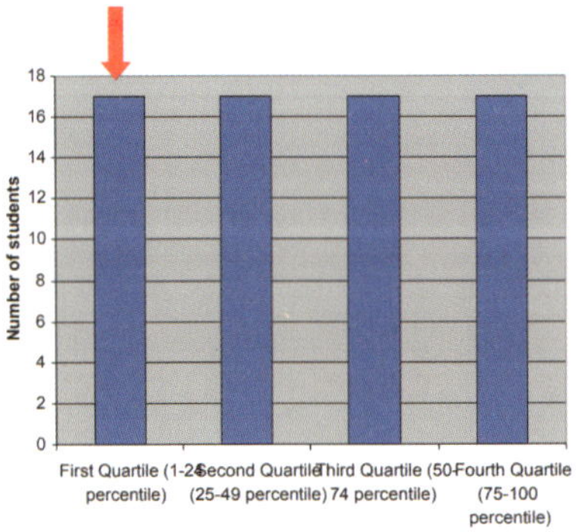

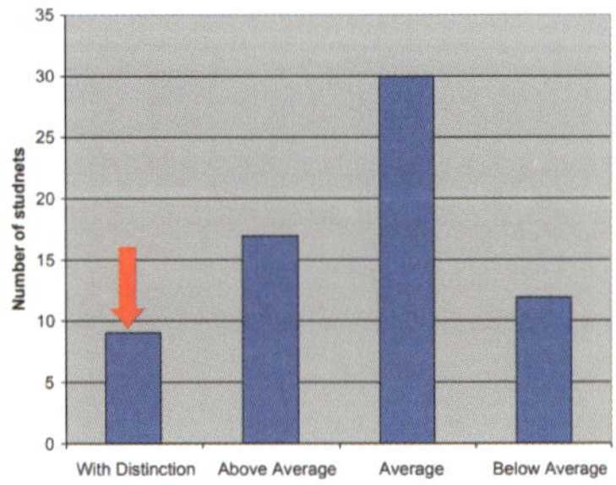

APPENDIX F

Medical School Information

Yeungnam University College of Medicine (http://yumc.yu.ac.kr)

Goal of the Medical School:

A graduate of the M.D. program, Yeungnam University College of Medicine, is expected to function as a competent, ethical and intellectual physician and contribute to Health promotion and academic improvement.

At the end of the program, students will be able to:

1. Perform preventive, therapeutic, and rehabilitative services to the community.
2. Develop attitudes to continue life-long self-learning in any specialized medical field based on social requirements and medical development.
3. Acquired basic capabilities for medical education and creative medical research.

Special Characteristics of the Medical School's Educational Program

1. Emphasis on More Laboratory Work and Clerkship over Lectures:
   The curriculum stressed laboratory work, tutorials, demonstrations and clinical clerkship rather than steretotypical formal classroom lectures.
2. Comprehensive Learning system:
   A specific organ or system-based learning was applied to preclinical courses.
3. Problem based learning:
   The students were organized into small-group and discussed cases designed to integrate information across the basic sciences in the context of medicine. PBL is a student-centered, self-directed learning experience that promotes a variety of educational objectives.

Average length of enrollment (initial matriculation to graduation) at the medical school:

4 years

Description of the Evaluation System used at the Medical School:

Yeungnam University College of medicine is a four-year school that offers training in both basic and clinical sciences. We use both a scoring system and a ranking system. We also have a five-letter grading system, which includes A, B, C, D and F. The GPA is based on the following sub-grading system. A 4.0 (90-100), B 3.0 (80-89), C 2.0 (70-79), D 1.0 (60-69), and F 0 (below 60).

Medical School Requirements for Successful Completion of USMLE Step 1, 2:
USMLE Step 1: Not required
USMLE Step 2: Not required

Medical School requirements for Successful Completion of Objective/Observed Structure Clinical Evaluation (OSCE) and Medical School. OSCE are used:
□ Completion of course
□ Completion of clerkship
□ Completion of third year
■ Graduation
□ Other:

Utilization of the course, clerkship, or elective director's narrative comments in composition of the MSPE. The narrative comments contained in the attached MSPE can best be described as:
□ Reported exactly as written
■ Edited for length or grammer, but not for content
□ Edited for content or included selectively

Utilization by the medical school of the AAMC "Guidelines for Medical Schools Regarding Academic Transcripts" This Medical School is:
□ Completely in compliance with Guidelines' recommendations
■ Partially in compliance with Guidelines' recommendations
Exceptions:
□ Not in compliance with Guidelines' recommendations

Students are permitted to review the MSPE prior to its transmission:
■ Yes
□ No

당시 학장님께도 부탁 메일을 보냈다.

Jong Ryeol Eun <dreundavis@gmail.com>
yhlee에게

이영환 학장님께,

그동안 안녕하셨는지요?
지난번 도와주셔서 캘리포니아 레터를 의외로 쉽게 받았습니다.
감사합니다.
여전히 대부분의 외국인 지원자들이 캘리포니아 레터를 받는 절자상의 어려움과
캘리포니아 지역이 외국인을 받지 않는 분위기 때문에 캘리포니아 지역은 지원하지 않고 있습니다.
저도 캘리포니아 지역 병원에서 인터뷰 받을 기대는 하지 않지만
최선을 다한다는 생각으로 미국전역 병원에 지원하려고 합니다.

이제 레지던트 지원일(9/15)이 한달 반 앞으로 다가왔습니다.
이력서, 자기소개서, 주천서, 의대성적표 등 많은 서류를 준비하고 지원사이트에 업로드하고 있고
한편으로는 개인튜터를 통해 인터뷰와 영어연습을 하고 있습니다.

다름이 아니라, 지원서류 중에 MSPE(Medical Student Performance Evaluation)를 부탁드리고자 메일을 드립니다.
알고 계시리라 생각합니다만, 김민지 선생님은 신경과에 매치되어 지금 뉴욕(?)에서
내과인턴 1년한 후 내년에 University of Florida로 자리를 옮겨 신경과를 할 예정입니다.

저희 대학을 포함하여 한국 의과대학이 MSPE를 발급하지 않으므로, 지원자들이 MSPE를 자기가 만들어서
학장님 서명을 받은 후 서류를 제출하는 것으로 알고 있습니다.
같은 대학 출신은 같은 양식을 사용하는 것이 좋으므로 저는 김민지 선생님이 사용한 양식을 대체로 따랐습니다.

한번 봐주시고, 큰 결함이 없으면 4페이지 끝에 학장님 서명을 부탁드립니다.
전체 MSPE를 하나의 PDF파일로 변환해서 올려야 하는데 하나의 PDF파일로 변환해서 보내주셔도 좋겠고,
4페이지 서명부분만 JPEG 또는 PDF파일로 보내주셔도 감사하겠습니다. 그러면 제가 하나의 PDF파일로 변환해서
지원사이트에 업로드하겠습니다.

USMLE 시험도 힘든 과정이지만 지원서류 준비 또한 참 힘든 과정인 것 같습니다.
그리고 영어 한마디 못하면서 미국의사하겠다고 덤벼든 것 부터가 미친 짓인데,
너무 뒤늦게 깨달았습니다. 이제는 어떻게되든 하는 데까지 한번 해봐야 할 듯 합니다.

지난번 너무 기꺼이 도와주셔서 다시한번 감사드리고,
이번에 또 번거롭게 해 드려 죄송합니다.
지난번에도 말씀드렸지만, 제가 미국 제도권에 들어가고 미국에서 자리를 잡게 된다면
미국을 생각하는 영남의대 후배들에게 기꺼이 등대와 같은 역할을 하고 싶고, 꼭 도움을 주겠습니다.

감사합니다.

은종렬 드림

5. 레지던트 프로그램 지원

각 병원별로 엑셀 파일로 정리된 자료가 usmlekorea에 있었다.

	A	B	C	D	E	F	G	H	I
1	FREIDA	ST	HOSPITAL IM PROGRAM COPYRIGHT 2005 FMG AMERICA	EXAMS	CLINICAL EXPERIENCE	REQUIREMENTS	# FMGs	DEADLIN	SPONSORSHIP
2	140-01-11-024	AL	University of South Alabama Program	pass	2-3 Months US clinical experience preferred.	none		31-Dec	Sponsor J-1 only
3	140-01-21-020	AL	Baptist Health System Program	step I&II first attempt pass	U.S. Clinical Externship Preferred				Sponsor J-1 only
4	140-01-21-022	AL	University of Alabama Medical Center	Step 1: >79 on 1st attempt preferred	US clinical experience helpful	None	0.9	Dec. 1st.	H-1/J-1
5	140-01-21-447	AL	University of Alabama Medical Center (Montgomery) Program	Pass first attempt	Don't require but strengthens application	Graduated in last 5 years		Dec. 31st.	H-1/J-1
6	140-01-31-021	AL	Carraway Methodist Medical Center	200	6 months training in ACGME program	None	Some	Dec. 31st.	Accept H-1/J-1
7	140-03-11-026	AZ	Maricopa Medical Center	83 (205), 1st attempts	U.S. Clinical Externship Preferred	None	~50%	Dec. 31st.	Do NOT sponsor
8	140-03-11-027	AZ	St Joseph's Hospital and Medical Center Program	220 I&II	1 yr hands on US clinical experience	None	some		J-1
9	140-03-21-025	AZ	Banner Good Samaritan Medical Center Program	Pass	1 Year clinical experience in a teaching hospital.	None	~25%	Dec. 31st.	Do not sponsor
10	140-03-21-029	AZ	University of Arizona	75	U.S. Clinical Experience Preferred	None	25 out of 78	Nov. 15th.	Accept J-1 Only
11	140-03-21-512	AZ	Mayo Clinic Scottsdale	80, 1st attempts	1 Year US clinical experience	None	2	Dec. 15th.	Sponsor J-1 only
12	140-04-21-030	AR	University of Arkansas for Medical Sciences	213 (if without US experience)	US clinical experience required if USMLE scores<213	Graduated within 7 years	4-11 / Year	Nov. 15th.	H-1/J-1
13	140-05-11-040	CA	Cedars-Sinai Medical Center	Average Match score ~220	Not required but preferred	None	2	Dec. 15th.	J-1 Only
14	140-05-11-045	CA	Charles R Drew University	Pass	U.S. Clinical Externship Preferred	None	0.4	ASAP	Do not sponsor
15	140-05-11-046	CA	University of California at Los Angeles Med. Ctr.	240	U.S. Clinical Externship Preferred	None	<1%	Dec. 1st.	Sponsor J-1 only
16	140-05-11-049	CA	White Memorial Medical Center Program		U.S. Clinical Externship Preferred				
17	140-05-11-056	CA	Huntington Memorial Hospital Program	pass	U.S. Clinical Experience Preferred	none 3 LOR's	3 out of 24	38322	Do NOT sponsor
18	140-05-11-057	CA	Scripps Mercy Hospital Program	Pass 1st attempt	U.S. Clinical Externship Preferred				
19	140-05-11-070	CA	Los Angeles County-Harbor-UCLA Medical Center	Pass; residents way above average.	U.S. Clinical Experience Preferred	None	0	Dec. 15th.	Do not sponsor
20	140-05-12-042	CA	Kaiser Permanente Southern California (Los Angeles)		U.S. Clinical Externship Preferred				
21	140-05-12-052	CA	Kaiser Permanente Medical Center, Oakland	Pass, higher the better	Not required but preferred	None	4 out of 11	Jan. 31st.	J-1 Only
22	140-05-12-060	CA	Kaiser Permanente Med. Ctr., San Francisco	Pass, but 200 is preferred	Not required but preferred	None	6	Dec. 31st.	Do NOT sponsor
23	140-05-12-062	CA	California Pacific Medical Center	Pass	U.S. Clinical Experience Preferred	None	5	Jan. 15th.	Do not sponsor
24	140-05-12-069	CA	San Joaquin General Hospital Program	At least 80's 1st attempt	Not required but preferred	Graduated within 3 years	18 out of 19	Nov. 30th	Do NOT sponsor
25	140-05-21-032	CA	University of California (Davis) Health System Program	Pass	2 Years US clinical experience	None	2	Nov. 15th.	Accept J-1 only
26	140-05-21-036	CA	University of California (Irvine) Program	215 I&II	Recommended but not required/supporting LOR	None		dec.10th	Do NOT sponsor
27	140-05-21-038	CA	Loma Linda University Program	200 I&II	1 year USCE or passing of CSA	none		Dec.31st	j-1
28	140-05-21-044	CA	University of Southern California LAC+USC Medical Center Program	Pass	U.S. Clinical Experience Preferred	None	0.27	Dec. 1st.	Sponsor J-1 only
29	140-05-21-047	CA	UCLA-San Fernando Valley Program	220-230 I&II	U.S. Clinical Externship Preferred				
30	140-05-21-058	CA	University of California at San Diego	220+ Parts I & II, no failures permitted.	U.S. Clinical Externship Preferred	Graduated within the last 5 years	3	Dec. 1st.	Sponsor J-1 only
31	140-05-21-064	CA	University of California (San Francisco) Program		U.S. Clinical Experience Preferred				
32	140-05-21-067	CA	Kaiser Permanente Med. Ctr., Santa Clara	Pass on 1st attempts	Not required but helpful	None	16	Dec. 31st.	Do NOT sponsor
33	140-05-21-068	CA	Stanford University	Pass	Currently in U.S. fellowship program or research	Graduated within 2-3 years	2	Nov. 15th.	Do NOT sponsor
34	140-05-21-465	CA	David Grant Medical Center Program		U.S. Clinical Externship Preferred				
35	140-05-21-490	CA	Scripps Clinic Scripps Green Hospital	82	U.S. Clinical Externship Preferred	None	0	Dec. 12th.	Do not sponsor
36	140-05-22-063	CA	St Mary's Hospital and Medical Center	200, without failures	US clinical exper or postgraduate studies desirable.	Graduated within 5 years	11 of 37 in	Dec. 1st.	Do not sponsor
37	140-05-22-066	CA	Santa Barbara Cottage Hospital	Pass excellent scores	US clinical experience helpful	Very recent graduate preferred.	1	Dec. 31st.	Sponsor J-1 only
38	140-05-31-031	CA	Kern Medical Center Program		U.S. Clinical Experience Preferred				
39	140-05-31-033	CA	University of California (San Francisco) Fresno	Pass on 1st attempts	US clinical experience is not required by very helpful.	None	Have IMGs	Jan. 4th.	Do not sponsor
40	140-05-31-039	CA	St Mary Medical Center Program	Pass	U.S. Clinical Externship Preferred	None		Jan 31st	Do NOT sponsor
41	140-05-31-048	CA	UCLA-VA Greater Los Angeles	None	U.S. Clinical Experience Preferred	None	0.2	Dec. 31st.	Sponsor J-1 only
42	140-05-31-051	CA	Alameda County Medical Center - Highland Hospital	80	U.S. Clinical Externship Preferred	None	~60%	Jan. 31st.	Do NOT sponsor
43	140-05-31-065	CA	Santa Clara Valley Medical Center Program	Pass	Not required preferred	None		Dec.30th	Sponsor J-1 only
44	140-07-21-073	CO	University of Colorado	80-85 and above	Clinical experience on our campus	Graduated within 5 years.	~10	Dec. 1st.	Accept J-1 only
45	140-07-31-072	CO	Exempla St. Joseph Hospital	205, 1st attempts	2 Months inpatient ward experience (see note)	Graduated within 5 years	1out of 10	Dec. 31st.	Accept J-1 Only
46	140-08-11-074	CT	Yale University (Bridgeport)	85	3 Months US clinical experience or (see notes)	Preferably graduated within 5 years	Majority	Jan. 1st.	H-1 J-1
47	140-08-11-075	CT	St. Vincent's Medical Center	200	Not required, but desirable	Graduated within 10 Years OR (see note	>50%	Dec. 15th.	H-1/J-1
48	140-08-11-076	CT	Danbury Hospital	>82 more likely get selected	Some US clinical experience preferred	None	Majority	Dec. 1st.	J-1 but H-1 possibl
49	140-08-11-087	CT	Stamford hospital Colum.Univ.college of Phys.& Surgeons		U.S. Clinical Experience Preferred				
50	140-08-21-079	CT	Greenwich Hospital Association Program	86 I&II	U.S. Clinical Externship Preferred				Sponsor J-1 only
51	140-08-21-085	CT	Yale-New Haven Medical Center Program		U.S. Clinical Experience Preferred				
52	140-08-21-496	CT	Yale-New Haven Medical Center (Waterbury) Program	85 I&II	2 months US clinical hands-on experience	3 years			Sponsor J-1 only
53	140-08-21-499	CT	University of Connecticut (New Britain) Program		U.S. Clinical Externship Preferred				
54	140-08-31-077	CT	Griffin Hospital Residency Program	<85 unlikely to get interview	1 Year US clinical exper is preferred not required	None	na	Dec. 31st.	H-1 J-1

내과 레지던트를 뽑는 병원이 230개로 추려졌다. 그 가운데 나와 기본조건이 맞지 않는 병원들을 또 추려냈다. 각 병원 홈페이지마다 들어가서 모든 조건들을 확인해 보았다.

Hawaii

0. University of Hawaii

Alkansa

10. University of Alkansa >220 or >2m 1st attempt CS

Arizona

115. Maricopa Medical Center Program

118. College of Medicine, Mayo Clinic (Arizona)

CA

92. Kern Medical Center recent graduate preferred

93. Kaiser permanente Southern California

96. Scripps Green Hosp

97. Loma Linda Uni

98. St. Mary's Medical center, SF recent graduate or current USCE, US citizenship or GC holder 힘들지만 지원은 가능

99. Cedars-Sinai Medical Center

100. UCLA medical center Cat or primary care track 둘 중 하나 지원해야 함.

103. UCLA Olive view

104. UC Riverside

102. Kaiser Permanente. North California/Oakland 자국에서 레지던트 마쳤는가? 리서치 및 발표논문 등 중요

105. Alameda County Medical Center

~~106. UC Irvine USCE strongly recommended <3yr preferred 힘듦~~

~~107. Huntington Memorial Hospital Pasadena <5yr, USCE 힘듦~~

~~108. Eisenhower Medical Center Prelim(6)~~

~~108. Scripps Mercy Hospital San Diego <5yr, USCE preferred~~ 힘듦

109. UC San Diego Physician-Scientist Training (PSTP)
= research residency pathway.
과거 research experience에 대해 outline 하는 short essay.
publications, 관심분야, subspecialty, research and faculty laboratories which suit your interests
2-day interview (day1: residency training program.
day2: research program faculty lab)
general academic performance, clinical performance, LORs,

110. Kaiser Permanente Northern California, SF

110. California Pacific Medical Center 조건명시 없음

110. UCSF Cat, Primary care track, General primary care track, score>230

111. St. Mary Medical center.

111. Santa Clara Valley Medical Center 구체적 조건 없음

12. 15. St. Mary's (Waternury) hospital (지원은 가능) USCE>2mo (strongly preferred)

13. Danbury Hospital, Yale New Haven 지원조건명시없음

123. Bridgeport Hospital/Yale University >85+ 레지던트수료, 1st author

124. St. Vincent's medical center USCE>2mo, strong interest in IM as evidenced

126. Greater Danbury Community Health Center (Connecticut Institute for Communities) 정보없음

128. Greenwich Hospital Association Program (Yale New Haven Health) 정보없음

Washington DC

16. Medstart Washington Hospital center 특별조건명시없음

133. Georgetown University Hospital/Washington Hospital center program

134. Georgetown University Hospital program

136. Providence Hospital 요건 없음

137. Howard University

Delaware

138. Jefferson Medical College/Christiana Care Health Services: publications, honors,관심분야, 계획

Florida (FL)

17. Florida hospital 특별조건명시없음

139. University of Miami Miller School of Medicine/Palm Beach Regional Campus

140. University of Florida step2>250+ >1yr post-graduate clinical training

141. University of Florida college of Medicine Jacksonville Program

142. Collge of Medicine, Mayo clinic (Jacksonville) diploma copy

145. Orlando Health Program

146. Florida Hospital Medical Center

Georgia (GA)

151. Emory University <5yr but cut off (X)

152. Morehouse school of Medicine

Illinois

2. University of Illinois College of Medicine at Peoria 3LORs USCE(x)

18. St. Francis hospital of Evanston (Resunection Health Care) <5 선호 (지원은가능)

20. Louis A Weiss Memorial Hospital >3yr preferred, USCE (지원은 가능)

21. Advocate Illinois Masonic Medical Center <5 선호 (지원은 가능)

22. University of Southern Illinois

23. Rosalind Franklin University USCE 필요(research포함)

24. New Cook County Hospital (John H. Stronger Jr. Hospital of Cook County) <5 선호 (지원은 가능)

160. MacNeal Hospital Program, IMG step3, 1st attempt, <5yr preferred

161. Mercy Hospital and Medical Center 명시없음

162. Rush University Medical Center 조건명시없음

Alkansa

10. University of Alkansa >220 or >2m 1st attempt CS

Arizona

115. Maricopa Medical Center Program

118. College of Medicine, Mayo Clinic (Arizona)

CA

92. Kern Medical Center recent graduate preferred

93. Kaiser permanente Southern California

96. Scripps Green Hosp

97. Loma Linda Uni

98. St. Mary's Medical center, SF recent graduate or current USCE, US citizenship or GC holder 힘들지만 지원은 가능

99. Cedars-Sinai Medical Center

100. UCLA medical center　Cat or primary care track 둘 중 하나 지원해야 함.
103. UCLA Olive view
104. UC Riverside
102. Kaiser Permanente. North California/Oakland
자국에서 레지던트 마쳤는가? 리서치 및 발표논문 등 중요
105. Alameda County Medical Center
106. UC Irvine　USCE strongly recommended. <3yr preferred 힘듦
107. Huntington Memorial Hospital. Pasadena　<5yr, USCE 힘듦
108. Eisenhower Medical Center　Prelim(6)
108. Scripps Mercy Hospital. San Diego <5yr, USCE-preferred 힘듦
109. UC San Diego　Physician-Scientist Training (PSTP)
= research residency pathway.
과거 research experience에 대해 outline하는 short essay.
publications. 관심분야, subspecialty, research and faculty laboratories which suit your interests
2-day interview (day1: residency training program.
day2: research program faculty lab)
general academic performance, clinical performance, LORs,
110. Kaiser Permanente Northern California, SF
110. California Pacific Medical Center 조건명시 없음
110. UCSF　Cat, Primary care track, General primary care track, score>230
111. St. Mary Medical center.　significant clinical experience in US (힘듦)
111. Santa Clara Valley Medical Center　구체적 조건 없음
112. Santa Barbara Cottage Hospital 구체적 조건 없음

병원들 홈페이지를 찾아보면서 미국 주들과 병원 이름을 많이 알게 되었다. 특히 현대자동차가 있어 한국인이 많은 조지아주의 귀넷 병원에 한국어를 잘 하는 의사를 구한다는 공고를 보고 이메일을 보냈다. 지금 보니 얼굴이 달아 오를 정도로 부끄럽지만 그때는 절실했던 모양이다.

Dear Dr. Darrow,

It's a great pleasure to have a chance to write to you.
I have come to know that Gwinnett Medical Center will open internal medicine residency program in 2014. I am preparing to apply for internal medicine this September. I am very interested in your program. I'm writing to inquire a few questions about the program.

First, let me introduce myself. I am a 41-year-old physician from Korea. I've worked as a faculty in GI/Hepatology, Internal Medicine, Yeungnam University Hospital, Daegu, South Korea over the past 7 years. I graduated from Yeungnam University in 1997, and finished 5 years of intern and internal medicine residency in 2002. After 3 years of army service and one and a half years of GI/Hepatology fellowship, I became a faculty in 2006. I came to the US in February, 2012 for research about liver cancer stem cells. Now I've been working in Dr. Mark Zern's lab, GI/Hepatology, Internal Medicine, UC Davis Medical Center, Sacramento, CA.

I have two questions. Does your program have year of graduation cut-off? If not, I really want to apply for and be a resident in your program. Do you provide observership opportunities? I would like to have opportunities of observership in Gwinnett Medical Center.

I am kind of old applicant. But I have been working in clinical practice and teaching students and residents. I believe my clinical experiences might contribute to your residency program. Besides, I don't need a visa. I'm going to get a green card in one month or so. I got ECFMG certificate this year (Step 1 223, Step2CK 251, Step2CS pass, Step3 216 - all first attempt).

I can't attach my full CV and other my credentials at this email. I wish I have an opportunity to provide you my CV and other documents.

Thank you very much.
I look forward to your kind reply.
Sincerely yours,
Jong Ryeol Eun, M.D.

물론 바로 거절 메일을 받았다.

Susan L. Hill <shill01@gwinnettmedicalcenter.org> 2013년 8월 16일

Thank you for your interest in our Internal Medical program. Our program is currently in the development phase and we will not be ready to accept residents until at least 2014 or later, we are not yet in the 2014 Match and do not recruit housestaff out of Match. When the time comes, our application wil be assessible through the ERAS resident selection system. For mor information regarding the program, please check our webside in the near future for further developments and answers to yoru questions. Thank you

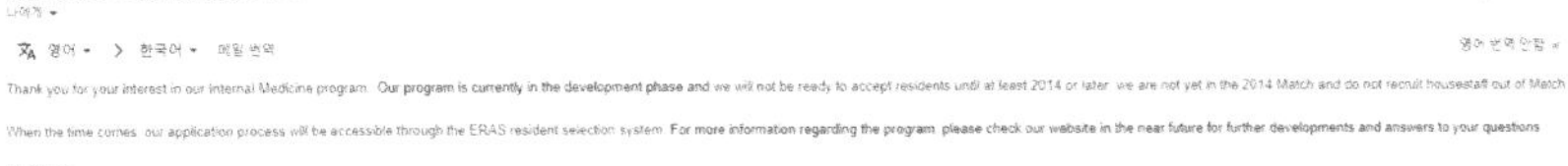
Susan L. Hill

Thank you for your interest in our Internal Medicine program. Our program is currently in the development phase and we will not be ready to accept residents until at least 2014 or later. we are not yet in the 2014 Match and do not recruit housestaff out of Match. When the time comes, our application process will be accessible through the ERAS resident selection system. For more information regarding the program, please check our website in the near future for further developments and answers to your questions.

Thank you

2013년 9월 15일, 드디어 레지던트 지원일이 되었다. 지원하는 병원 숫자에 따라 계단식으로 비용이 늘어난다. 정확히 기억은 나지 않지만 지원비로 600만 원 이상 들었던 것 같다.

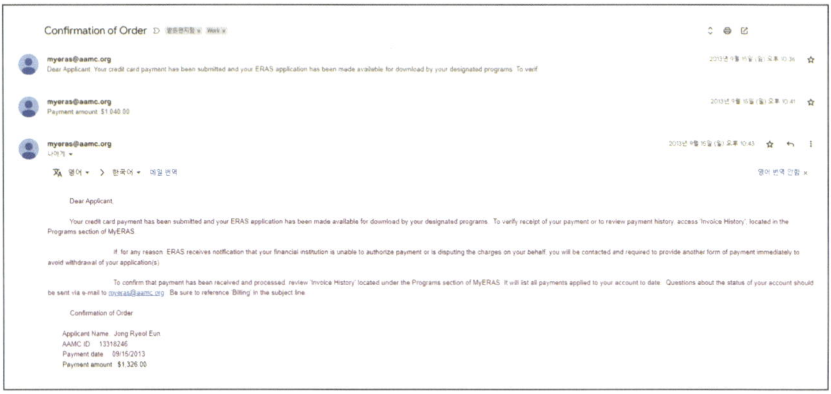
Confirmation of Order 받은편지함 Work

myeras@aamc.org 2013년 9월 15일 (일) 오후 10:36
Dear Applicant. Your credit card payment has been submitted and your ERAS application has been made available for download by your designated programs. To verif

myeras@aamc.org 2013년 9월 15일 (일) 오후 10:41
Payment amount $1,040.00

myeras@aamc.org 2013년 9월 15일 (일) 오후 10:43
나에게

영어 > 한국어 메일 번역 영어 번역 안함

Dear Applicant,

Your credit card payment has been submitted and your ERAS application has been made available for download by your designated programs. To verify receipt of your payment or to review payment history, access 'Invoice History', located in the Programs section of MyERAS.

If, for any reason, ERAS receives notification that your financial institution is unable to authorize payment or is disputing the charges on your behalf, you will be contacted and required to provide another form of payment immediately to avoid withdrawal of your application(s).

To confirm that payment has been received and processed, review 'Invoice History' located under the Programs section of MyERAS. It will list all payments applied to your account to date. Questions about the status of your account should be sent via e-mail to myeras@aamc.org. Be sure to reference 'Billing' in the subject line.

Confirmation of Order

Applicant Name: Jong Ryeol Eun
AAMC ID: 13318246
Payment date: 09/15/2013
Payment amount: $1,326.00

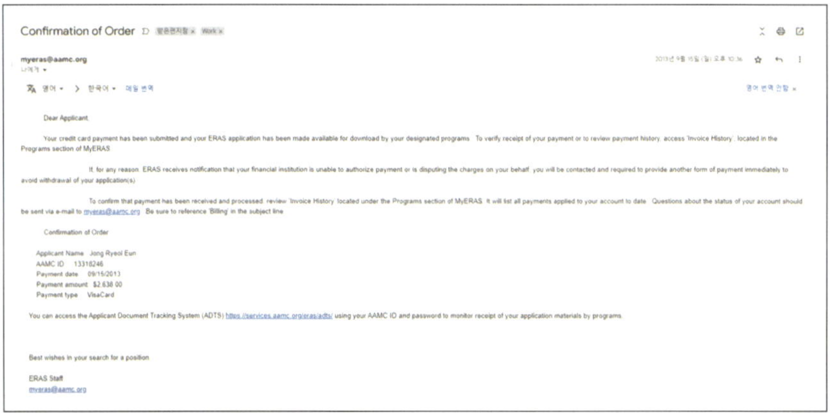
Confirmation of Order 받은편지함 Work

myeras@aamc.org 2013년 9월 15일 (일) 오후 10:36
나에게

영어 > 한국어 메일 번역 영어 번역 안함

Dear Applicant,

Your credit card payment has been submitted and your ERAS application has been made available for download by your designated programs. To verify receipt of your payment or to review payment history, access 'Invoice History', located in the Programs section of MyERAS.

If, for any reason, ERAS receives notification that your financial institution is unable to authorize payment or is disputing the charges on your behalf, you will be contacted and required to provide another form of payment immediately to avoid withdrawal of your application(s).

To confirm that payment has been received and processed, review 'Invoice History' located under the Programs section of MyERAS. It will list all payments applied to your account to date. Questions about the status of your account should be sent via e-mail to myeras@aamc.org. Be sure to reference 'Billing' in the subject line.

Confirmation of Order

Applicant Name: Jong Ryeol Eun
AAMC ID: 13318246
Payment date: 09/15/2013
Payment amount: $2,638.00
Payment type: VisaCard

You can access the Applicant Document Tracking System (ADTS) https://services.aamc.org/eras/adts/ using your AAMC ID and password to monitor receipt of your application materials by programs.

Best wishes in your search for a position

ERAS Staff
myeras@aamc.org

무수히 많은 광탈 이메일을 받다가 2013년 10월 18일 뉴욕에 있는 코니 아일랜드 병원으로부터 처음으로 인터뷰 메일을 받았다. 2013년 지원에서 유일하게 받은 인터뷰였다. 인터뷰 날짜는 2014년 2월 3일로 정해졌다.

Interview Confirmation - Coney Island Hospital

Jamie Vigliotti

Dear Dr. Eun,

This e-mail will confirm your interview at Coney Island Hospital on February 3, 2014. Please report to the Medical Services Office, Room 4N98, no later than 7:30 a.m. At that time you will attend Morning Report with our housestaff. At 11:00 a.m., you will tour the hospital with one of our Chief Residents, lunch with him/her and then attend our teaching lecture at 12:00. Interviews will begin at 2:00 p.m.

Please bring with you the following documents (copies are sufficient): Medical School Diploma, ECFMG Certificate, USMLE score report (front and back), Transcript, Dean's Letter and a copy of your Visa (if applicable).

If you have any questions, please call me at (718) 616-3779. Looking forward to meeting with you. If you need overnight accommodations, the closest motel is – The Comfort Inn, in Sheepshead Bay and their phone # is (718) 368-3334.

Please be advised that if you park in our parking lot, **we cannot** validate your parking ticket.

Jamie Vigliotti

Jamie Vigliotti
Coordinating Manager
Internal Medicine Residency Program
Coney Island Hospital

인터뷰 하루 전에 미리 뉴욕으로 가서 병원 위치를 확인했다. 우리나라 대학병원에 비하면 초라해 보이는 지역병원이지만 당시에는 정말 간절했다. 하필 인터뷰 당일에 폭설이 내렸다. 자고 나니 차가 눈에 파묻혀 보이지 않을 정도였다. 앞 창문에 붙은 눈만 쓸어내리고 엉금엉금 기어서 겨우 병원으로 갔다. 어떻게 인터뷰했는지는 잘 기억이 나지 않는다. 다만 인터뷰하러 병원 입구를 지나가는데 건장한 흑인 시큐리티가 어디 가느냐고 물어서 레지던트 인터뷰하러 왔다고 대답한 것, 대기실로 올라가 순서를 기다렸던 것, 인터뷰는 아주 간단했다는 것만 기억난다. 그리고는 숙소로 돌아오니 오후가 되어 있었다. 비행기는 다음날 오전 첫 비행기였다. 할 일이 없어 저녁에 공항에 가서 렌트카를 반납했다. 게이트 앞에서 밤을 샐 작정이었는데 밤이 되니 공항이 폐쇄되어 쫓겨났다. 어쩔 수 없이 나와서 건물을 이동하는데 정말 뼈에 사무칠 정도로 지독하게 추웠던 게 기억난다. 외투 없이 양복만 입고 있었는데 밤 12시에 건물과 건물 사이만 이동하는데도 처음 경험해 보는 추위였다. 공항 1층 로비에서 달달달 떨다가 새벽 5시에 체크인이 열리자마자 다시 수속을 밟았다. 그런데 항공권에 색연필로 체크 표시가 되어 있어서 어젯밤 쫓겨난 일을 설명하느라 진땀을 뺐다. 오전에 샌프란시스 공항에서 프로펠러 비행기로 갈아타고 새크라멘토 공항으로 왔다.

가진 돈이 바닥나고 생활비가 없었다. 아르바이트 할 병원을 알아본 뒤 혼자 한국으로 급히 귀국했다. 아르바이트를 하는 동안 매치되기를 기대하며 조

급한 마음으로 기다리는 외로운 시간이 지나가고 있었다. 2014년 3월 셋째주, 드디어 발표 날이 되었다. 기대와는 달리 탈락을 확인하고 2014년 3월 20일 절망감으로 UK에 다음과 같이 후기를 적었던 게 기억난다. 다시 읽어보니 너무 부끄럽지만 당시에는 솔직했던 감정이므로 소개한다.

> **2014년 3월 20일**
>
> 매치되신 분들 진심으로 축하드립니다. 실패하신 분들은 저처럼 많이 힘드실 줄 압니다. 위로가 전혀 되지 않겠지만 빨리 털고 일어나셨으면 합니다. 매치 결과를 기다릴 때는 실패하면 하늘이 무너질 것 같은 절망감을 느끼지 않을까 두려웠습니다. 매치에 실패했다는 이메일을 보고 기분이 괜찮다고 하면 거짓말이겠지요. 당연히 실망스럽고 어찌해야 할 바를 몰랐습니다. 이제 3일 정도 지나서 감정을 추스르고 현실을 직시하고자 합니다. 그동안의 제 시험 과정을 풀어보려고 합니다.
> 저는 졸업 17년차의 old graduate로 영어 한마디도 못하는 상태에서 정확히 3년 전 USMLE 시험에 뛰어들었습니다. 지방 대학병원 소화기내과에 근무하는 상태로 2년 전 미국 연수길에 올랐습니다. 연수 가기 전(2011년) Step 1, 2CK 보았고, 연수 1년째(2012년) 말에 CS, 영주권 취득, 연수 2년째(2013년) step 3를 보고 9월에 지원했습니다. 10월 중순까지 인터뷰를 하나도 못 받았습니다. 그러다가 인터뷰를 겨우 하나 받았는데 영주권자 이상만 주는 뉴욕 병원이었습니다. 인터뷰 하나로 되는 경우도 있다고 하여 나름 최선을 다했지만 안 되었습니다. 그래서 3년이란 노력을 쏟은 것이 물거품이 된 것 같아 좌절감을 잠시 느꼈습니다. 그렇지만 다른 측면에서 한번 제 처지를 돌아보았습니다.
>
> 1. 요행히 매치되었더라도 환자를 진료하기엔 역부족인 영어 실력이었습니다. 그래서 낙방한 것은 지극히 자연스러운 일일지 모릅니다.
> 2. 저는 평생 영어공부라고는 해본 적이 없었고, 기본적인 인사말도 못하는 상태에서 미국연수를 떠났습니다. 미국의사가 되어보겠다는 강한 동기가 없었다면 영어를 공부할 의욕도 없었을 것입니다. 지난 2년간 열심히 영어공부를 했습니다. 매일 공부, 연습하고 튜터링도 받고 나름 많이 는 것 같습니다. 지금 한국으로 귀국했는데, 습관이 들어서 영어책, 단어숙어장이 옆에 없으면 불안할 지경입니다. 2년 전 영어는 소음이었는데, 이제 영어신문은 읽는 데 그렇게 어렵지 않은 것 같고, 드라마는 못 알아듣지만 영어뉴스는 좀 들리는 것 같기도 합니다. 단기적으로는 3년, 길게는 나이 오십이 되기 전에 영어를 완성하는 것이 이제 목표가 되었습니다.
> 3. 오로지 병원 지원에 조금이나마 도움이 되고자 영주권을 받았습니다. 그런데 이제 나에게는 필요 없게 되었고, 대신 아이들이 미국에서 계속 학교를 다니게 되어 꼭 필요한 아이러니한 상황이 되었습니다.
>
> 이제 뭘 하나 하고 절망하고 있는데 종병과 컨택이 되어 취직하려고 합니다. 월급을 많이 줄 것 같습니다. 그렇다고 지금 아주 해피한 것은 아닙니다. 미국이 여전히 정말 그립고 한국에서 일하면서 계속 기회를 보려고 합니다. '여우의 신포도'처럼 제 불쌍한 처지를 합리화해 보려고 주접을 떨었습니다. 실패하신 분들 힘내시기 바랍니다. 저는 어제를 마지막으로 그만 울기로 했습니다.

포기할까 하다가 한 번 더 도전하기로 마음을 바꾸었다.

지성배 선생님과의 인연

지성배 선생님을 한 번도 뵌 적은 없다. 검색해 보면 현재 메사추세츠 베스 이스라엘 디콘세스 메디컬 센터Beth Israel Deaconess Medical Center에 근무하시는 걸로 나온다. USMLE Step 2CS와 레지던트 매치 준비를 하면서 많은 선생님들로부터 도움과 조언을 받았는데, 특히 지성배 선생님으로부터는 이메일로 많은 조언을 받았다. 주고받았던 이메일을 지성배 선생님의 허락을 받아 소개한다.

2013년 8월 23일

은종렬 선생님께
선생님 NIW로 영주권을 취득하신 걸로 압니다만 residentswap은 꼭 '갑자기 그만둔 레지던트 자리 채우는' 곳만은 아닙니다. 새로 문을 연 프로그램이 타이밍이 늦어 레지던트 매칭에 참여 못했을 경우 여기 공고를 올리기도 하고, TO가 늘어난 프로그램에서 매칭에 이 자리를 못 올릴 경우에 올리기도 합니다. 이런 자리들은 대개 비자 서포트를 안 하는 경우가 많아서 영주권자가 확실히 유리하고요. 90달러를 날린다고 생각할 수도 있으시겠지만. 만약 이 돈 없어도 된다 싶으시다면 가입하고 꾸준히 모니터링 하면서 그때그때 지원서류를 날려 보는 것도 나쁘지 않은 것 같습니다. 저도 90달러 세 번째 낸 시즌에 결국 지금 자리를 찾았으니까요. (저는 residentswap과 아무 관계가 없답니다 ㅎㅎ) 한 해 한 해 지날수록 더 힘들어지는 게 사실인 것 같고. 아무쪼록 요번 해에 꼭 뜻을 이루셨으면 좋겠습니다.

2013년 8월 23일

고생이 많으십니다. 매치라는 게 참 묘해서 그런 조건들을 내세우더라도 뭔가 자기들이 원하는 것과 맞아떨어지는 사람이 있으면 그런 것들은 순식간에 아무것도 아니게 되어버리기도 하는 것 같습니다. 특히나 선생님처럼 엄청난 백그라운드를 가지신 분이라면 그 점을 널리 어필하셔야 하지 않을까 싶네요. 지금 미국에서 정확히 어떤 기관에 몸담고 계신지는 모르겠으나 지금 계신 곳을 발판으로 다음 스텝을 노려보는 게 정석인 것 같고요, 제가 소개해 드릴 수 있는 자리는 Miami의 Transplant House Physician인데 내년 6월부터 시작하게 됩니다. 이번에 매칭이 여의치 않을 경우 차선책 정도로 생각해 두시면 좋을 것 같고요. 내년에 매칭 발표 시즌쯤 되었을 때 필요한 경우 제가 직접 그쪽 프로그램으로 연락드리겠습니다. 참고로 올해에도 한국 내과 보드 선생님 한 분을 소개 했었는데 한국에서 ID fellow까지 하신 분이라 아무 문제없이 뽑아줄 줄 알았습니다만 (간이식 인턴으로 ID fellow라니 뭘 더 바란단 말입니까.) 경쟁이 치열한 가운데 결국 안 뽑아 주더라구요. 제가 들어갈 때만 해도 이 정도는 아니었고 한국 어텐딩이 한 분 계셔서 수월했는데 이젠 그렇진 않은 것 같습니다. 지금 일하는 사람 중 몇 명이나 매칭되어 나가느냐가 문제인데 지금으로서는 기다려 보는 수밖에 없겠지요. 아무쪼록 매칭이 잘 되어서 마이애미 오실 일이 없기를 빌고요. 궁금하신 것이나 필요하신 것 있으면 알려주시기 바랍니다. 행운을 빕니다 선생님.
지성배 올림

2013년 8월 24일

지성배 선생님,
친절한 답장 감사합니다. 선생님의 조언대로 residentswap 가입해서 빈자리 모니터링 하겠습니다. 그리고 Transplant House Physician 자리도 좋은 기회일 것 같습니다. 한국에 있을 때 간이식에 관심이 많았고, 이곳 UC Davis Medical Center에 연수 온 것도 이식에 관심이 있어서 Institue of Regenerative Medicine (IRC)이라는 기관의 Transplant research program에 오게 되었습니다. 결국 와서는 cancer stem cell research하고 있지만요. 일단은 금년은 매칭에 전념해 보고자 합니다.
한 가지 더 조언을 부탁해도 될런지요?
제 졸업연수와 USCE 없는 것이 가장 red flags라는 것을 잘 알고 있습니다.
그래서 cut-off가 명확한 곳 제외하고 내과 categorical 만 243군데 프로그램을 서칭해
두었고, 지원 계획입니다. 요즘 인터뷰를 한 군데도 못 받는 악몽을 꾸고 있습니다.

인터뷰를 받는다 해도 영어가 문제이므로, 사실 서류들은 일찌감치 완료(수정은 계속)하고, 인터뷰 문답집 수정작업도 계속하면서 인터뷰 연습에 올인하고 있는 실정입니다.
암튼 걱정이 많고 비공인 프로그램이라도 좋으니까 자리가 있었으면 하는 바람입니다.
제 CV, 지원서, PS, MSPE에 대해 조언 있으시면 부탁드립니다.
은종렬 드림

2013년 8월 24일

안녕하세요? 지성배입니다. 보내주신 자료 잘 읽어보았습니다. 경력도 화려하시고 점수도 좋으셔서 제 느낌엔 잘 되실 것 같은데요 ^^ 충분히 자신감 가지셔도 될 듯싶습니다. 아래는 제가 PS 읽어보고 몇 가지 comment를 첨부한 건데요, 제가 전혀 이런 쪽으로 professional하지 않으니 참고만 하시기 바라고요. 혹시 전문가의 교정을 제대로 받으셨는지 궁금합니다. CV는 잘 짜여진 것 같습니다. 그냥 제 포맷도 한 번 참고해 보시라고 제 CV를 첨부파일로 보냅니다. CV나 PS는 (믿을 만한) 여러 사람들에게 보내서 의견을 물어보시는 것이 좋은 것 같습니다. 여러 가지 서로 다른 view에서 조언을 얻으시면 더 나은 product를 만드실 수 있을 거라 생각됩니다. 별 도움은 안 되겠지만 궁금하신 것 있으시면 언제든 연락주세요. 고맙습니다.

p.s. 제가 인터뷰 다니며 꼭 들었던 질문이 너 나이도 많고 경력도 많은데 우리 레지던트, 펠로들이랑 잘 지낼 수 있겠니? 였습니다. 이 질문 반드시 들으실 겁니다. 미리 답을 한 번 생각해 보시고 PS에 한 줄 넣는 것도 나쁘지 않을 것 같습니다.

NAME: Jong Ryeol Eun

Looking back at my life in Korea, over the past 41 years, every step I came across was challenging, even though it looked easy to others. I have always tried my best and finally overcame every hurdle. Now I am going to try a new, amazing challenge to become a physician in the U.S.

I used to be a little shy and introverted in medical school. I enjoyed studying. I liked most subjects, except anatomy. In particular, I liked internal medicine. It was exciting to learn pathophysiology, diagnosis and treatment. Internal medicine was logical. That's why I did not hesitate to become an internal medicine resident. Five years of intern and residency training gave me invaluable experiences. **Traditionally, resident training in Korea is really tough. At that time my only desire was to sleep soundly.** (이 부분이 꼭 필요한지 잘 모르겠습니다) But overall I was happy and enjoyed the residency life. I had a lot of hands-on experiences. I also participated in many procedures, including cardiac catheterization as an assistant. Meanwhile, I was interested in abdominal ultrasonography and echocardiography. **I studied them by myself** (한국적 사고로는 좋은 일일지도 모르겠지만 미국식으로는 "왜 supervision없이 그렇게 하는지, 위험할 수 있다"고 생각할지도 모르겠습니다) I became familiar with the equipment and could read the findings of liver, pancreas, biliary system, and kidneys. I also could measure cardiac wall motion and valve area, even though I was not an expert. In my 4th year residency, I spent much time preparing for the board exam. I summarized all the 15th edition of Harrison's Textbook of Internal Medicine and uploaded the notes on my personal blog for Korean medical students and resident doctors. Online visitors recorded more than 100,000 hits on my blog. Although the website is not available now, the contents are still available on other websites. Many Korean medical students have used the contents for studying. That's why I am kind of a celebrity among Korean medical students. (이부분은 아주 좋은 것 같습니다)

My most valuable experience, however, was how to communicate well with patients, their families, and hospital staff. **I think** (I think가 꼭 필요할지요.. 너무 구어체 같은 느낌이라서요)that is the most invaluable asset in my career. **I was not mature enough and lacked a lot of communication skills when I was an intern and during 1st year of residency.** (제가 뽑는 사람이라면 이부분에서 흠칫 놀라서 인터뷰 리스트에서 뺄지도 모르겠습니다 굳이 이런 말이 필요할지요) Through many trials and errors I became more mature and learned all the skills I need to do my job efficiently.

I was **academically interested** (academically는 사족이란 생각이 듭니다만...) in Gastroenterology and Hepatology and became a staff physician in Yeungnam University Hospital in 2006. I did my best in teaching students and residents, writing papers, and presenting my data at academic meetings as well as taking care of outpatients and inpatients. Taking care of patients was fruitful. Sometimes, however, I was frustrated when I could not help grave patients, like those with advanced liver cancers or severe alcoholic hepatitis. That's why I focused my research on liver cancers and alcoholic hepatitis. For advanced **HCC**s, (줄임말은 항상 full term을 앞에 적고 나서 괄호 안에 넣어야 한다던데 잘 모르겠습니다) our protocol based on hepatic arterial infusion chemotherapy improved tumor response rate by 40-60%. It increased survival by around 1.5 years in treatment responders. Four of my patients were cured by the chemotherapy alone or curative surgical resection after downstaging. I always felt happy whenever I met any of them in my office. On the other hand, I gathered the data about the HCC incidence in chronic hepatitis B patients treated with antiviral agent. I published the data in a high quality journal, Journal of Hepatology. I felt like walking on air when I saw my name on the paper. In addition, I paid attention to a drug called Cilostazol, a widely used antiplatelet drug. There are two options available for the treatment of severe alcoholic hepatitis at the moment, steroid and pentoxifylline. The main pathophysiology is related to an increased TNF-alpha in Kupffer cells. I found that Cilostazol significantly inhibited TNF-alpha in Kupffer cell-like macrophages. I got a patent based on the data. It was an interesting experience. I would like to continue my research to establish a possible clinical use. (patent 있다는 부분은 좀 더 강조하셔도 좋을 듯...)

I have been doing research about liver cancer/cancer stem cells at UC Davis Medical Center, Sacramento, California since I came to the U.S. in 2012. I have been enjoying life with my family. My children love their friends, school and life in America. **I realized that I was a frog in a pond before I explored the outside world.** (한국식 사고로는 충분히 할 수 있는 말이지만 선생님의 경험 같은 것을 비추어 봤을 때 이 문장은 빼시는게 어떨까요... 제 짧은 경험으로는 ... 미국은 겸양이 그리 미덕스럽지는 않은 곳인거 같습니다) I am strongly motivated to be a doctor in a bigger world. I would like to build a new career in the U.S. with my family. I know it will be really tough and there are many obstacles to overcome. I will do my best and overcome challenges as before. I believe my clinical, research and teaching experiences, and academic accomplishments will contribute to your internal medicine residency program.

내가 작성한 PS를 읽어보시고 수정하고 도움을 주셨다. 보내주신 이력서를 참조해 나의 이력서를 만들었다.

2013년 8월 24일

한 말씀 더 덧붙이자면... 미국 추천서를 더 얻으시면 좋을 것 같고요 (미국 2 + 한국 1 조합으로 가시죠 ㅎㅎ) 지금 계신 기관에서 외래 또는 입원환자 observation이라도 할 수 있는 기회를 얻으실 수는 없는지 궁금하네요.

2013년 8월 25일

주옥같은 지적 감사합니다.
랩 친구와 튜터와 여러 번 상의하고 수정작업 하고 있는데, 그분들도 미처 발견하지 못한 점들을 지적해 주셔서 감사합니다. 말씀대로 수정해서 튜터와 상의해 보겠습니다.
선생님의 경력도 정말 화려하신 것 같네요.
Observership이 없는 게 마음에 걸리긴 하는데, 제가 있는 곳은 금지하고 있어서 좀 힘드네요. 다른 곳을 알아보려면 할 수도 있었겠지만 제 의지의 문제였겠지요.
이젠 현재 조건으로 PS 마지막 고치고, 그냥 인터뷰에 최선을 다해야 할 듯합니다.
영어가 짧으니 예상문답집을 만들어 반복 연습하는 수밖에 없네요.
인터뷰 예상 질문 중요한 야마 감사합니다^^
혹시 예전에 인터뷰 준비할 때 사용하신 자료(예상질문항목) 있으면 부탁드려도 될런지요?
다시 한 번 감사합니다.
은종렬 드림

2013년 8월 26일

딱히 예상 문답을 준비하진 않았습니다. 영어가 짧지만 "인터뷰 답을 외워서 한다"는 인상을 주고 싶지 않았기 때문이기도 하고 (아무래도 티가 납니다) 그럴 시간적 여유가 없기도 했습니다. 질문을 못 알아 듣거나 크게 실수한 일은 여태껏 없었던 것 같고요. 실제 해보시면 아시겠지만 인터뷰어들에게도 꽤나 스트레스 많이 받고 떨리는 과정이긴 사실 매한가지이기 때문에 너무 걱정하지 마시고 긴장하지 마시고 이 사람이랑 얘기 좀 한번 해보자라는 마인드로 하시면 별로 스트레스 받을 일도 없을 거라 생각됩니다. 한 가지 주의하실 점은 인터뷰 과정에서 상대방의 리액션(?) 같은 것에 너무 일희일비하지 마시라는 겁니다. 누구한테나 "오 너 정말 엑설런트한 캔디뎃이구나"라는 사람도 있고, 마음에 들어도 뚱~한 사람이 있으니까요.
아, 그리고 거기서 항상 "질문 없니?"라는 역공?이 들어오니까 적절한 질문은 준비해 가시는 게 좋을 겁니다. 선생님 경력과 관련해서 뭐뭐 할 수 있는 기회가 있니? 이런 거 물어보면 좋아합니다. 저는 디너자리가 젤 힘들던데요. 하하. 저도 워낙 introverted에다가 지들끼리 떠드는데 말 끼어들기도 어렵고 참 거시기하더라구요. 저도 그건 딱히 드릴 말씀은 없지만, 디너 때 참석한 레지던트들에게 패컬티들이 rule out할 사람이 누구냐고 물어본다고 하니 중간만 가도록(?) 잘 하셔야 하겠습니다. 또 궁금하신 것 있으면 알려주세요 :)
Sung Bae Jee

지성배 선생님의 조언에 따라 옵저버십observership을 해야겠다는 생각을 했다. 2014년에는 UC 데이비스 메디컬 센터에서 한 달간 옵저버십을 했다. 결국 매치에는 실패했지만 옵저버십 자체는 미국 병원을 체험해 본 좋은 경험이 었다.

2013년 10월 17일

선생님 안녕하세요, 지성배입니다.
매칭 잘 되어가시는지 궁금해서 안부차 연락드립니다.
제가 도울 일 있으면 꼭 알려주시고요.
아무쪼록 행운을 빕니다.
지성배 드림.

2013년 10월 17일

지성배 선생님,
이런 기막힌 우연이 있을까요? 지금 샘께 이메일 쓰고 있었습니다.
아래와 같은...

안녕하세요? 선생님께서는 리틀락에서 어느덧 레지던트 생활의 4개월째를 보내고 계시겠군요. 부럽습니다^^
저는 안타깝게도 인터뷰를 하나도 받지 못했습니다.
경쟁이 치열한 점도 있겠으나 무엇보다도 저의 능력이 부족한 탓이 가장 크겠지요.
인터뷰를 못 받은 이유로 가장 큰 문제점은 졸업 16년째라는 점과 USCE가 없다는 점이라고 생각합니다.
한국에서 뭘 했든 이곳에서는 중요하지 않은 것 같습니다.
아직 인터뷰 시즌이 남았지만, 냉정하게 보면 제가 남은 기간 인터뷰를 하나라도 받을 가능성은 매우 희박해 보입니다. 그래서 다음 계획을 생각해야만 할 것 같습니다. 한국으로 돌아가거나, 여기에서 내년을 기약해 보거나.
한국으로 돌아가지 않을 수 있는 방법이 있다면 가장 좋겠지요.
그 가운데 선생님께서 지내신 마이애미 Transplant House Physician 자리에 들어갈 수만 있다면 너무 기쁠 것 같습니다. 그마저도 경쟁이 치열해서 많이 어려울 것으로 생각합니다. 지금 생각으로는 그곳에 들어갈 수만 있다면 내년에 housestaff 뽑기 전, 지금이라도 들어가서 observership이나 unpaid intern으로 경험을 쌓고, 내년 3월쯤 정식으로 apply하고 싶습니다. 이 점을 상의드리고자 이메일을 드립니다.
올해 미리 그곳 프로그램에 연락을 하고, 미리 지원할 수 있는 방법은 없을런지요?

제 장점을 굳이 어필하자면,
영주권이 있다는 점과, 미국 리서치 랩에서의 2년간의 경험을 통하여 미국문화를 약간이나마 배웠다는 점, 그동안 영어공부에 나름 최선을 다해서 아직 많이 부족하지만 기본적인 의사소통은 가능하다는 점, 비록 나이를 많이 먹었지만 한국에 있을 때 많은 입원환자, 중환자실 환자를 돌본 경험이 많다는 점 정도가 되겠습니다. 선생님의 조언 기다리겠습니다.
은종렬 드림

2013년 10월 17일

안녕하세요, 선생님. 갈수록 매칭이 터프해지는 것은 어느 정도 예상한 일이고요, 꼭 정공법이 다가 아니고 다른 곁가지 길을 꼭 노려보시기 바래요.
http://residentswap.org/how_it_works.php
제 기억으로 여기에도 매칭 외로 뽑는 자리들이 띄엄띄엄 떴던 것들을 기억하거든요. 갑자기 TO가 늘었다든지 누군가 사직한 경우가 있거든요. 서류 준비해 놓으시고 정기적으로 모니터링하다가 바로바로 지원해 보시면 기회가 있지 않을까 합니다. 선생님께서 미국에 계시고 영주권이 있으시니 확실히 유리하리라 봅니다. 주제 넘는 말씀인지 모르겠지만 내년 6월까지 좋은 소식이 없을 경우 어떻게 하실 것인지 여러 가지 경우의 수와 계획들도 최대한 구체적으로 갖추어 놓으시는 게 좋다고 보고요. 아! 그리고 현재 계신 프로그램의 컨넥션을 이용하는 것이 가장 좋은 수단입니다. 안면이 있으신 모든 사람들에게 한 번씩 꼭 물어보셔요. '안 되면 말고' 정신이 정말 중요합니다 ^^
그럼 행운을 빕니다!

From: Sung Bae Jee <bodhjee@gmail.com>
Date: 2013/10/16
Subject: I have a candidate for you...
To: "Fan , Ji" <JFan@med.miami.edu>
Hi, Dr Fan!

I hope everything is going well with you. Recently I got in touch with a Korean doctor who is interested in House physician position. He is an associate professor at Yeungnam University Hospital in Korea and now he is doing research at UC Davis. His major field of interest is HCC. He is 41 yrs old and now he is trying to match (yeah, maybe a little more courageous than average guys) and want to do House physician as a US clinical experience. He has green card. I will attach his CV. 530-304-5754 is his phone number. Please let me know if you have any questions. Thank you so much and take care!
Sincerely,

2013년 10월 17일

감사하고 감사합니다.
언젠가 미국에 자리 잡아서 선생님을 뵐 날이 오게 되기를 바라겠습니다.
은종렬 드림

2013년 10월 17일

아이구 별말씀을요, 선생님 꼭 좋은 일이 있길 빕니다.
Dr. Fan은 중국 사람이고요. 거기서 펠로 2년하고 작년에 어텐딩이 된 사람입니다. 마이애미에서 고생 많이 했죠 ㅎㅎ 아랫사람 잘 챙기고 '따거' 기질이 좀 있습니다.
인터뷰 연락이 올 때쯤이면 제게도 꼭 알려주세요. Dr. Tekin이라고 선발을 담당하는 어텐딩에게도 연락을 따로 하겠습니다. 이 양반은 아주 입지전적 인물인데요, 터키에서 흉부외과 하고 마이애미에 와서

house physician 2년 하고 외과 레지던트 들어가서 마치고 다시 간이식 펠로 2년하고 어텐딩까지 된 사람이거든요. 사람 착하고 제가 외과 인턴 들어가는 데 결정적인 도움을 준 사람입니다. 이 사람은 너무 바빠서 지금 얘기하면 까먹을 게 분명하니 임박해서 제가 연락을 해볼까 합니다.
가장 중요한 건 지금 버티고 있는 애들이 매칭돼서 자리가 많이 비어야 그 틈으로 들어가시는 거거든요. 걔들이 잘 되길 비는 수밖에 없습니다ㅎㅎ 체력적으로도 좀 힘드실 수 있고 교수님 하시던 분께서 하시기에는 좀 거시기한 면도 많습니다만 미국 시스템을 이해하고 경험을 쌓기에는 좋은 기회임이 분명합니다.
Sung Bae Jee

이메일 이후 뉴욕 코니 아일랜드 병원에서 인터뷰 하나를 받았다. 지성배 선생님께서 인맥을 동원해 자리를 알아봐 주셨지만 잘 되지 않았다.

2014년 3월 18일

그동안 안녕하셨습니까?
저는 인터뷰 한 개 받고 매칭에 실패했습니다. 지금은 매우 낙담한 상태입니다.
졸업연수 17년이라는 객관적인 핸디캡이 있지만, 실패의 원인은 저 자신에 있었던 것 같습니다. 엉성한 영어실력과 소심한 성격 등.
지금은 희망을 많이 잃었습니다.
2월 말 한국에 입국해 지금은 대진 아르바이트를 하고 있습니다.
혹시라도 매치되면 미국에 다시 들어가려고 했었는데, 실패하는 바람에 취직해야 할 것 같습니다. 작년 인터뷰를 못 받아 낙담하고 있을 때 포항의 한 병원과 접촉했습니다.
그때 이사장이란 분이 미국의 일이 잘 되면 가라, 안 되면 꼭 우리병원에 와 달라, 원하는 거 다 들어주겠다고 이야기되었습니다. 2월 입국했을 때도 마찬가지였구요. 포항에서 ERCP 할 줄 아는 의사가 잘 없는 것 같아서 ERCP만 적극적으로 해주면 페이나 조건을 다 들어줄 듯합니다. 지금까지 기다려준 이사장님께도 미안한 마음도 들구요.
선생님께서 소개해 주신 마이애미 프로그램에도 제게 너무 과분하고 감사한 일이지만, Dr. Fan에게서 연락이 오면 어떡할지도 고민입니다. 무작정 인터뷰 연락이 오기를 기다리고 연락 오면 미국으로 인터뷰 받으러 가야 할지...
2년간의 미국생활을 하면서 미국이 너무 좋았고, 너무 그립습니다.
생계와 관련된 현실적인 문제, 진료현장에서 너무 오래 멀어지는 데 대한 두려움 등으로 어떻게 해야 할지 잘 모르겠습니다.
아직 영어가 매우 부족하므로 영어를 늘리고, 돈을 벌면서 후일을 도모해야 할지
좀 더 과감하게 한국의 모든 것을 버리고 미국에 올인해야 할지.
두서없이 말씀드려 죄송합니다.
어떤 결과든 선생님을 알게 된 것은 행운이고 감사하게 생각합니다.
고민 있거나 힘들면 또 연락드리고 조언을 구해도 될런지요?
은종렬 드림

2014년 3월 18일

연락 주셔서 감사합니다, 선생님.
선생님의 그 고민 십분 이해합니다. 뭐라고 위로의 말씀을 드려야 할지 모르겠습니다. 저도 매칭은 두 번 다 실패해 본 경험만 있기에 그 기분을 잘 알 것 같습니다. 저는 그렇게까지는 하고 싶지 않았고 처자식을 계속 고생만 시킬 수도 없었기에 "여기까지 해 보고 안 되면 돌아간다"는 생각을 한편으로는 항상 가지고 있었던 것 같습니다. 기약 없는 프레림을 2년 동안 할 생각은 없었는데 가정의학과에 자리를 얻으면서 마침내 마음의 평화와 안정을 얻게 되었지요. 제 처까지 저랑 같은 생각을 가지고 있었다면 어쩌면 기회가 없었을지도 모르겠습니다만, 저를 믿고 항상 용기를 주면서 더 버텨 보라고 푸시(?)해준 덕에 버티다 보니 저도 기회를 얻은 것 같은 생각입니다. 첫 번째, 두 번째 매칭 실패하면서 얼마나 힘들었는지 모릅니다. 한국으로 돌아가 뭘 해도 이 짓은 더 못하겠다 싶었지요. 어쨌든 제 포인트는, 미국에 꼭 남아야 끝내주는 성공이고 한국에 남으면 뭘 하든지 실패다, 이런 생각은 좀 아니라는 겁니다. 저는 어찌 됐든 우리 가족이 함께 행복하느냐가 더 중요한 포인트였고 그걸 위해서라면 한국에 가서 응당 알바를 해도 뭐 그렇게 억울할 것 같지는 않았습니다. 미국보다 맘은 편할 테니까요.
결국은 선생님의 가치판단과 가족들의 합의가 중요할 것 같습니다. 선생님 혼자만의 생각으로 밀어부칠 수 있는 일이 아닌 것 같고, 그렇게 되기도 힘드니까요. 어느 쪽이든 너무 극단적으로는 생각하지 마시고요. 어찌됐건 어서 지금의 기분에서 벗어나시길 바랍니다. 길게 보면, 또 한 번 기회를 노려보실 수도 있는 것 아닐까 합니다. 제가 이렇게 하시라 저렇게 하시라 감히 말씀드릴 입장은 아닌 것 같습니다. Dr. Fan에게는 분위기가 어떤지 한번 넌지시 물어보겠습니다. 올해부터 PA를 뽑아서 쓰겠다는 말을 얼핏 들은 것 같아서 확인해 봐야 할 것 같습니다.
그럼 이만 줄이겠습니다.
지성배 드림.

2014년 3월 18일

다시 한 번 감사합니다.
제 진로가 어떻게 되든 선생님과의 인연은 이어가고 싶습니다.
선생님은 참 따뜻하고 좋으신 분인 것 같습니다.
은종렬 드림.

2014년 3월 18일

마이애미에서도 이제 arnp를 뽑아서 쓰기로 결정했다고 합니다. 여기서는 기회가 없을 것 같네요.
Sung Bae Jee

2014년 3월 20일

연락 감사합니다.
불확실성이 없어져서 제가 결정하는 데는 더 잘 된 것 같습니다.
또 이곳 한국 소식 전해드리러 연락 한 번씩 드릴게요.

2014년 3월 20일

네, 선생님. 일단 어디서든 마음의 안정을 찾으시면서 또 기회를 노려보시면 좋겠다는 생각이 듭니다. 마이애미에서 몇 년 일하고도 매칭 안 되는 사람도 많았습니다. (정말 최악의 케이스죠. 일 년 이상 하는 게 아무 도움도 안 되는데 말이지요). 힘내세요 !!
Sung Bae Jee

이후로 지성배 선생님께 더 연락을 드리지 않았다. 사람이 간사한 게 내가 필요할 때만 생각나는 것 같다. 주고받은 이메일을 정리하다 보니 지성배 선생님을 한 번 뵙고 싶었다. 책을 내는 데도 허락을 받아야 해서 이메일을 또 보내게 되었다.

뜻밖에 바로 답장을 주셔서 너무 기쁘고 반가웠다. 가족사진도 보내주셨다.

2025년 2월 1일

선생님, 정말 오랜만입니다. 연락 주셔서 감사드립니다. 저는 직장을 뉴햄프셔의 Dartmouth-Hitchcock에서 매사추세츠의 베스 이스라엘로 옮긴 지 벌써 5년이 넘었습니다. 눈 깜짝 할 사이에 어느새 대학생 학부모가 되어 있지 뭡니까 아...
보내주신 원고 감사히 잘 보았고요, 의사로서 가장으로서 힘든 시간을 묵묵히 버텨 내신 데 대해 존경을 보냅니다. 여러모로 뜻깊은 저서가 될 것 같고요, 제가 감히 책에 들어가도 되는 건지 모르겠지만, 아무튼 저로서는 영광입니다.
저는 매사추세츠 주 렉싱턴에서 살고 있고, 제 전화번호는 603-203-xxxx 입니다. 보스턴 오시면 연락 주세요!
지성배 올림

미국연수 3년차 그리고 귀국

2014년 2월 3일 월요일

코니 아일랜드 병원 인터뷰를 하고 혼자 한국으로 귀국했다. 생활비가 떨어져 가고 있어서 아르바이트를 할 수밖에 없었다. 2012년 첫해는 대학으로부터 급여가 나와 충당이 되었고, 2013년에는 퇴직금 1억 원으로 생활했다. 수입 없이 통장 잔고가 줄어드는 것을 보는 것은 몹시 불안한 일이었다. 3월 한 달간은 순천에서, 4월 2주간은 김천에서, 5월 한 달은 영천에서 대진을 하면서 생활비를 마련했다. 일기를 보니 잊었던 기억이 조금씩 떠오르는 것 같다.

2014년 3월 18일 화요일

매치 결과를 열어볼 때 가슴이 터질 듯했다. 실패. 하늘이 무너지는 듯하다. 감정을 추스르고 지성배 선생님과 아흐마드, 유유, 핼리, 닥터 전에게 이메일을 보내야겠다. SK 엔카를 통해 마티즈를 149만 원에 구입하기로 했다.

* USMLEKOREA에 올린 후기를 지금 읽어보니 너무 부끄럽다.

2014년 3월 21일 금요일

취직할 병원을 알아보고 있다. 미국 입국 시 필요한 서류도 알아보고 있다.

2014년 3월 25일 화요일

I-131 재입국 허가서Reenry Permit에 대해 알아보았다.

~2년 발행일로부터from the date of issuance

2-2-1년 (지난 5년 중 4년 이상 외국에 있었으면 다음은 1년으로 제한)

DHSdepartment of Homeland Security, 국토안보부

* I-131
  - type or print legibly in black ink
  - If an item is not applicable or the answer is none, print or type N/A
  - driver's license
  - Green Card
  - I-551 전후면 copy (or)
  - passport copy + permanent resident
* Expedite
  - severe financial loss
  - extreme emergent situation
  - humanitarian situation

Where to file? www. uscis.gov/I-131
Filing fee $360
Biometrics services fee $85 total $445
check payable to U.S. Department of Homeland Security

2014년 3월 27일 목요일

4월 11일에서 19일, 8일 동안 김천에서 아르바이트를 하기로 했다.

5월 1일에서 31일, 한 달간은 영천에서 아르바이트를 하기로 했다.

2014년 3월 28일 금요일

올해 한 번 더 레지던트 도전을 하기로 했다. 옵저버십을 하기로 했다.

6월 1일, 미국으로 돌아간다.

6월 10일부터 8월 3일은 레지던트 지원 준비를 하고

9~12일은 참관 계획을 잡았다. 8월은 닥터 전 만나기.

* 옵저버십
닥터 전에게 부탁해 허락 받았다. UC 데이비스 소화기내과 다른 교수들께는 모두 거절당하거나 회신이 없었고 내시경 의사인 우라야마에게만 허락 받았다.

2014년 4월 2일 수요일

UCDMC 소화기내과 스탭들에게 옵저버십을 부탁하는 이메일 초안을 작성했다.

* Gastroenterology email

LORs Dr. Zern, Dr. Urayama

2014년 4월 8일 화요일

핼리, 닥터 전, 닥터 우라야마에게 줄 선물로 서문시장에 가서 자개필함과 보석함을 구입했다(100,000원).

2014년 4월 10일 목요일

김천 K외과에서 아르바이트 대진을 시작했다. 의사랑 프로그램을 익혔다.

2014년 4월 18일 금요일

환자가 없어서 대기실로 나왔는데 TV를 보다가 충격적인 세월호 침몰사고를 보았다.

2014년 6월 1일 일요일

오전 10시 45분에 아시아나를 타고 SFO 터미널에 도착해서 바트BART를 타고 30분 걸려 시빅 센터/UN 프라자에 오후 4시 40분에 도착했다.
바로 3342번 버스를 타고 55분 걸려 에머리빌Emeryville CA EMY에 오후 5시 35분 도착했다.

저녁 7시 2분, 데이비스 742 캐피틀 코리더Capitol corridor에 도착했다.
집사람이 마중을 나왔다.

2014년 6월 5일 목요일

준성이 어린이집 졸업식이다.

2014년 6월 6일 토요일

한국에서 아르바이트를 마치고 지난 일요일에 데이비스로 돌아왔다. 월요일에는 데이비스 커뮤니티 클리닉에 보험문제로 갔다. 집사람과 CCFS에도 면담하러 갔다. 수요일 아침에는 Mr. 핼리를 만나 안부 인사를 전했다. 우라야마를 만나 옵저버십에 대해 이야기를 나누었다. 나이스한 분이었다. 닥터 전도 만났다. 아침에는 준성이 어린이집 졸업식이 있었다. 금요일에는 첼로를 반납했다.

2014년 7월 17일 목요일

내과 매니저인 마리아에게 옵저버십 관련 이메일을 보냈다.

2014년 7월 20일 일요일

핼리와 식사했다. 집사람과 애들은 한국에 있는 청송 과수원에 가 있다. 집사람의 친정이다.

* 핼리는 은퇴한 치과의사로 은퇴 후 데이비스 욜로 라이브러리를 통해 외국인 대상으로 영어 튜터를 무료로 해주셨다. 나와 매치되어 미국에 있는 동안 영어를 가르쳐 주셨다.

코로나 전 크루즈 여행사진(2021년 핼리에게 이메일로 받음)

2014년 7월 21일 월요일

마리아한테 답장이 왔으면 좋겠다. 오늘 할 일은 PS 작성, CV 입력 끝내기, 영어공부다.

2014년 8월 1일 금요일

병원 리뷰하고 지원할 병원 120개를 추렸다.

2014년 9월 2일 화요일

닥터 전과 닥터 우라야마 클리닉에서 옵저버십을 시작했다.

우라야마 선생님이 내시경 시술하는 것을 참관했다.

내시경실 가는 날은 UC 데이비스로 가서 셔틀을 타고 새크라멘토 UC 데이비스 메디컬 센터에 내렸고, 시내 클리닉 가는 날은 집 근처에서 욜로 버스를 타고 갔다.

인터뷰 2개를 받았다. 뉴욕의 리치먼드 대학교Richmond university, 킹스브룩 유대인 의료센터Kingsbrook Jewish medical center였다. 이번에는 최대한 빨리 인터뷰를 하고 귀국해 취직하기로 했다. 그래서 10월 16일과 17일로 인터뷰를 예약했다.

2014년 10월 14일 화요일

오후 1시 샌프란시스코 공항을 이륙하여 저녁 7시 35분, 미네아폴리스에서 환승했다. 밤 11시 13분, 라구아디아 공항La Guadia airport에서 허츠Hertz 자동차를 렌트한 후 재키로빈슨 파크웨이Jackie Robinson Parkway를 11.2마일, 16분 달려 렉싱턴 인Lexington Inn에 도착했다.

2014년 10월 15일 수요일

어젯밤 뉴욕에 도착했다. 2개의 인터뷰가 예정되어 있다. 킹스브룩 의료센터와 리치먼드 대학병원. 여기저기 돌아다니고 병원으로 가는 길을 체크하는 도중에 물을 사기 위해 CVC 앞 길가에 주차하고 잠시 들어갔다 나왔는데 차가 사라졌다. 주차할 때는 보이지 않았던 '소화전Fire hydrant' 표시가 보였다. 주차 가능parking permit 표지와 주차 요금 징수기parking meter만 보았던 것이다. 패닉 상태가 되었다. 차는 견인되었다. 지나가는 사람에게 도움을 요청했더니 311에 전화해 보라고 했다. 바로 전화했는데 말이 너무 빨라 알아들을 수가 없었다. 어찌어찌 견인사무소에 연결이 되었는데 위치를 알 수 없었다. 그때 또 지나가는 사람에게 부탁했는데 매우 친절하게 도와주었다. 가게에서 종이를 빌려 주소를 적어 주고, 택시를 불러 요금도 대신 내주었다. 전화번호를 물어보았어야 했다. 어떻게 감사 인사를 전달해야 할지 모르겠다. 경찰서에 도착해서 서류를 작성하고 차를 되찾았다. 벌금은 끔찍했다. 견인비 185달러, 주차위반 115달러, 총 300달러였다. 망했다. 호텔로 돌아오는 길에 킹스브룩 메디컬 센터에 갔다. 지쳤고 뉴욕이 싫다. 우울하다. 벌금 때문이 아니라 내 영어 때문에.

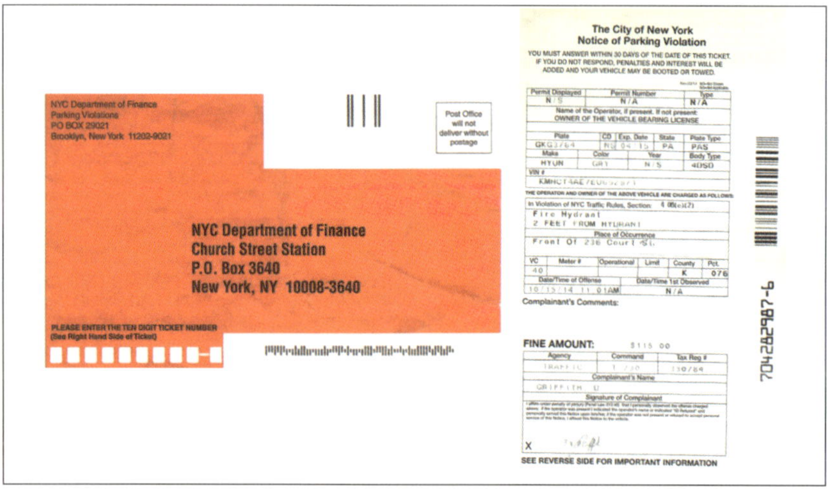

2014년 10월 16일 목요일

5시 30분 기상, 6시 출발, 7시 30분 도착, 8시 30분 오피스 리포트

> Richmond university medical center
> 8:30AM Dr. Bloomfield conference room
> Villa Building, 355 Bard Avenue, Staten Island, NY
> 355 Bard Avenue. Dept of Medicine - Villa Building, 1st floor
> Staten Island, NY 10310 718-818-2419
> Parking: Bard Ave Main building 2nd driveway on the right

블룸필드 회의실Dr. Bloomfield conference room

오전 8시 30분~9시 치프 레지던트와 미팅

오전 9시~10시 30분 교수진과 인터뷰

10시 30분~ 병원 투어

11시 30분 점심

12시 15분 Dr. Jay Nfonajin, Program director

귀가

Richmond University Medical Center
An Affiliate of The Mount Sinai Hospital and School of Medicine
Jong Ryeol Eun
Internal Medicine Residency Program

명찰을 패용하고 병원 투어를 했고, 레지던트 교육 컨퍼런스를 참관한 후 레지던트들과 점심 식사를 같이 했는데 좋은 경험이었다. 치프 레지던트는 아프리카에서 왔는데 레지던트 생활이 매우 만족스럽다고 했다.

2014년 10월 17일 금요일

킹스브룩 유대인 의료 센터

7시에 기상, 8시 30분 출발

오전 9시 30분 킹스브룩 도착. 마치는 데 6시간 걸림.

인터뷰 약속

캐츠 빌딩Katz Building, 4층 9시 30분부터 6시간

2자리 점수2 digit score KJMC 지원서

유효한 ECFMG 자격증, 영주권 카드permanent residency card,

의대 졸업장medical school diploma

KINGSBROOK
JEWISH MEDICAL CENTER
Department of Medicine

October 7, 2014

Re: Internal Medicine Residency Program Application

Dear Applicant:

In regard to your application for a residency position in Internal Medicine, please contact this office between ***1:00 PM to 4:00PM Mon-Fri*** at telephone number (718) 604-5415, to arrange for a personal interview. Please ensure that you contact us as soon as possible, but no later than October 20, 2014.

All interviews will be conducted in the Department of Medicine office located in the Katz Building, 4th Floor. Please arrange to arrive at 9:30 AM. The entire process will take approximately 6 hours. Your day will include: processing of the application, general orientation, the interview, and a tour of the Medical Center.

It is essential that you bring the following original documents with you on the day of your interview along with a photocopy of each document.

1) **If you did STEP 1 and STEP II before 2013 please upload your two digit score report to ERAS.**
2) Completed enclosed KJMC Application
3) Valid E.C.F.M.G. Certificate , if applicable
4) Eligibility to work fulltime in the U.S.A. as of the date of your employment (e.g. US Passport, Permanent Residency Card, EAD, etc.)
5) Medical School Dean & Three (3) Faculty letters of reference (if not already uploaded into ERAS)
6) Medical School diploma

Alternate side street parking rules apply in this area, but for your convenience, there is paid parking at the hospital. The parking lot is located on Rutland Road between Utica Avenue and East 49th Street.

Thank you.

Department of Medicine

2014년 10월 18일 토요일

오전 11시 40분 LGA 이륙 – 오후 2시 01분 환승Cincinnati – LAX 오후 5시 48분(8:00) – SMF 4시 8분(9:22)

2014년 10월 19일 일요일

핑거프린트Fingerprint 예약(10/29, 수)

2014년 10월 31일 금요일

혼자 귀국했다.

2014년 11월 4일 화요일

김해 ○○병원에서 면접을 보고 집으로 오던 중 명지병원으로부터 전화를 받았다.

면접 보러 오지 않겠냐고.

2014년 11월 6일 목요일

명지병원에 면접 보러 갔다. 병원은 괜찮았다. 근무하기로 했다.

2014. 11월 11일 화요일

고양시 덕양구 화정동 한화오벨리스크로 이사했다. 500만 원에 월세 50만 원.

중개수수료는 35만 원.

500만 원이 없어서 대출을 받았다.

2014년 11월 17일 월요일

명지병원으로 첫 출근했다.

* 그로부터 10여 년 명지병원에서 근무했다.

2014년 11월 23일 일요일

11월 17일부터 명지병원 첫 근무를 시작했다. 첫 주는 많이 긴장했지만 지금은 매우 행복하다. 어제 경복궁에 가보았다. 청와대와 청와대 주변 길도 걸었다. 평화롭고 좋았다.

2014년 12월 3일 수요일

지난 토요일에는 일했고, 일요일에는 병원에서 차로 5분 거리에 있는 행주산성에 갔다. 어탕국수를 먹었는데 맛있었다. 오늘 점심에는 전체 교수회의가 있었다. 회의 때 내 소개를 했다. 오후에는 대장내시경 검사를 2명 했는데, 두 번째 케이스는 어려워서 한 시간이나 걸렸다. 마른 체형이어서 힘들었는데 그래도 간호사 보기가 좀 부끄러웠다.

2014년 12월 7일 일요일

길병원에서 간 관련 세미나가 있어서 인천에 갔다. 사무치듯 추웠다. 김영석 교수님과 권오상 교수님을 만났다.

2014년 12월 8일 월요일

몽골에서 온 중환자 한 명이 입원 중이다. 말기 간경변과 간암 환자다. 환자 상태가 매우 걱정이 된다. 환자의 딸이 영어를 할 수 있어서 영어로 상태를 설명해 주었다. 유창하지는 못하지만 대화에 불편함은 없었다.

2014년 12월 11일 화요일

데이비스 집 인터넷에 문제가 생겨서 월요일 예약이 걱정이었는데 잘 해결되어 다행이다. 라이브 챗으로 재예약했다. 오늘 오후 집사람으로부터 전화가 왔다. 인터넷이 다시 개통되었다고 했다. 고맙다고 말했다. 마음 한 켠으로는 입원해 있는 몽골 환자가 걱정이다. 지난 금요일 입원했는데 상태가 점점 나빠지고 있다. 병원에서 사망하게 될까 걱정이다.

화정역 오피스텔에서 본 해지는 전경

2015년 3월 셋째주

명지병원에 근무하면서 매치 결과를 기다렸다. 매치 발표일에는 숨이 막힐 듯이 떨렸다. 두근거리는 마음으로 클릭을 했는데 매치되지 않았다는 내용이 떴다. 절망적이었다. 그날 밤 입천장에 심한 궤양이 생기는 등 한동안 힘들었다.

2015년 6월

명지병원에서 서남대 인수를 추진하면서 우선협상 대상자가 되었다. 그때 잠시 서남의대 부학장을 하면서 의대 관련 일을 하고 학생들과도 잘 지냈다. 그러나 얼마 후 서남의대가 폐교되었다.

보직 임명 및 면직자 명단

임 명

직 위	성 명	소속학과	직 급	임 기	비 고
연구기획과장		경찰행정법학과	조교수	2015. 6.15.~2015. 8. 31	겸직
의학부장		의 학 과	교수	2015. 6.15.~2015. 8. 31	
의학부교학과장		의 학 과	조교수	2015. 6.15.~2015. 8. 31	
교무부학부장	은종렬	의 학 과	부교수	2015. 6.15.~2015. 8. 31	
교육부학부장		의 학 과	부교수	2015. 6.15.~2015. 8. 31	
학생부학부장		의 학 과	부교수	2015. 6.15.~2015. 8. 31	
연구부학부장		의 학 과	교수	2015. 6.15.~2015. 8. 31	
의학과장		의 학 과	조교수	2015. 6.15.~2015. 8. 31	겸직
기초의학과장		의 학 과	조교수	2015. 6.15.~2015. 8. 31	겸직
임상의학과장		의 학 과	부교수	2015. 6.15.~2015. 8. 31	
의학도서관장		의 학 과	조교수	2015. 6.15.~2015. 8. 31	
학생생활연구소장		사회복지학과	조교수	2015. 6.15.~2015. 8. 31	아산캠퍼스 겸직
교수학습지원센터장		항공비즈니스영어학과	조교수	2015. 6.15.~2015. 8. 31	아산캠퍼스 겸직

2015년 8월 20일

하계휴가 때 미국에 갔다. 라센Lassen으로 여행을 갔다.

LASSEN
VOLCANIC

Lassen
Peak

2015년 어느 날

아이들 등굣길 사진을 집사람이 보내왔다.

2015년 10월

할로윈 때 집사람이 찍어서 보내주었다.

2016년 8월 말

가족들이 영구 귀국했다. 아래는 귀국 전 보내온 사진들이다.

2017년 6월

몽골에 의료봉사 및 국립암센터와의 조인트 심포지엄으로 다녀왔다.

2017년 8월 19일

평창으로 놀러갔다.

2020년 1월 19일~2월 1일

2주간 휴가를 내어 미국으로 추억여행을 떠났다. 쉐보레 서버번을 렌트해 미국 서부와 동부를 다녔는데 데이비스가 가장 좋았다.

오랜만에 다시 가본 타겟

오랜만에 장도 보고

데스밸리에서

디즈니랜드에서

다시 가본 몬테레이

귀국하는 날 비행기에서 내리면서 핸드폰을 열었더니 명지병원이 실검 1위여서 놀랐다. 코로나가 시작되는 날이었다. 금방 끝날 줄 알았던 코로나 기간이 3년 이상 지속되었다. 병원은 특히 더 힘든 시간을 보냈다.

에필로그

명지병원에서 지난 10여 년간 진료에 전념했습니다. 그리고 동국대학교 일산병원으로 옮겨 진료한 지 2년째입니다. 이제 내 나이 50이 훌쩍 넘었습니다. 나의 40대가 어떻게 지나갔는지 기억이 잘 나지 않습니다. 고통스런 기억을 잊으려고 더욱 일에만 몰두했는지도 모르겠습니다. 어느새 첫째와 둘째 아이는 대학에 진학했고, 막내도 사춘기가 찾아와 질풍노도의 시기를 보내고 있습니다. 미국의사를 준비하고 도전한 4년 여의 시간을 회상하면 가슴이 아려옵니다. 한편으로는 미국에서 보낸 시간이 가장 행복했던 기억으로 남아 있습니다. 집사람과 가족들도 미국 데이비스에 또 가보고 싶어 합니다.

이제 인생의 후반부에 접어들었습니다. 마흔이 되기 전에는 뭘 해도 해낼 수 있을 것 같은 자신감과 무모함이 있었습니다. 그때로 돌아간다면 다시 도전할 수 있을지 확신이 들지 않습니다. 지금 생각하면 이제 다시는 못할 것 같습니다. 과정 하나하나가 너무 힘들었습니다. 다만 그때 도전해 보지 않았다면 지금, 그리고 평생 후회와 아쉬움을 가지고 살아갈 거라는 걸 잘 알게 되었습니다. 분명 대단한 경험이었고 나를 한 단계 발전시키는 계기였습니다.

실패한 사람이 이제 도전하려는 의대생이나 젊은 의사 선생님들에게 조언을 하는 게 주제넘은 일일 수도 있습니다. 그럼에도 불구하고 젊음은 좋은 것이고 희망은 현재를 견딜 수 있게 하는 원동력이라는 점을 말해 주고 싶습니다. 또 해볼 만한 도전이지만 '대충 해보고 안 되면 말지'라는 생각으로는 절대할 수 없는 험난한 과정이라는 점도 분명히 말해 두고 싶습니다.

실패하고 낙오한 사람의 입장에서는 매치에 성공하여 미국에 계신 선생님들이 진심으로 존경스럽습니다. 실패하신 분들께는 위로를, 또 도전하는 분들에게는 응원의 마음을 보냅니다.

그동안 아내 혜영, 큰딸 예린, 둘째 지우, 막내 준성이에게 아빠의 지난 무모한 도전으로 힘들게 한 점에 대해 사과하고, 앞으로는 남편과 아빠로서 가족을 위해 성실한 삶을 살 것임을 다짐합니다.

2025년을 보내며

일산에서 은종렬

동국대학교 저서출판 지원사업 선정도서

이 저서는 2024년도 동국대학교 연구비지원을 받아 수행된 연구결과물임.
This work was supported by the Dongguk University Research Fund of 2024

USMLE, 미국연수
그리고 영주권

2026년 1월 12일 초판 1쇄 인쇄
2026년 1월 19일 초판 1쇄 발행

지은이 은종렬
발행인 박기련
발행처 동국대학교출판부

출판등록 제1973-000004호(1973.6.28)
주소 04626 서울시 중구 퇴계로36길2 신관1층 105호
전화 02-2264-4714
팩스 02-2268-7851
Homepage https://dgpress.dongguk.edu
E-mail abook@jeongjincorp.com

디자인 위드
인쇄처 건영프린테크

ISBN 978-89-7801-788-6 (13510)
값 18,000원